"Health and wellness guru Kathryn Scoblick attacks conventional wisdom about diets. In *Health Inspires*, she makes it clear that there is so much more people can do to master their wellbeing. Anyone who has worried about diets, or the obesity problem in our society, or simply health in general will find value in this engaging book."

—Elizabeth F. Loftus, PhD
Distinguished Professor, University of California, Irvine

"*Health Inspires* is a transformational read for anyone on a weight loss mission. Kathryn Scoblick loads this book with evidence-based and practical advice for mastering your health and wellbeing. She changes the way we look at our weight loss, offering wisdom from positive psychology that will catalyze each reader's journey to a healthier lifestyle."

—Daniel Ivankovich, MD Co-Founder & Medical Director, OnePatient - Global Health Initiative

.health inspires!™

Sarah,

Inspiration is everywhere!

Kathryn
Scablick

.health inspires!™

Your Way to | Sustainable Weight Loss

Kathryn Scoblick

© 2017 Kathryn Scoblick

Published by
Health Inspires Publishing
Austin, TX

Health Inspires: Your Way to Sustainable Weight Loss by
Kathryn Scoblick. Austin, TX: Health Inspires Publishing, 2017.

Library of Congress Control Number: 2017907721

Publisher's Cataloging-in-Publication Data
Scoblick, Kathryn.
p. cm.

ISBN-13: 9780692885338
ISBN-10: 0692885331
1.   Health and wellness—Current trends and foundations 2. Food industry and marketing—United States 3. Positive Psychology methods—United States 4. Health Inspires, LLC—Kathryn Scoblick I. Title.

Edited by Pam Bixby
Cover design by BigBlueDesigns

Printed in the United States of America
1 2 3 4 5 21 20 19 18 17
Second Edition

www.healthinspires.com

Table of Contents

Note: Download your free *Healthy Weight Success Journal* at healthinspires.com

Introduction

Talking about nutrition is like talking about religion or politics. We all have different beliefs about foods and diets. I know that you have had conversations about specific diets or about what foods are healthy or not healthy, and that people have stridently different feelings about these things. There is a wide spectrum that includes scientific validation, anecdotal evidence, old wives' tales, and everything in between. I suspect the confusion over what is true is one of the very *reasons* that you have not been successful at losing the weight and keeping the weight off. To get us on the same page, I want to share two things about which I think we can all agree:

1. We should eat more fruits and vegetables.
2. We should eat fewer processed foods.

I have not yet found anybody who disagrees with these two statements. In addition, there actually is a no fail diet. In 2005 Consumer Reports magazine published a diet survey that rated nine diets followed by nearly 8,000 successful dieters. What was the most frequent and consistent response from successful dieters regarding the most effective strategy for their sustainable weight loss? The survey said: "My own diet and exercise regimen." Surprising? Not at all.

The National Weight Control Registry (NWCR) offers support for this diet "breakthrough." Established in 1994, the NWCR is the largest prospective investigation of long-term weight loss maintenance. The NWCR is currently tracking more than 10,000 individuals who have lost significant amounts of weight and have kept it off for long periods of time. Registry members have lost an average of 66 lbs and have kept it off for an average of 5.5 years.

Not to mislead, some of these registrants have lost 30 pounds and some 300 pounds, some have kept it off for just one year and some for more than 65 years. Some have done it slowly and some rapidly. Successful dieters can voluntarily become part of this database, contributing to our understanding of how and what people do to lose weight and keep it off. The NWCR reports of successful dieters include these statistics:

- 80 percent of the registrants are women and 20 percent men
- 98 percent of registry participants report they have modified their food intake in some way to lose weight
- 94 percent increased their physical activity, and walking is the most frequently reported form of activity

- Most people report that they maintain a low calorie, low fat diet and engage in high levels of activity

In addition:

- 78 percent eat breakfast every day
- 75 percent weigh themselves at least once a week
- 62 percent watch fewer than 10 hours of TV per week
- 90 percent exercise, on average, about an hour per day
- 45 percent of registry participants lost the weight on their own
- 55 percent lost weight with some type of program

What I find to be the most significant piece of information found in these people's stories is that *they report that their weight loss benefits other facets of their lives as well.*[1] That is powerful. Making healthy choices will put that bounce back in your step, clear your mind, make you feel better and stronger mentally, emotionally and physically. *When you feel strong, you act strong.* When you start to lose weight, good things start to happen in other parts of your life as well. There is a reason for this. Your confidence increases, and you have a higher energy level. When you feel good, you are more likely to engage in positive activities. Success breeds success in so many ways! To this point, weight loss may be a byproduct of your focus on something else that is positive, such as living a life with purpose. That is the premise of this book.

DIETS ARE NOT HEALTHY

The average dieter ends up 11 pounds heavier than when he started his diet. By now, we all know that extreme diets and yo-yo diets are not good for us. But do you really know what that means? I mean REALLY not good for us:

- There is a causal relationship between dieting and eating disorders (anorexia and bulimia)[2]
- Overweight individuals who refrain from eating may develop tendencies to binge eat
- Nearly 65 percent of dieters gain their weight back within three years (Yo-Yo dieting)[3]
- Those who lose weight and gain it back time and time again have a higher mortality rate[4]
- Losing muscle mass affects your heart (which is a muscle), and muscle helps you burn fat
- Losing muscle mass affects your metabolism

We know that diets fail for many reasons. You most likely know that it is not all about the food. **Here are some reasons why diets eventually fail:**

1. Beliefs and stories: You reinforce your beliefs over time by telling yourself stories that you come to believe. These stories serve a purpose, allowing you to be who you say that you are. Your story creates your identity.
2. All or nothing approach: Once you have one misstep, you throw up your hands and give up.

3. Resistance: When you focus on what you can't have, that is exactly what you will want.
4. Resentment and blame: Blaming somebody else for your weight gain keeps you stuck in the past. This is a negative and self-defeating emotion.
5. Being right: We like to be right. This comes from our need for consistency and certainty. The need to be right gives you every reason not to succeed and not to take responsibility. If you have failed at weight loss in the past, then you "get" to say, "See, I told you so, I cannot lose weight! I have tried everything!" We like to be right. This goes hand in hand with the stories we tell ourselves.
6. Habits and thoughts: Habits are of the subconscious mind. Habits from years past have been reinforced in the nerve impulses in your brain. You revert to engrained rituals the minute you encounter an obstacle.
7. Confusion: You haven't found the "right" diet and exercise program that works for you and one that you can stick with. The market is sending confusing messages and you have fallen into a trap. Confusion is an excuse.

We create inner struggles rife with self-sabotaging and berating behavior. Our brains are wired to make our stories come true, whether consciously or subconsciously. We are the most intelligent species and yet we rationalize, make excuses and do things that are not in our best interests. What is most remarkable is that we recognize that we do these things! We ask, "Why do I do that!?"

Unfortunately, we can and often do apply these psychological gymnastics to many things that keep us from being the best we can be, instead of *simply* choosing healthy foods; making time for essential daily physical activity; pursuing our dreams; investing time in a healthy and meaningful relationship; and most importantly, choosing kindness, love and gratitude.

If you think you have *tried* everything, every diet and every way imaginable to lose weight and haven't been able to keep it off, consider that merely "trying" to lose weight lacks traction. "Trying" leaves open all possibilities, except the possibility of losing weight. Losing weight, like anything else that you master in your life, requires consistency. In this case, it is a consistent pattern of food choices and physical activity, over time. You either do it, or you choose not to do it.

I enjoyed the original Star Wars as a girl and all the prequels with my children, and I like what Yoda says: "Do. Or do not. There is no try." He also says, "You must unlearn what you have learned." If you think the movie quote is hokey, then how about a quote from Henry Ford? "Whether you think you can or think you can't—you are right."

It all starts with our beliefs and how we process our world. We believe first, and we back into making our beliefs true through our perceptions, what we read, and the need to be right.

This book is divided into three parts.

Part 1 is about understanding how our belief system is the core from which our experiences, perceptions and thoughts emanate—and thus, reinforces our beliefs. We create our "stories" out of our beliefs that then psychologically and emotionally rule what we believe to be true. If you tell yourself you cannot lose weight because it is impossible, then that is your truth. But you can change it by first changing your belief system (I know I can lose weight) and then habitual thought patterns, feelings, emotions and behaviors will follow. You will learn how to change your beliefs using practical tips and proven tactics drawn from the science of positive psychology.

Part 2 is where you create your vision, goals and strategies for your healthy weight. This is where you find your meaning and motivation to make your dreams come true. You will learn the secrets and strategies that you must implement in order to be successful in your weight loss and maintain a healthy weight for life. This is the no-fail approach you have not fully implemented in the past. This game is mostly psychological and one that you will win. The plan is designed especially for you.

Part 3 provides all the facts on food, nutrition, portion control, how to enjoy your favorites, the food industry, diets, government policies and guidelines, and clinical studies. I also share practical tips on how to realize your plan within the busy-ness of life. I will show you how to get through each day and week healthy and happy and successful, and that includes when you derail! You will be back on track, no problem, no regret, with your game face on. You'll learn about the obesity epidemic in our country and its implications, providing industry awareness and inspiration to control what you can so that you become part of the solution.

You have tried everything else; now it is time for you to take control of your health with Health Inspires and learn that weight loss is sustainable.

Before we begin, complete this inspiring exercise:

Journal Exercise: (download your free *Healthy Weight Success Journal* at healthinspires.com)

1) **On Page 1 of your Health Inspires™ Healthy Weight Success Journal, write down your weight loss goal.**

It is important how you think about this and how you write it. You must write it as if it were already true. It will look something like this…

I am 60 pounds lighter and weigh 134 pounds.

2) **List all of the reasons you want to be this weight. You can list as many things as you like. Always write what you want for yourself as if you have already achieved it.**

It will look something like this…

I have confidence

I have greater self-esteem

I feel good

I have good energy, feel great and I have cute new clot
My husband/wife/partner tells me how sexy I am
My (health) numbers are good and my disease risk is zero
I will run the half marathon

This is an exercise to get your head in the right place and is a nice prelude to Part 2 when we work on your vision, goals and strategies to succeed.

Focus on what you want. You can have it and it is achievable. You can.

les

Part 1: How You See It

1

Power of Belief: Your Reality

"The thing always happens that you really believe in; and the belief in a thing makes it happen."

— FRANK LLOYD WRIGHT

For a long time, through the 1940s and early 1950s, running a four-minute mile was considered physiologically unreachable, which naturally fueled the psychological belief that it was *impossible*. Physiologists of the time *believed* running and training to beat this time was dangerous to the health of any athlete who attempted it.

But on May 6, 1954, Englishman Roger Bannister became the first person to break the "four-minute barrier," clocking 3.59.4 at the Iffley Road track in Oxford, running for the Amateur Athletic Association during its annual match. He was a medical school student at the time. Before that, Australian John Landy held the record for the fastest time, at just over four minutes. Prior to Landy's record, no one had broken the world record in eight years![5]

Within two months of Bannister's breakthrough, Landy surpassed his record with a 3:57.9 in Finland. That same year, a race called "Miracle Mile of the Century" was staged on the last day of the British Empire & Commonwealth Games in Vancouver to determine the fastest miler. Bannister won with 3:58.8 to Landy's 3:59.6, and this was the first time two men in one race had broken the four-minute barrier.

Bannister had the ambition to win a gold medal. He couldn't understand why Landy could run a 4:02 minute mile three or four times, and somebody else could run 4:01, yet no one could break four minutes. For Landy, "It was like a wall." His perception was his limitation. But Bannister knew it was just a matter of time. He believed that someone would "inevitably come along, train a little better, know that there's a target to be beaten, and beat it," he said. "So that was my mental approach to it." He broke it down into achievable measures. He determined that a four-minute mile on a quarter-mile track, is four, one-minute laps. And he was very clear that this was psychological training first, and then physiological training and technique second.[6] It is no wonder that Bannister was the first to break it.

BY THE END OF 1957, 16 RUNNERS HAD LOGGED SUB-FOUR-MINUTE MILES!

The four-minute mile story is a perfect example of how beliefs are integral to what we can and can't achieve. Once athletes realized it was possible, they were able to achieve! That is the power of belief.

There is evidence that we choose what we believe, regardless of scientific evidence. We believe first.[7] We believe what we want to believe, and then we reinforce it with what we read, our life experiences and how we perceive those experiences. This is the very reason why some of us believe in ghosts and some of us don't. It is the very reason some of us believe in UFO's and some of us don't. It is also the first reason why most of us believe in God, a higher power, and some of us don't. Belief is the first ingredient in determining whether a person succeeds at fulfilling his or her dreams. When we believe we can achieve, we take action to make it our reality. Each of us reinforces our beliefs through our thoughts and actions—and from the resulting outcomes (proof), perceptions or rationalizations—regardless if those beliefs are scientifically valid.

Our minds are very powerful and can open opportunities or close them. We have the power to decide what we want to believe and to take that achievable first step to reinforce it.

Our belief systems begin developing at a very young age, influenced by our upbringing and what our parents believe, and then our life experiences pile on through the years. Personal temperament matters as well. Through our experiences, we create emotional connections that are meaningful to us. These are called neuro associations, and they can be positive or negative. So feelings are built upon each individual's life experiences.

Sugar provides a simple and relatable example of how emotional connections, or neuro associations, work. Our past experiences with sugar have a lot to do with these associations. If you associate drinking a soda with a happy childhood memory that made you feel good, like going to the park with your dad, then your neurotransmitters, or your "happy chemicals," cement those positive connections in your brain. Coke® ads play to your memories. Seeing or hearing a Coke® ad, for the sake of this example, will be your cue, and you will find yourself feeling nostalgic and wanting a Coke®. You associate it with feeling happy, and this reinforces your beliefs and your actions.

These neuro associations are our truths because we have created meaning around them. The soft drink industry knows this and exploits it. In 2006, of the $870 million spent on marketing junk foods to kids under 11 and the $1 billion spent on advertising to teens, 65 percent of those dollars were used to promote carbonated sweetened beverages, fast food restaurants and breakfast cereals.[8] In 2013, Coca-Cola and PepsiCo spent $3.3 billion and $3.9 billion, respectively, on advertising and marketing activities.[9]

These companies want you to be a life-long consumer of their products. Once you know this, you may be less likely to fall prey to their marketing game. You can change how you feel by creating new meanings around soda and, therefore, create new neuro-associations. In this example, perhaps you can choose to see soda ads as manipulative and not in your best interests, only in the interests of the soft drink industry. I have much to add to this conversation in Part 3.

Perception is reality. It simply is. Your perception will influence how you view people, places and all things you see or hear. Perception reinforces your beliefs because you see it the way

YOU see it. Your perception is why you believe you are right, no matter what. Two people can share the same experience and reflect on that experience from two completely different perspectives, coming to two completely different conclusions about what just happened.

But perception is subjective. As this relates to your health and past weight loss efforts, your beliefs and the story you have been telling yourself are keeping you stuck in a pattern. Your inner struggle will dissipate once you decide to open your mind and believe that your weight loss is achievable once you change your perception about weight loss.

Anything you could ever want is possible. The only reason it hasn't been available to you before now is because you have limited your own potential through your beliefs, reinforcing thoughts, experiences and actions. Change what you believe about weight loss, and your weight loss story will change.

What makes a person believe he can change is *merely* the decision and willingness to believe he can, from his very core and being. Realize that you have everything you need right now in this very moment to succeed, and this is the moment you will *know* it is possible for you.

Scientific studies consistently demonstrate that people who believe they are worthy and capable, and have the drive and desire, will do better than those who do not. People who believe they will be successful perform better than those who doubt they will be successful. Your success has everything to do with your personal beliefs about your capabilities, and not your actual skills.[10]

In 2004, Clifford Mallett and Stephanie Hanrahan conducted a study of five male and five female elite track and field athletes from Australia who had finished in the top 10 at either the Olympic games or World Championships in the six years prior. The researchers were interested in determining what drives some athletes to achieve at the highest level while others fail to reach their physical potential. This study was a psychological review, collecting data by way of surveys and interviews. The analysis "revealed several major themes associated with the motivational processes of elite athletes: (a) they were highly driven by personal goals and achievement, (b) they had strong self-belief and (c) track and field was central to their lives."

In coming to their conclusions, the researchers reviewed motivation theories such as Self-determination, Hierarchy of Motivations and Achievement-goal Theories. It was clear that the athletes subscribed to self-determined forms of motivation. When they accomplished their goals, their perceptions of their own competence were enhanced and that, in turn, promoted more self determination.[11] The elite athletes were highly driven, they believed they would succeed, and track and field was extremely meaningful to them.

The study clearly confirmed the "success breeds success" cliche. Achieving even small successes inspires us to keep moving forward and aiming for more success.

Consider the last time you lost weight. Once the number on the scale started to decline, you felt good and were motivated by your achievement; then those feelings inspired more weight loss. When you feel strong, you act strong. That is how humans are wired.

In the world of psychology, this power of belief is called "self-efficacy." Albert Bandura coined Self-efficacy Theory in a 1977 Psychological Review article, "Self Efficacy: Toward a Unifying Theory of Behavior Change." Bandura developed his theory within the framework of Social Cognitive Theory, originally a clinical treatment for anxiety. What clinicians found, however, is that Bandura's theory applied to just about *anything* requiring psychosocial functioning, including health and exercise behavior.

Self-efficacy, as Bandura explained, means that "people's beliefs in their capabilities produce desired effects by their own actions."[12] These beliefs are about what individuals think and know they can do, *regardless of their skills.*

To apply self-efficacy theory in your weight loss context, your ability to lose weight and keep it off may be limited only by your thought processes and your view of yourself.

Your beliefs have been reinforced by past performance, experiences, verbal persuasion and physiological states, which all fuel your emotions and the meanings and associations that drive those emotions. Believing in yourself gives you the power to take action in the direction of your desires and to overcome the things that are holding you back.

DECIDE

If you want to accomplish something, then you must first expect it of yourself.

Essentially, it is all in your head. The stories you replay over and over again make them real, whether they are or not. We want to be right. We distort our truth with generalizations, we label ourselves and take an all or nothing approach.[13] We fabricate some really good stories that we tell ourselves and believe, and this is called rationalization.

Instead, believe that you can have good health, be your ideal and happy weight, and feel and look amazing. If you are reading this book, then you most likely have struggled with your weight in the past. You are reading this book because you want to lose weight and keep it off. You want to match the picture you have of yourself in your mind. You want to learn to enjoy healthy foods, stop your unhealthy food cravings and enjoy your life.

You can. You can start now.

Presuming that one of your obstacles is that you are waiting for the perfect time to "start a diet," then I say the perfect time is now. "Starting a diet" is not what you think it is, and it certainly is not what it has been in your past. This is not a "diet." This is making healthy choices in all things, and treating yourself with the great respect that you deserve. This is wellbeing.

Many diets take an all or nothing approach by eliminating food groups or restricting your favorite foods, and that is difficult to maintain over time. You may have been enticed in the past by a promise of quick weight loss. The ads, the marketing, the peddlers and product distributors are selling you hope and products. Hope is a necessity for a healthy mind, but "products" not so much. Diets like this don't work in the long run, and they are not constructive for your mental or your physical health. There is enough evidence now to suggest that it might even be better to be consistently overweight than to gain and lose over and over:[14] what is infamously called "yo-yo dieting."

Starting today is easier than you might think. Ask yourself right now, what one thing will you do today that makes you healthier than you were yesterday? You can choose anything at all that makes you feel or act healthier. You can take one step today toward your healthier, happier, ideal weight.

For example, it could be any of these actions:

- Decide to make your self-talk positive and say and think only kind words to yourself (cognitive task)
- Decide today to drink one extra glass of life-giving water than you normally would. (We are physically made of between 60 and 70 percent water, and a higher percentage is related to lean muscle mass. Water helps us gauge hunger better and, therefore, control our weight better. It plays a role in most bodily functions such as transporting nutrients and ridding our bodies of toxins, and keeps fatigue at bay.)
- Decide to drink one less soda today
- Decide to have an apple for an afternoon snack today instead of a cookie
- Decide to go for a 10-minute walk today

I do not know what you are willing to do today; but *you* know. Say what you *will* do, and not what you *won't* do. So for example, if you want to drink one fewer soda because you have three each day, then you would say, "I am going to have water with my lunch today." If you say that you are not going to have a soda at lunch today, guess what you will want? The fact is that you get more of what you focus on, so don't focus on the soda. All that you have to do in this moment is make one decision and act on it. Decide and act quickly. Once you go back to doubting or disbelieving, you will waver. Decide and act.

Journal Exercise: (download your free *Healthy Weight Success Journal* at healthinspires.com)

1) **Take this time to write the one thing in your *Healthy Weight Success Journal*, that you have complete control over and are willing to change right now. Be specific.**

I am_____

Tricia

A 120-pound weight loss started one year prior with Tricia's new lifestyle regimen. As I sat in her office to hear her story, she proudly told me, "No diet tricks, gimmicks or quick fixes. I cook every night or I turn the previous night's leftovers into sandwiches or a salad, and I exercise almost every day."

For 20 years Tricia had told herself a story that kept her stuck and believing that weight loss was not for her. That story had years of reinforcement and became her absolute truth and reality. It took Tricia many years to get to her "aha" moment: to realize she had everything she needed to succeed at weight loss and keep it off.

Up until now, Tricia played the psychological game of "I told you so" by losing 20 pounds at most on any one weight loss attempt, and then gaining it back. Her inevitable return to her previous weight reinforced her belief that losing and maintaining a healthy weight was not possible for her. This is a predictable human game that ensures that we are "right" and is simply a form of self-sabotage.

Tricia could not lose weight in the past, and she will tell you that is exactly what she believed, and she had good reasons to justify her beliefs. She has a physiological issue that makes it difficult for her to lose weight. Her grandmother had a similar clinical history, and constant comparisons between Tricia and her grandmother as she was growing up brought her to the inevitable con- clusion that losing weight was not for her. She had been overweight as a child and had a genetic predisposition for hanging on to her weight, she believed. Since the age of 15 she had tried every diet imaginable over the years: Weight Watchers, the cabbage diet, the Atkins diet and the South Beach diet, to name a few.

Tricia's breakthrough moment was based on fear. Crises have a way of forcing change.

A close family friend was diagnosed with tongue cancer from a longtime smoking habit. She was there to support her friend and observed the treatment, complications and suffering. This experience caused her pain (fear), and it was then and there that she decided it was time to quit smoking! She quit cold turkey and says it is the hardest thing she has ever done.

Kicking the habit came with an additional 50 pounds that she didn't need, and her next conclusion was obvious. It was time to figure out weight loss...again. She was motivated and believed that if she could quit smoking cold turkey, then she could accomplish anything! She established a positive neuro-association, connecting her belief in herself to the capability to lose weight, and she completely changed her story... just like that.

The meaningful achievement of her first 10-minute walk led to 60 minutes of walking a day, which then led to a passion for cycling. She said there was no way she was getting on a bike until she lost some weight, and when she had finally lost some weight, she bought a new bike!

She approached her weight loss differently this time and committed to invest in herself and to make permanent lifestyle changes. She searched for free resources and used them as motivators. She used the MyFitnessPal app for calorie tracking and awareness, and Endomondo for her cycling tracking.

Overall, Tricia lost 120 pounds, all on her own. She believed.

Tricia's story perfectly demonstrates the need to observe what story you have been telling yourself. If you have not been able to lose and keep the weight off in the past, it is time to reframe your story and your vision and see that you can. Recognize the story you have been telling yourself and replace the negative reinforcement with positive reinforcement. Decide. Decide that you are going to take amazing care of yourself and take the necessary steps according to a plan you create. To intentionally create change, BELIEVE THAT YOU ALREADY ARE WHAT IT IS THAT YOU WANT TO BE.

You will gain momentum and ease with even the smallest of wins if they are meaningful to you. Your motivators will change, because you change, your goals change, your life changes, and this is all part of the process. Losing weight is fun once you see the numbers on the scale drop.

Once you hit your target weight and you are maintaining for a while, then it may get hard again. This is because the meaning changes, and you will absolutely need new motivators. Those old habits are hardwired in your subconscious mind, and it is a decision every day to tell yourself the right story for your success; over and over and over until it becomes the new hardwiring. When I say *every day*, this means every day, every moment. Practice, practice, practice.

You wrote down in your Healthy Weight Success Journal the weight you want to be. That weight is achievable, and you will be able to maintain a weight range close to that number. We all fluctuate, and I suggest you give yourself a small range, determined by what is acceptable to you. Some people I know choose a five-pound range or a 10-pound range. Ten pounds would be a huge swing for me, so my range is small at about three pounds, and maybe four if I am really cutting loose. That is what works for me.

Take one single day at a time, and I mean one day and today only as you keep your eye on what you want for yourself and why you want it. This approach keeps you from getting overwhelmed, and all you have to do is focus on right now. Plan for tomorrow, of course, yet this moment is where you are now. All you need to do is make it through one day. That is it. One day. *The journey of a thousand miles begins with a single step.* This is your health and wellbeing journey and not a diet. This is a series of decisive and meaningful actions that become your new rituals and your new normal.

LEARN AND GROW

The 20th century psychologist, Erik Erikson, had a clear understanding that our convictions strengthen through our life span; the repetitive stories that we tell ourselves become more true over time. Erikson defined eight psychosocial stages through which we progress as we age, develop deeper convictions and solidify our identity.[15] Those convictions become our belief systems.

With each experience that life brings you, you choose to learn and grow—or not. You may have experience with diets that did not work for you in the long run. Gain wisdom and learn from those failures. Believe that you can be a healthy weight and that your past approaches may not have been the right way for you. Trying to wrap your brain around starting a restrictive diet is difficult enough, and embarking on such an endeavor immediately creates resistance. You may gain momentum and hit your number, but then, gaining weight is much easier than losing it, and the number on the scale starts to creep back up. It is insanity to keep doing this over and over again.

It does take EFFORT and DISCIPLINE and PLANNING and DECISION and ACTION to make changes in any area of your life. Could you try making a few changes that, over time, will create new habits and rituals?

Sometimes we are far from knowing who we are and what we are capable of. Sometimes it takes a crisis to push us to change. Just knowing that heart disease is the leading cause of death and that one in four of us will die from it each year isn't personal enough to push us to take immediate action to protect our health. We continue rituals that damage our health until the day comes when we no longer have a choice but to take immediate action.

A NOTE ABOUT RATIONALIZATION

A friend told me during the summer of 2015 that both his wife and son were concerned about his weight. He told his son that he didn't have a choice because, "I have to go eat Mexican food with my out-of-town clients because they always want Tex-Mex when they come to Austin." In the same conversation, he shared with me that he *would* work out *if* there were a gym by his office; but there isn't one so he could not exercise. I suggested going for walks with his wife. He replied, "But we cannot leave our child at home alone to go for a walk." Then I asked him if he could walk with a neighbor. He said he tried that, but his neighbor walks with his own wife, and so that was not an option.

I listened to my friend with complete empathy and non-judgment. It was easy to hear the self-limiting thinking—when looking from the outside. I observed the normal humanness of the conversation. Humans rationalize to make themselves right. He was not ready to change. He had a response that negated every possibility for change. He had reasons, excuses and rationalizations.

Each of us has played this game at some time, and many of us have played it more than once. We get so stuck that we cannot hear our own excuses. We believe what we say…until we choose to tell ourselves the truth. When we choose to tell the truth, we finally start to *really* hear the story we have been telling ourselves. Sometimes it helps to have our stories reflected back to us.

Journal Exercise:

2) **What has kept me from losing weight in the past or losing it and gaining it back? These are your**

obstacles as well as the stories you have been telling yourself. List your obstacles.

As you complete the obstacle exercise, I want you to recognize the strengths you have that will help you overcome these obstacles. In Part 2, we will dive deeper into this concept, but for now, I want you to become aware of the story you have been telling yourself, and then identify one or two things you can do today to begin to change your story.

Journal Exercise:

3) **I recognize that I have many strengths to overcome obstacles. The strengths I will use to overcome my obstacles are: List your strengths.**

People have asked me to tell them how to eat, and they promise they will do exactly what I tell them to do. That doesn't work long term. Telling people what to do creates resistance, and you know you really don't want anybody telling you what to do.

The truth is that you know what to do—you just haven't done it yet, or at least done it consistently. If I told you what to do, you would say, "I knew that!" We each have to decide what we are willing to do for ourselves. Brainstorming is a good exercise because it provides "suggestions for consideration," which is completely different from being told what to do. That one thing you committed to doing today (#1 in this Chapter and in your journal) is the way to your success. You deciding what you will do for you is more powerful than me deciding for you.

During one of my health awareness presentations, a member of the audience shared her Zumba instructor's method of maintaining a healthy weight. She said that her Zumba instructor keeps a bowl of fresh raw veggies out on her counter, and she munches on those as a way to keep her from less healthy choices. So, when she is hungry, she fills up on healthy foods, drinks water, goes for a walk…then she no longer wants the less healthy food she may have craved. I like this. I suggested that this is one of the "games people play." At home, *always* have fresh food prepared, available and ready to eat. Otherwise, you may come home ravenous after work and do some serious caloric intake damage. Planning and prepping are necessary strategies to healthy eating that I will discuss in Chapter 13.

Some people are thin because they truly don't think too much about food. They eat when they are hungry and stop eating when they are satisfied, and they are wired that way. Food is not their issue. For many of us, maintaining a healthy weight does take a conscious effort to make the right choices. It is a choice to eat just enough and not too much. It is a choice to eat the apple and not the cookie. It is a choice to make time for exercise. It is a choice to decide that you want to match the vision you have for yourself. This becomes easier as these choices become routines.

If being healthy is of great value to you, then attaching meaning to your health goals will help you believe that you can be healthy. YOU CAN. This is the first step toward creating the new and healthy habit. Most importantly, sometimes you might simply decide to have the damn cookie! You can have a few cookies from time to time. A few cookies are not the issue. It wasn't a few cookies that caused your weight gain. It was a culmination of choices and rituals over time: too much food, the wrong foods and not enough exercise.

Having the desire and passion to lose weight, and believing that you can, is most of the game. The other pieces are planning, action, repetition of healthy choices, gaining momentum and your actual weight loss. All of these parts are mostly psychological. Recognize and believe that the benefits of losing weight outweigh the benefits of continuing to be overweight, and create meaning around that. You are whole and complete today, and you have everything you need to take that first step to be better today than you were yesterday.

Michael Shermer, author of *The Believing Brain*, discusses "how we construct our beliefs and reinforce them as our truths" in contexts from faith to politics. He ends his book by saying how and what we choose to believe "depends on your own belief journey and how much you want to believe."[16]

Only you can decide.

Journal Exercise:

4) I believe I can: _____

_____

Believe that you can have what you want for yourself and in your life. Write what you can to do inspire and energize yourself and to focus on what you want.

2

Your Thoughts: Feelings and Emotions

"Your thoughts create your emotions, therefore, your emotions cannot prove that your thoughts are accurate."

- David D. Burns, M.D.

Cinnamon

Cinnamon hadn't realized how negative her self-talk had become. Her confidence was lacking, and it wasn't until she began her weight loss journey that she realized it.

As a newly hired employee of YMCA of Austin, she thought she would take advantage of the free gym membership to get into shape...and then soon discovered that just because she walked into a gym every day didn't mean she would use it. She found herself gaining weight and making excuses.

At the age of 39, Cinnamon decided her 40th birthday gift to herself would be her weight loss. She told herself, "You have one year to do this," and she jumped in. She called the 10 years leading up to this moment the "neglect of self-care," and believed that, like many women who become mothers, she put herself last for the sake of family. In 10 years she had tried either diet or exercise, but never both simultaneously. Now she recognized she needed both.

Her reflections captured my attention. She homed in on her confidence and self-talk.

She said, "I realize now how shallow my conversations were with (YMCA) members before my weight loss. I lacked confidence and felt that I was being judged all of the time. It was so emotional and difficult. Now I have meaningful conversations with members, and I have a story to tell to inspire them. I have so much more confidence."

She also recognized that her self-talk had completely changed. She said she realized that how you talk to yourself and tell yourself what you can and can't do is very important. Some mornings, for instance, she just *doesn't feel like working out. But instead of saying to herself, "There's no way I can do this," she now says, "I take it one minute at a time, and before I know it, I have completed the warmup, and I'm ready to go."*

Cinnamon made a personal commitment to success and built accountability into her plan by scheduling workouts with a YMCA personal trainer two mornings a week. She also added a layer of accountability and support by recruiting a fellow co-worker to join those early morning workouts. Cinnamon said that her workout buddy has come to the 6:00 a.m. workout with a migraine, and has gotten sick in the middle of the workout, and then returned to the floor to finish! That is commitment!

Even with that support system in place, the morning came when Cinnamon missed her workout. She simply didn't show up and didn't let her trainer or her co-worker know that she wasn't coming that morning. Her son needed her and she didn't want to let him down. When she got to work that day, unable to dodge her trainer, of course, Cinnamon told her "reason for missing." The trainer kindly let Cinnamon off the hook, suggesting that there are differences between reasons and excuses. That kindness made Cinnamon realize for herself, that she had counted on her son being the reason she had to miss her workout, so in actuality, that was her excuse.

In hindsight, she realized that her 14-year-old son could have helped himself, and she could have made it to her workout, honoring her personal commitment to herself and strengthening her integrity. She admits that some mornings are still hard, but she has support and accountability and focuses on her motivators to get through the hard mornings.

Cinnamon's motivators are unique to her, and she knows exactly what they are: She wants to be an inspiration for others to have a healthy lifestyle, and she wants to feel good about putting her health first and being a good role model for her family. Being an inspiration to others makes her feel good. Feeling good is the real motivator. She knows getting to her workout makes her feel good, makes her better for herself, her family and her job, and she doesn't want to disappoint her workout buddy by not showing up.

You may find it surprising that Cinnamon does not have a weight loss goal! I know that it surprised me! She isn't finished losing weight and isn't sure where she will end up, but she does know what is important to her. This is a healthy approach and it works for her. The number on the scale will not be what makes her feel good or bad about herself. Her "knowing" is a deep understanding of who she is and what motivates her.

FOCUSING ON THE POSITIVE

Work in psychology, psychoanalysis and neuroscience has come a long way since the 1960s. We now know that the human brain is a complex and fascinating organ with more than 100 billion nerves that communicate to our mind and body through connections called synapses where nerve impulses pass. Neurotransmitters are the chemical substances that transfer impulses through the synapses.

We know which part of the brain controls our emotions (limbic system), which is involved in both short- and long-term memories (temporal lobe), as well as what constitutes the executive function (frontal lobe) and analysis. The brain scans now available show which parts of the brain light up with each thought process and emotion. You can be certain with each thought comes a signal that is carried from one nerve cell to another. These signals affect our hormones and moods and change our very physiology and emotions. A thought is that powerful.

Understanding these functions enables professionals to better understand human behavior and help people get through rough patches in their lives. There are developmental and other predictable stages that occur as people age, and when a professional can explain that what a person is going through is normal, he may feel supported and, thus, be more resilient and better able to cope with his situation.

It was psychoanalyst Dr. Aaron Beck who gave us Cognitive Therapy (now known as Cognitive Behavior Therapy) back in the 1960s. Dr. Beck designed and carried out several experiments while at the University of Pennsylvania to test his theories about the origin and mechanics of depression. He learned that his depressed patients had spontaneous streams of negative thoughts that he called "automatic thoughts," and he could consistently stack them into three categories: negative ideas about 1) themselves, 2) the world and/or 3) the future. The Cognitive Therapy he developed was a new way to analyze his patients and help them change their underlying beliefs about themselves, the world and other people. This therapy brought about long-lasting change in these patients.[17]

Another psychoanalyst of the same era who worked with severely depressed patients, Dr. David Burns, attended Beck's seminars to learn this new therapy. Burns used this technique on his patients and found that it worked! His suicidal patients—who had felt worthless and told themselves that they never amounted to anything—got better. When Burns asked them to write down everything they had accomplished in their lives, he observed their positive feelings and emotions, and these patients began to realize that it didn't make sense why they felt worthless in the first place. Their previous negative thoughts and the stories they had been telling themselves did not match the real life story they wrote out in the assignment.[18]

From his observations, Burns found that depressed patients had three things in common. They 1) label themselves, 2) have an unrealistic view of what is going on in their lives (make their problems bigger than they are) and 3) take an all or nothing approach.[19]

Telling yourself a story that is not true, and believing it, is the perfect way to limit yourself. The more you tell yourself that you can't do something, the more likely you are to believe it and feel bad, and then get stuck in those negative emotions. The more you think those thoughts, the bigger the emotional hole you are digging for yourself. Labeling yourself and giving up because nothing works reinforces your belief.

Burns observed, "Your thoughts create your emotions, therefore, your emotions cannot prove that your thoughts are accurate."[20] Said even more succinctly, *your feelings are no indication that your thoughts are accurate.*

Adding to this body of thought, Dr. Carl Jung, founder of analytical psychology, discovered that his clients who focused on what was working in their lives fared better than those who focused on their problems. He found that when we focus on the positive, our horizons expand, and we see opportunities and potential. Dr. Jung wanted his clients to understand that everyone has problems, they are simply a part of life. Jung counseled that focusing on what is working in our lives doesn't make problems disappear, but it does make them lose their sense of urgency. Focusing on what you want and what is working in your life is magical.

Journal Exercise: (download your free *Healthy Weight Success Journal* at healthinspires.com)

1) **Focus on the positive. Write all of the things that are working in your life.**

We all have moments of self-doubt, anxiety and emotions that make us feel less than good, and we each experience some negative feelings to varying degrees every day.

Also, depending on how things are presented to us or how we perceive them, our brains are more likely to focus on the negative and get stuck in the negative longer. Therefore, once focused on the negative, it is more difficult to return to the positive.[21]

If I told you, for example, that there is a diet that will help you lose 50 pounds in two months, but that most people gain back 25 pounds in the following two months, you might decide not to try that diet. However, if I told you that you could lose 25 pounds in four months, and I guaranteed that you would keep it off, you would view this diet quite differently, wouldn't you? You would most likely say "yes!" If I presented you with the first scenario and then the second, research shows that you are more likely to still say "no" to the first option, or it will take you longer to get back to "yes."[22]

There are techniques we can practice that make positivity the normal tendency rather than negativity. We can train our brains to focus on the positive. It takes effort, just like any regular exercise. Some of us are naturally wired to be more positive than others, and these people are naturally in the habit of practicing positivity, which reinforces the positive.[23]

The energy that drives your every emotion, whether it is happiness, joy, sadness, depression, anxiety, fear, anticipation, disgust, courage, resilience, shame or something else, comes from the way you process your thoughts. According to the Laboratory of Neuro Imaging (LONI) at the University of Southern California, one of the foremost neurological research centers in the U.S., we have an average of 70,000 thoughts each day.[24] You have direct control over your conscious thoughts, but subconscious thoughts are less identifiable and flexible and more complex, controlling, deliberative or action-oriented than your conscious thoughts.[25]

You can be absolutely certain that the vast majority of your conscious thoughts plant seeds in your subconscious mind. There is even greater certainty that those unconscious thoughts are there because of your conscious beliefs to begin with. We process our thoughts based on what we believe to be true.

Barry Gordon, M.D., Ph.D., a professor of Therapeutic Cognitive Neuroscience and of Neurology at John's Hopkins, said, "The intrusive thoughts you may experience throughout the day or before bed illustrate the disconcerting fact that many of the functions of the mind are outside of conscious control. Whether we maintain true control over any mental functions is the central debate about free will." He added, "We exert some power over our thoughts by directing our attention, like a spotlight, to focus on something specific."

The author or co-author of more than 150 scientific articles and book chapters, Dr. Gordon shared that even though thoughts sometimes seem to suddenly pop into our awareness, it is more likely those thoughts have "been simmering for a while" in the subconscious. He said, "Controlling the thoughts that you can will eventually help the subconscious thoughts that fuel your fears and your emotions that are not beneficial."[26]

Your subconscious is your involuntary *sleeping* mind that responds automatically. Your conscious mind is your *waking* mind of voluntary thoughts that feed your subconscious. This is to say, if you are thinking peaceful, kind, loving, happy and positive thoughts, then you are creating the conditions for a harmonious subconscious mind. Your subconscious mind responds to the conditions you consistently plant with your conscious thoughts. Thus, you create your reality through both your conscious and unconscious thoughts.

You have complete control over your conscious thoughts. That means you can decide to stop your thoughts, change your thoughts or redirect your thoughts. You simply have to decide that you want to do it and focus on what you want, specifically.

The internationally renowned self-help author and motivational speaker Dr. Wayne Dyer said, "Your subconscious mind rules your world." Your thoughts, whether you realize it or not, make you feel a certain way, and your body and mind respond to that feeling. It is in your best interest to take an active role in rewriting your thoughts—the story you tell yourself. You can do that by making sure what you are telling yourself is the actual truth, not an exaggeration or a version that twists the facts. Controlling your conscious thoughts will help you override subconscious ones.

Become aware of your thoughts, and allow only healthy, positive ones to process. This will enable you to create new habits and new beliefs that rewire your subconscious mind. Habits are things you do and think without even realizing it, they are *automatic* and of the subconscious mind. Learn to recognize your habits, rituals and consistent behaviors that have gotten you where you are today. You can change your rituals by knowing what you want, by reframing your story, and by saying and writing what you want in the present tense as if it were already happening. Creating a plan is also part of this process. More on planning in Part 2.

MANAGING MOODS

"Where an emotion is a single note, clearly struck, hanging for a moment in the still air, a mood is the extended, nearly inaudible echo that follows."[27]

Every now and then I feel like being grumpy, and I give myself a short amount of time to "enjoy that." Then, I get over it. I have practiced that for years, and it works for me. Sometimes I just want to be left alone for a bit. That self-awareness quickly moves me through a mood that benefits no one.

A mood is typically a state of mind that surfaces after the events of your day have played with your emotions. Moods don't always have an explanation; sometimes they just seem to come over us. As we know more about physiology and brain function, we learn that moods also have much to do with your natural circadian rhythms, your hormone fluctuations throughout the day (more fluctuations for women of course), how much sleep you are getting, your stress level, your physical activity, your sex life, your social life, the last time you ate (and what you ate). Sugary snacks can bring you up and bring you down and make you crave more sugary snacks. Too much alcohol, saturated fats, processed and refined foods are not good for you or your mood. Stressors play a role in your moods, and exercise helps you cope with stress, and so does sleep. Yep—diet and exercise.

Contemporary neuroscience research continues to yield new and exciting discoveries. For a long time, scientists believed that we are born with a certain number of brain cells and that we do not generate new ones, but that theory has been disproven. Neuroscientists have discovered that new nerve cells continually develop in the hippocampus, an important part of the limbic system and the brain's center for *mood* and emotion. We can generate 700 new neurons per day in the hippocampus![28] What was once thought to be something that occurred only prenatally is now discovered to occur in the adult brain as well. This is called neurogenesis—the growth of nervous tissue, and in this case, brain neurons.

But whether you are generating new brain cells every day depends completely on your diet (rich in colorful plant foods), exercise (most days if not every day), whether you are building new neural pathways by being curious and constantly learning new things, as well as how you process your thoughts. Mood, emotion and memory are all affected by this same self-care just described, which helps you build new brain cells.

If you have a positive mindset, and stimulate your mental and physical health in the ways described, then you will stimulate brain cell growth. If you maintain a negative outlook, then you lessen your potential for brain cell growth. We know that exercise will elevate your mood, and we know that exercise is one factor that stimulates brain cells. If you are choosing less than healthy foods with artificial ingredients and refined sugars, then your brain is not firing on all cylinders, and this can affect your mood with hormone highs and lows. Everything is connected.

Be aware of your daily routines and how they affect your highs and lows. You may be a night owl or a morning person, depending on when your energy wanes during the day. When you are tired, you are likely to have lower tolerance for stress and experience greater stress related to things you typically handle well. When your stress level is high, hormones like cortisol and norepinephrine wreak more havoc on your mood, not to mention your physiology. Production of these hormones has been tied to weight gain, and now we know that this affects your neurogenesis.

You may already realize that stress impairs your cognitive functioning, but now you know it can also impair your ability to "grow" new brain cells. I don't know about you, but I'll take all of those that I can get! The best strategy to keep those cells regenerating is to invest in self-care, making healthy choices in mind, body and spirit that prevent debilitating or destructive moods, and choosing happiness every day.

Be aware of your natural circadian rhythms and what times of day you experience predictable energy lows. Know what times of day you are more susceptible to making poor food choices or engaging in less than healthy behaviors when you feel an energy low. What are your natural tendencies or habits at those times? Also, know when your best times are, when you are freshest and sharpest.

Journal Exercise:

2) **What times of day are my natural energy lows?**

3) **What are my tendencies during these times?**

4) What are the times of day when I am naturally sharp, fresh and at my best?

REGULATING MOOD

My energy wanes in the late afternoon, and by about 3:00 or 4:00 p.m., I am getting hungry and a little tired. If I haven't packed a healthy snack, I will be edgy on my drive home through traffic. Very edgy. This mood is preventable and so is being that hungry! I have learned to always have a whole food snack with me, in my purse or in my car, such as an apple, almonds, peanuts or clementines. I never leave home without something.

Prevention is always the best strategy, as there are constructive ways to get through those lows. Planning how you will get through these daily energy lows will help you create healthier habits. If you turn to food and choose unhealthy snacks, caffeine, sugary drinks or alcohol to get over your low, then planning a better strategy will help. Better strategies include taking a power nap, reading a book, calling a friend, going for a brisk walk or engaging in any type of exercise. Any of these solutions will get you through the low or stressful part of your day, and exercise is shown to be the best mood regulator.

Exercise sends blood to the brain and increases your energy. It changes your physiology immediately and promotes a positive mood and thoughts. Getting enough exercise, sleep and rest is as important to your good health as anything else. I discuss these healthful habits in more detail in Chapter 13. Taking a short power nap can make all of the difference in your mood and cognition: Fewer than 30 minutes of sleep will give you a power boost, while more than that might make you groggy.

Supported by clinical evidence, eating right and exercising are at the top of the list of the best mood regulators, stress coping mechanisms, body-shaping and -changing, mind- and life-altering things you can ever do for yourself. Exercise is medicine for those suffering from depression, and not exercising is a depressant. The problem is, when one is depressed, finding motivation to exercise is not an easy task. Those who engage in these mood boosters will get better sooner.[29]

Whether you are exercising now or remember how great it felt when you *were* exercising, write in your journal how you feel/felt when you are/were exercising. It is good to remind yourself of the emotions and feeling of strength and energy that accompany exercise.

Journal Exercise:

5) How do I feel when I exercise?

Presuming that you feel energized when you are exercising, discover why feeling that way is important to you.

6) Why is feeling this way important to me?

The next time you are having a daytime low, could you take a break and go for a brisk walk? Can you leave your desk at work for five or 10 minutes to take a brisk walk along the hallways or outside for a bit? Get blood flow to the brain, relieve a little tension, and the quick refresh will make you feel better and ready to work again once you come back to your desk. This is also a great strategy to stop the tendency to go to the cafe for a sweet treat. A walk will help you break that habit.

7) The next time I have a daytime low, I will _____ to take care of myself.

HANDLING STRESS

We have each learned from personal experience that stress is exhausting! We know now—thanks to the research of Hans Selye, MD, the endocrinologist who discovered and studied the effects of stress on the human body—that stress plays a role in all disease. He discovered that when he exposed his lab animals to persistent agitations like blaring lights and loud noises, they all develop the same pathological responses that humans present when under stress, such as kidney disease, stroke, heart attacks, inflammation of the adrenals, shrinkage of the lymphoid tissue and even rheumatoid arthritis.[30] Not coping well with stress can result in cognitive impairment, withdrawal, depression and changes in physiology.

All of these bad things happen because of your body's chemical response to stress. When you are stressed, your brain sends a biochemical message to your body to release cortisol, norepinephrine and adrenaline. This is the automatic fight or flight response mechanism that prepares us to confront or flee danger. This is a helpful life-saving response when you are faced with an imminent threat; but in modern times, this mechanism is responding not to a short-term, life-or-death situation but to chronic stress, which can wreak havoc on your physiological and mental health. When the stress hormones signal, your heart races, your blood pressure spikes, your muscles tense, blood retreats to your core, and your body breaks down glucose and fatty acids for quick energy. With chronic stress, you are turning those mechanisms on and off for days or sometimes weeks at a time. Scientists believe the unused energy that is now running through your blood potentiates blood clotting, increases your triglycerides, lines your arteries with LDL (lousy) cholesterol and helps to increase your risk for heart disease. We know that in high moments of stress, heart irregularities are more likely to occur.[31]

The American Heart Association says that stress does not cause high blood pressure, but it does cause your blood pressure to spike. High blood pressure (hypertension) damages your arteries. It puts pressure and strain on your artery walls, causing damage with every heartbeat. Clinical research has not yet pin-pointed the way stress affects the heart, but studies do show that stress contributes to heart disease, as it affects behaviors that increase heart disease risk, some of which I just mentioned. Stress is harmful to your mental, emotional and physical health.

The role stress plays in emotional eating has a lot to do with a habitual response (your subconscious mind and trigger) to stressors, and then your hormones get out of whack and you get caught in a vicious cycle. The release of hormones hurts the regulation of your appetite, and you may seek food as your emotional response. Choosing to believe that your thoughts, diet and exercise can change this cycle is much more to your benefit than believing that your genetics and hormones are dictating your choices. We are talking about what is and is not within your control. In many cases, if not most, your hormones are a mess because of the state of your health and not the other way around.

It might interest you to know that people of average weight have less of a tendency to cope with stress by overeating. This tendency is found more in the overweight population to begin with.[15] People have conditioned themselves to respond to stress in good and bad ways: Know that you can manage stress through the way you process your thoughts.

Learning to handle your stress starts with altering your beliefs, thoughts and rituals; changing toward a tendency to positivity; watching your diet; and getting enough physical activity and sleep. Your self-care comes first, and then you will handle stress better. You have to feel good first and then you take action.

Dr. Selye, the researcher who coined the term "stress," once said, "Only the dead have no stress." He believed that we need to learn to handle problems that we can control and not concern ourselves with those that are just part of life and are unsolvable. This is similar to Jung's prescription. Selye recognized that acute stress is completely subjective, and that two people can have the very same experience yet process it quite differently. How we perceive and process our world comes from a culmination of our life experiences. We all have stress, and life will hand us all crisis situations. How we choose to handle the crises that face us is completely up to us.

When presented with a problem, assess the situation for what it is. Stop and take a few really deep breaths. Breath in deeply through your nose for several seconds, hold your breath for a few seconds and then exhale through your mouth. Breathing deliberately has a calming affect that directly counters the physiological responses to stress. Breathing techniques decrease your blood pressure, relax your muscles and enable you to think more clearly. Then take a walk to clear your head. It works. There are solutions and resources for many of our problems; all you have to do is decide to take the first step. Once you take the first step, it is easier to see the light at the end of the tunnel.

We cope better with crisis when we have support and when we take control of the things that are able to be controlled. But do not wait for the crisis! If you start making healthy choices today, you are less likely to face a health crisis.

And don't forget that some stress is good stress. Good stress (eustress) helps you be more productive on a deadline, for example. You will feel good stress when you are accomplishing a task that is evenly matched with your skill set and has the right amount of challenge. Too much of a challenge or a project not matched with your skill set will cause awful stress. If you feel this way in the early stages of a project, it is a good time to ask for help. The way we handle stress largely impacts our life satisfaction.

What we have learned about coping with stress is that it starts with how we process our thoughts. Dr. Abraham Maslow, who developed the Human Hierarchy of Needs, said that a peaceful approach to tackling problems within our control is to simply handle them and to not concern ourselves with the things that are not in our control. This sounds like the philosophy of Drs. Jung and Selye. It also sounds like the Serenity Prayer, authored by the American theologian Reinhold Niebuhr.

Serenity Prayer
God, grant me the serenity to accept the things I cannot change,
Courage to change the things I can,
And wisdom to know the difference.

There is no value in worrying. You simply must work it out and solve the problem at hand.

Stress is inevitable, and we need to learn to better manage it. Listen to and learn from the experts—from Beck to Burns, from Selye to Maslow and Seligman (more to come on Seligman)—and heed the wisdom of spiritual leaders from any peaceful faith.

APPROACHING CHANGE
In the same way there are predictable stages of grief with the loss of a loved one (denial, anger, bargaining, depression and acceptance), there are predictable stages of change. You are reading this book because you are thinking of change. You are either thinking about losing weight, or ready to lose weight now. If you are contemplating weight loss, then keep thinking about it! The more you think about it, the closer you get to

doing something about it. You get what you focus your attention on.

The stages of change are:

1) Pre-contemplation - You are not ready or thinking about change
2) Contemplation - You are thinking about change
3) Preparation - You are preparing to take action
4) Action - You are taking action
5) Maintenance - You are maintaining a good practice

I like to remind you that it is important to feel good. You can feel good by recognizing all of the things that are working well in your life while you are making changes in the areas of your life that need changes. This helps to keep you in a healthy mindset. If you are reading this book, you are most likely in stage 2 or 3 of your weight loss journey.

The breakthroughs we eventually have do not happen out of the blue or overnight, although they may seem that way. Change comes typically after much contemplation, and then BOOM! One day you take action! When you DECIDE is when change happens.

In Chapter 1, I shared that Tricia contemplated weight loss her entire life. She had prepared and taken action numerous times, but not every weight loss journey needs to take a lifetime. Contemplation does not need to be a long process at all. However, in order to take action and be successful, you have to focus your thoughts on what you want and not on what you don't want. Your desire is to lose weight, and you are working on changing your thoughts (stage 3, preparation) so that you may take action.

In order to get to stage 4, you need to start framing things in a positive way. Once you focus on what you want, you will attract that very thing into your life. The moment you have self doubt, or focus on what you don't want, you will immediately be challenged. Resistance is a guarantee to get more of what you don't want. It is a negative emotion, and it conjures up many other negative emotions. Any negative approach or type of avoidance of any kind will naturally trigger your inhibitions. This is how our brains are wired. The minute you focus on what you do not want, i.e., "I do not want to be overweight," or "I cannot have chips," then I promise you, that is exactly what you are going to get. You are going to crave chips, and think about chips, and struggle with those darn chips! You will focus on the fact that you are overweight and you will be in an unnecessary struggle with yourself.

On the other hand, focusing on what you do want, such as being thin, looking and feeling good, and having confidence, will keep you going in that direction. Feel-good neurotransmitters, dopamine and serotonin, are associated with the reward center of your brain, and those kick in with positive thoughts and actions. Taking action toward what you want is rewarded, and it releases these happy and motivational neurotransmitters. Stephen Covey, author of the Seven Habits of Highly Effective People, told us to *begin with the end in mind*. Thinking this way clears the path, provides clarity, and gives you strength, direction and energy to act.

Jeremiah

My friend Jeremiah approached his 50-pound weight loss simply. He treated it like a problem he wanted to solve. He knew what he had control over and took the necessary steps to "check off his list" each task to be completed. He said that he had been thinking about weight loss (contemplation), so when he went for his annual biometric screenings and saw results that he did not like, he moved immediately into stage 3 of change: preparation.

When this lean man with a great sense of humor told me that he had lost 50 pounds, I couldn't believe it! I couldn't even picture his frame any differently from what I saw at that moment. Of course, I asked him how he did it, and he told me as matter of factly as I am sharing this with you. He said, "I didn't like my numbers, so I thought about what I was willing to change. I don't care too much about dessert, so I won't have dessert. I love my coffee, so I am not giving up coffee. I drank it with a lot of cream and sugar, so I stopped putting cream and sugar in it, and now I drink it black. I enjoy a drink sometimes, so I am not giving that up." He went down his list of things he was willing or unwilling to change.

Jeremiah's weight gain happened over time as part of aging, lack of exercise and retaining the eating habits from his youth. His breakthrough moment was seeing his numbers, and that moved him from stage 2, contemplation, to stages 3 and 4, preparation and action, respectively. It took him about seven months to lose 50 pounds with this approach, and he is successfully maintaining his lower weight now (stage 5, maintenance).

His long-term success includes Saturday morning weekly meal planning and grocery list creating with his wife. He said that his entire family eats healthier with meal planning, and they also waste less food.

Jeremiah simply took the information he was given at face value, and handled it. He didn't like what he saw, so he changed it. He didn't make it bigger than it was, but he didn't minimize it either. He simply decided. I should add that he entertains in his role at work, and that means he eats out a lot. But Jeremiah figured it out and makes healthy choices. Notably, he took the path of least resistance by focusing on what came easy to him.

Now Jeremiah often invites our friends to join him in fun runs and other active events. His interest in events and activities that keep him healthy is a natural progression that follows any big change in life. As we achieve our goals, our motivators change because *what is meaningful to us also changes. We are NEVER the same person day after day, as long as we are learning, growing and experiencing life. Change one thing in your life that makes you better, and that will affect other parts of your life. Your emotions and energy change, you are happier, you begin to achieve other things as well. One change for the better makes everything better.*

CREATING HEALTHY HABITS

Anticipation is a positive mood booster. If you tend to be an emotional eater, then you might happily anticipate eating that cake you have at home when you walk through the front door at the end of a long and stressful day. (By the way, saying or believing that you are an emotional eater (labeling) also contributes to you being an emotional eater). If you recall, psychiatrist Dr. Burns said that if you label yourself, have an unrealistic view of what is going on in your life or take an all or nothing approach, it's a sure way to limit your potential, reinforce your belief and keep you stuck where you are or worse.

What if, instead, you create new things to joyfully anticipate upon walking in your front door after a long day? A new hobby or dream that you are chasing can change your life on a dime! What about a book you have been wanting to read? You may plan to take a walk as soon as you get home (shoes and shorts on and right back out the door before you go to the kitchen!), meet a friend after work, solidify vacation plans or go to the movies. Make a plan to do whatever it is that you look forward to so you can start creating new rituals and break your old habits.

"Mindless" eating takes you to the pantry where you pop snacks into your mouth just because the food is in front of you. This is a bad habit that results in poor health, unwanted weight gain and unhealthy thoughts and feelings that you don't need. Because most emotional eaters overeat due to perceived stress, the answer is to cope with stress better by recognizing the triggers and having a plan.

Two people can be exposed to the same stressor and respond to it differently. One walks to the pantry and one goes for jog. One calls a friend, and one grabs a drink. One is short tempered with a friend, and one gently asks for consult. How you respond to life's circumstances and events will make all the difference in your wellbeing. You have choices in how you respond to stressors, and the better choices you make will create your new and better habits that will eventually override the conscious and subconscious habits you have now. It starts with your thoughts, and repetition is key.

As Proverbs 23:7 reminds us - For as he thinks in his heart, so is he.

Pausing before speaking or taking action can save you from agony. Our thoughts process in milliseconds: individual neurons, active for only 20-30 milliseconds, mediate our perceptions.[32] That means by the time we finish a thought, it has already processed and resulted in a feeling, and we are ready to take immediate action on that emotion.

When a craving hits you, and you immediately desire the pleasurable feeling that you get from eating the sugary or fat-loaded carbohydrate comfort food you are craving, practice pausing first and immediately taking a different action.

The pause test will help you change your present behavior and is an exercise that helps you recognize your subconscious and conscious triggers that define your habits. Pausing will help you consciously make the right choices.

Before you speak or take action following a thought; ask yourself this question:

WILL WHAT I AM ABOUT TO DO OR SAY BRING ME PEACE OR DISCONTENT?

When you have the thought to walk to the pantry and have a snack that you are craving (or whatever the unhealthy habit is for you)—perhaps because you feel stressed, not because you're hungry—follow these three steps to start conditioning yourself for a better and healthier lifestyle:

- **Stop and observe yourself.** Realize that you are telling yourself you need something that you clearly do not need. Recognize how the human brain works, and decide that it is so ridiculous that we can tell ourselves we need what we don't need. This is called rationalization. And when we resist, it causes pain. Resistance lowers our inhibitions, and we are more likely to cave because we are focusing on what we can't have, and we get what we give attention to. So instead, focus on how you want to look by losing weight and the energy you want to feel and whatever else is meaningful to you. It could be CONFIDENCE that you want. SELF CONTROL is POWERFUL. It strengthens your integrity and strengthens you. So now, when you start to walk toward the pantry, you will stop and observe that you are telling yourself you need something you clearly do not need. Your thoughts control your reality, so it is your thoughts you must control.

- **Have a planned distraction** for these moments and act quickly! You already know what your rituals are, so you will be practicing this game of "when this happens, then I will do that." This is your pre-planned strategy. So, for example, when I walk to the pantry out of habit, I am going to recognize it and *immediately* turn about face and walk out the front door for a brisk walk around my block. You *must* have a plan for when you recognize a trigger and act on it immediately. You want to recondition yourself to create a new habit. The thought comes fast! You must respond quickly to the thought that comes right after your pause for observation. Take up a new hobby that keeps your hands busy, call a friend or sit down to read a book you have been meaning to read. Read outside or in a different room far from the kitchen.

  If you have children, it is more difficult to avoid the kitchen, but you must never blame them for snacks you prepare that you decide to munch on. You have full control of what goes in your mouth. Clean the kitchen and "close" it just like our parents did. Create the plan that will work for you. Remember that it is not all about the food. It is about the patterns you have created and that you can change. One woman I coached who wanted to lose weight discovered that putting her tea pot in the garage helped her to exercise in the morning. Why? Her pattern was to wake up, put the water on to heat for her tea, and then proceed to sit and enjoy her tea with a muffin and never exercise. Changing that ritual helped her get to her apartment gym three days a week. Plan a distraction.

- **Celebrate!** Every time you make the "right" choice is a reason to celebrate! Success breeds success. You rewrite your story by tying a positive emotion to your achievement. That positive emotion will keep you focused, engaged and happy to make these decisions every chance you can. Celebrating small, daily successes makes life more fun and creates meaning. You don't work all year—from January to December—before you reward yourself for hard work: You reward yourself along the way. You buy a new shirt or go to dinner at your favorite restaurant or take a vacation. Celebrate every day. Small achievements eventually turn into the largest accomplishments. Pat yourself on the back along the way. Do a happy dance, and scream,

"___ yea!"…or whatever it is for you. Make it a celebration. You only need one in a row to get the ball rolling. It is the small steps that lead to lasting change. Today is one in a row and then tomorrow is two in a row and every day is one more day. One day at a time, and you celebrate with each achievement until it becomes the new pattern, the new ritual, the new habit and the new you who is no longer counting days.

Think of something in your life that you made happen because of your focus, desire and discipline. Anything worthwhile takes effort and practice. Changing our bad habits takes discipline and time. We spend our time on the things that we value. Taking time for self-care makes you better for you and all of those around you.

Some psychological literature suggests overcoming emotional eating is not about discipline. It might not solely be about discipline, yet it does take discipline! You can overcome emotional eating by believing that you can, controlling your self-talk, processing thoughts and stressors in the right ways, and finally, being willing to change. We have learned that people who believe they are capable are more successful than those who focus on their perceived lack of ability.[33] Believing you are capable is the first step.

MASTERING WELLBEING

Wellness is the presence of wellbeing. Wellbeing is the practice of life- and health-giving habits and being in a state of healthy mind, body and spirit. That means that diet, exercise and sleep are as important to your wellbeing as having a sense of purpose and practicing gratitude, which we will talk about in the next chapter.

Your wellbeing encompasses your self-talk, the way you handle stress and the way you treat your physical body through restful and restorative sleep, proper nutrition and physical activity. It also includes your spiritual awareness, and knowing your true and authentic self. To master your wellbeing, you must practice these life- and health-giving habits every day so that healthy habits and rituals become your default way of thinking and behaving. This includes enjoying your favorite things in life, food among them. Practice, practice, practice.

As you move to changing your thoughts to achieve wellbeing and your healthy weight, I want you to fully realize that your weight loss is about much more than your weight. Your wellbeing includes your overall life satisfaction, to include meaning and purpose and the quality of your relationships. If food is your main focus, then I know that your needs are not being met. As humans we have the same basic needs for food, shelter and belonging; and then, because we live in an affluent society, we have higher level needs for self-fulfillment. How we approach those higher level needs is different for each of us, and we want those approaches to be constructive and not destructive.

The pioneer of self-actualization, Dr. Abraham Maslow, presented the Human Hierarchy of Needs in the book *Motivation and Personality* in 1954. At the very top of his hierarchy pyramid sits the self-actualized person, and I promise, that is where you want to be. When you are self-actualized, you are meeting your potential, you are fulfilled, content and have purpose in your life.

It is important that you take one step toward self-actualization today, in the right and healthy direction for you. One step is all you need to take, and it is as simple as deciding and believing that you can. I know that you can.

When I notice people's weight loss, I typically pay them a compliment and ask how they did it. I have heard responses like, "It is just coming off. I am eating a little healthier." Some respond with something like, "I don't know what I am doing differently," or "I started walking three miles a day and I lost 30 pounds in a year." When I hear those stories, I speculate that other things in those people's lives DID change—once they took the first step in the right direction. You do not walk three miles every day and stay the same physically, mentally or emotionally. You become a different person in the way that Carl Jung described. Your mind opens, your horizons expand and you see opportunities. You probably make healthier diet choices too.

It deserves repeating that Burns said your emotions are no indication that your thoughts are accurate, and as it says in Proverbs 23:7: For as he thinks in his heart, so is he. As reinforcement, the influential and successful Henry Ford once said, "Whether you think you can, or you think you can't—you are right."

3

Positive Psychology: Techniques and Peacefulness

Positive actions and outcomes stem from positive energy and emotion.

– THE POSITIVE PRINCIPLE

The science of positive psychology is the study of human virtues and strengths that enable us as individuals and communities to thrive. It is founded on the belief that each of us wants to live a meaningful and fulfilling life, that we each want to cultivate what is best within ourselves, and that we want to enhance our experience of love, work and play. This positive psychology philosophy or approach was pioneered by Dr. Abraham Maslow in his 1954 book *Motivation and Personality*.

The current leading authority in the field of Positive Psychology is Dr. Marty Seligman. He has written more than

250 scholarly publications and about 20 books on this science. He studies human character traits such as resilience, learned helplessness, depression, optimism and pessimism and is an expert on interventions that prevent depression and build strengths and wellbeing. Wellbeing, as described in the last chapter, is the practice of life- and health-giving habits, including a sense of purpose, the practice of gratitude, a positive outlook, good habits such as regular exercise and a healthy diet, healthy relationships and overall life satisfaction.

The science of positive psychology has three central precepts and those are:

1. Positive Emotions:
   - Contentment with the past
   - Happiness in the present
   - Hope for the future

2. Positive Individual Traits and Strengths, such as:
   - Humor
   - Playfulness
   - Resilience
   - Courage
   - Discipline
   - Positivity
   - Creativity
   - Analytic Strength
   - Strategic Vision
   - Relating Ability

3. Positive Institutions, such as:
   - Teamwork
   - Community
   - Tolerance
   - Leadership
   - Purpose
   - Sense of Justice

The very premise of positive psychology is that we first generate positive emotions and energy, and that energy and emotion result in positive actions and outcomes.[34] This is why giving attention to the way you process your thoughts is worthy of your time. We have to feel good first before we take positive action.

As part of a hospital-based health challenge I led with the help of many engaged volunteers, I sent pre- and post-surveys to participants to measure certain physical (objective) and emotional (subjective) factors. During the course of the challenge, we measured weight, waist circumference, height, BMI, blood pressure, HgA1C and blood cholesterol. Our 90-day challenge results were inspiring and life changing for many participants. The 23 participants who completed the health challenge lost a total of 219.25 pounds and 62.25 inches off their waists.

I thought most significant were the positive feelings, newfound energy and confidence that weight loss gave the participants. I wanted to focus on their subjective view of happiness, so I specifically measured *happiness* in the post-survey. The survey question simply read, "Do you feel happier?" Of the 23 participants who responded to the survey, 91 percent said they were happier at the end of the health challenge than before it started.

When I reported on the success of our health challenge to the CEO, I homed in on the happiness outcome, sharing the premise of positive psychology that positive emotion and energy (happiness) results in positive actions and outcomes. What that means for a CEO is that happier employees are more engaged and more productive. We get more done, more efficiently and with better energy when we feel good. And that is good for patient care, good for our hospital and good for the employees and every life they touch.

There is a very funny former Emergency Department RN, Liz Jazweic, who is on the healthcare speaker circuit. Liz is obese, and she lets audiences know she has struggled with weight her entire life, although weight is not her primary subject matter. She says that when she gets home from a business trip, she goes straight to the scale. If the number is higher or the same as before her trip, she heads for the cookies. On the other hand, if the number is lower, she does a happy celebration dance. Can you feel that? This is EXACTLY the energy that a thought process can catalyze. Seeing a higher number on the scale produces an emotion that does not feel good, and she proceeds to act on that negative emotion. When the number looks good, she has a positive thought that produces a positive emotion, and the resulting action is the happy dance!

We build on these emotions. This is why small successes are crucial to any success, and especially weight loss success.

Inch by inch it's a cinch, no pun intended. The all or nothing approach is hard to sustain, and then when you slip up, like we all do from time to time, you might feel like you failed and give up. The right approach is to start from that moment and get back on track. Those derailing moments will happen less and less often and in less significant ways as you reinforce your new habits. Taking small steps toward success keeps you on track and allows new habits to be formed.

In order to move forward and away from your past unhealthy habits, you need to tell your story the right way and move on. That means not *dwelling* on WHY you have failed, or *dwelling* on WHY you haven't been able to lose the weight and analyzing it to death. That will keep you stuck. It is okay to recognize why it hasn't worked for you in the past, to learn from it and decide what you are going to do about it today. You recognize the past as the past, then make choices today that give you hope for an amazing tomorrow. It is better to focus on WHY you want to lose weight. That is the positive approach. It makes you feel good, and it makes you focus on what you want and why it is meaningful to you. Then you want to enjoy the journey. When you go for a bike ride, for example, enjoy and focus on the bike ride, not weight loss.

You have everything you need in this moment to head in the direction of your dreams. You are complete as you are now and everything you are in this moment is because of every decision and choice and life situation that you have experienced up until this point. That is your past.

Your next choice, in the present moment, can change the direction of your future. It could be as simple as a choice about your next snack, or whether you drink water or soda in the afternoon, if you use kind words or not, if you go for a walk today or not. More significantly, it could be a major shift and life-changing choice that is constructive or destructive, or staying in a job or leaving for a better opportunity.

We will cover the first precept of Positive Psychology, positive emotions, in this chapter; then follow in Chapters 4 and 5 with positive individual traits/strengths and positive institutions. Positive emotions result from having contentment with the past, happiness in the present and hope for the future. These ideas have everything to do with the way that you look at things and how you process your thoughts and tell your story.[35]

Let's look at these factors as they apply to your weight loss and your thoughts.

POSITIVE EMOTIONS:
Contentment with the past

To find contentment with the past, it's necessary to rewrite the story you tell yourself. The purpose is to learn and grow from your past by determining what you gained from it and how it strengthened you. Finding the positive message from your past makes life more fulfilling. Contentment with the past means that you do not blame anybody for your weight gain, for your genes, your stress level or your current situation.

No matter what's in your past, you have allowed it to show up in some way through life choices, food choices, lack of exercise or high stress levels. Taking ownership of those factors, processes, stories and choices is a great place to start. Rethinking and reframing the way you tell yourself your story can open your mind to opportunities you may have missed before now. Blame is the worst and most negative emotion outside of regret. You cannot change the past. None of us have control over the past. The past is the past. It is what it is. You do, however, have complete control over your thoughts and how you want to process your story.

The reward center of the brain is associated with feel-good memories that create a sense of nostalgia, like when your mom or dad took you to McDonald's when you were a child. Recognize that this is a great memory and a nice story, yet it may also be part of the reason you created a fast food habit that contributed to your weight gain. It may have been a behavior you practiced over time because you associated it with happy times spent with your mom or dad. Focus on what you have learned and how it can make you better and stronger and more resilient. What you can take from this specific example is that your parents wanted to share some meaningful moments with you. That is good! Now you have the opportunity to make the right choices. You cannot change your past, yet you can change now.

Returning to Tricia's story from Chapter 1, she recognized the story she used to tell herself was one that had her believing weight loss was not ever going to be in the plan for her. She changed her story by going for that first 10-minute walk. She realized she needed to get back in the kitchen and cook for her family, and she took full responsibility. She changed her story. She didn't want to pay for Weight Watchers any more, knowing she would cheat on it anyway. Tricia decided that was in her past and she learned from it.

Dr. Marty Seligman helps us learn to tell ourselves the right stories and have contentment with our past. In his book *What You Can Change and What You Can't*, he explored whether childhood events influence our adult personalities and if we can blame our parents. He concluded after reviewing numerous studies, "If you want to blame your parents for your own adult problems, you are entitled to blame the genes they gave you, but you are not entitled—by any facts I know—to blame the way they treated you."[36]

I read that as a light-hearted and nice way to remind us not to blame others and to take every opportunity in the present moment to create the life that we want for ourselves. He suggests that you can't blame anybody for who you are.[37] We all have one thing in common, and that is free will to make our own choices. Blame is a nice way to keep yourself stuck right where you are. If it is something that you cannot control, then accept that for what it is and don't spend energy on it. There is nothing you can do about that or your past.

Contentment with the past simply means you cannot change something that happened one second ago or something that happened years ago in your childhood. No blame, no resentment, and it is time to give attention to the present moment, which fuels your future direction and opportunities.

Journal Exercise: (download your free *Healthy Weight Success Journal* at healthinspires.com)

To rewrite your story, write down all of your excuses (reasons, self limitations, any of your "buts") you have ever had that supported your weight gain, being overweight and staying overweight. Write down all of the past stories and phrases you can think of that supported unhealthy habits or that gave you permission to be overweight. These could be things like you were told to clean your plate, or your parents always said you were big boned, or your mom gave you snacks the size of meals, or you have sugar cravings and sugar calls your name.

1) **Write your story of past self-limitations. List all of the excuses you've used and the limitations you have put on yourself that have kept you from being who you want to be.**

Next, I want you to rewrite your story in a positive frame, in a way that tells you what you learned from the past. For example: I am lean and mean and maintaining a healthy weight. I look good and feel good. I am big boned and I am 20 pounds lighter. I make half of my plate vegetables, and eat a smaller portion of the main course. I eat slowly and pay attention to my internal signals, so that when I feel satisfied, I stop eating. I pack a healthy lunch, which makes my sugar cravings dissipate. I believe I can and know I can and I am_____.

2) **Write a true story about all that you are and all that you know you can be and achieve. Look at the phrases you wrote above and reframe them in a truthful and positive way that enables you to overcome limitations and achieve your goals.**

The point of rewriting your story is to rid yourself of any negative emotions you have held onto that contributed to being overweight. You have no control over the past, including one minute ago! Move forward. The clean slate starts now. It is a choice, and we make choices one moment at a time in the present moment.

Happiness in the Present

The second premise of positive psychology is finding happiness in the present. The more we attend to positive and present moments, the better and more positive our intentions will be for future moments. Focus on what you have control over in this moment and let go of what you don't have control over. It is a waste of time and energy to struggle with or spend emotional time on something outside of your control. Maslow said it, Jung said it, and you know it's true!

Happiness in the present is the strengths-based approach to cultivating what is best in yourself. Happiness in the present comes with attention to present moments that direct a positive future. Making choices that align your thoughts, feelings and behaviors results in a peaceful existence. Incongruence in your thoughts, actions and feelings is miserable. For example, if you want to lose weight and you are ready to go for a walk, and that thought makes you feel good—and you go for a walk—angels are singing! That is congruency and it feels amazing! But if you want to lose weight and you are ready to go for a walk—but instead you sit down and eat a big, heavy dinner and then lay down on the couch because it made you lethargic—that doesn't feel good at all. That is incongruence. You strengthen your personal integrity and bring yourself happiness when you keep promises to yourself. You can create good habits by associating pleasure with making the right choices. Making good present moment choices will bring you happiness.

Positive psychology holds that there are practices that can increase the long-term positive feelings of happiness. We may all have fleeting moments of happiness, but these practices aim to raise our baseline of happiness to a higher level.

These daily disciplines—including expressing gratitude, practicing meditation and breathing techniques and reciting mantras—are scientifically proven to promote a positive mood, relieve stress, enhance cognitive functioning and promote healthy behaviors. Such disciplines don't come in a pill, a bottle or from a doctor's office. They come from you, are executed by you and are done for you. They give you a choice in the present moment that helps you in each future moment. The same positive results can come from exercise, yet these consistent daily disciplines I am speaking of come from the mind.

EXPRESSING GRATITUDE

Gratitude is an emotion expressing appreciation for what you have instead of focusing on what you want or what you don't have.

Gratitude is getting a lot of attention these days, and that is good. It is a simple and free solution to many "problems." It is not a new concept at all, and in fact, it has withstood the test of time. Practicing the daily discipline of gratitude is the perfect way to focus on all that is working in your life. The practice of gratitude is more powerful and meaningful than "positive thinking." Positive thinking alone does not create change. Just because you tell yourself you can make it to the next gas station on an empty tank doesn't mean that you will.

Expressing gratitude promotes feelings that make you more likely to create, achieve, succeed, live in happiness and feel joyful. Expressing daily gratitude rewires your brain, promotes positive feelings and emotions, inspires and helps you see the opportunities before you. It proves to deliver long-lasting positive feelings and enhances emotional and interpersonal wellbeing.[38] It is a virtue to nurture.

Researchers Ken Sheldon and Sonja Lyubomirsky examined the motivational predictors and positive emotional outcomes of regularly practicing two mental exercises in a study published in *The Journal of Positive Psychology* in 2006. They looked at how expressing gratitude or "visualizing best possible selves" (VBS) might increase and sustain positive emotion over time, as opposed to fleeting moments of happiness. VBS is simply picturing yourself and focusing on that image of your very best self, how you look, how you feel, doing whatever you envision for your life, as if it were already happening. For this study, subjects were divided into three groups: one that practiced the discipline of gratitude every day, one that participated in a VBS exercise every day, and a control group that simply rehashed the events of their day (poor control group)!

What the researchers found was not surprising. The VBS and daily gratitude groups were much happier than those subjects who focused on daily task recitation. The VBS group actually faired a little better than the gratitude group, although the difference was not statistically significant. The reason I share this with you, even as we talk about the benefits of practicing gratitude, is to point out that, as individuals, we may have different preferences for approaching positive affect (how we subjectively experience positive emotions) in our lives.

The researchers recognized that there may have been some people sorted into either the VBS or the gratitude group who would have felt better in the opposite group. Perhaps an individual's preferences, temperament, beliefs, personality and motivation would have been better matched to the other group. Both methods proved to enhance mood far beyond a recall of daily events.[39] However, each of us needs to discover what works for us personally. Increases in feeling good about life are the highest when the method to boost appreciation fits your interests and values and when it is performed neither too frequently nor too seldom.[40]

To increase and sustain positive emotions, we must engage in appropriate strategies and practices that we perform with effort and habitual commitment.[41] This is consistent with the finding that the pursuit of personal goals boosts wellbeing only if the goals are actually achieved. Achievement is important.

In addition to the positive mental boost, gratitude impacts our physical health, as well. According to Robert A. Emmons, professor of psychology at UC Davis and a leading expert on the science of gratitude, the practice of gratitude can have dramatic and lasting effects in a person's life. Studies show that a practice of gratitude can:

- Lower blood pressure
- Improve immune function
- Facilitate better sleep
- Reduce lifetime risk for depression and anxiety
- Reduce substance abuse
- Decreases LDL (bad cholesterol)
- Increase HDL (good cholesterol)
- Act as a resiliency factor in the prevention of suicide
- Help people engage in more exercise
- Encourage better dietary behaviors[42]

All of these factors lead to a happier, more fulfilling life.

In her keynote address to the American Heart Association's (AHA) 2014 Austin "Go Red for Women" event ("Go Red for Women" is the AHA's fundraising campaign for women's cardiovascular disease awareness and prevention), Kristin Armstrong said that she practices gratitude every day and takes it one step further. She adds WHY she is grateful. She said in a full year of this practice, "I have not had one bad day." I promise you, you will not have one bad day, because that is what gratitude does. It makes you the person that Maslow said we could be. You face and handle your problems that are within your control, check them off your list and focus on all the good things in your life.

Journal Exercise:

3) **Write down 10 things that you are grateful for. Then, each day, write at least three things that you are grateful for and why you are grateful for them. Make this a consistent daily discipline**.

Saying *the two words* "*Thank you*" is powerful. We all like to feel appreciated, and those who appreciate are appreciated in return. You just might find that being grateful will help you see opportunities that you may not have seen before.

PRACTICING MINDFULNESS TECHNIQUES: MEDITATION, PRAYER, BREATHING AND MANTRAS

Mohandas (Mahatma) Gandhi is quoted as saying, "I have so much to accomplish today that I must meditate for two hours instead of one."

Practicing meditation and prayer are good "mindfulness" techniques that help calm the soul and provide clarity in your life as well as help you with attention to the present. Eastern philosophies have recognized the health benefits of meditation for thousands of years. Meditation produces a deep state of relaxation and a tranquil mind and seems to enhance physical and emotional wellbeing.

Meditation techniques are now more widely practiced in the West as peaceful ways to reduce stress and anxiety. When you practice being in a calm state you start to become calmer overall. Breathing techniques, yoga, sitting quietly, practicing a mantra and praying all give you time to clear your mind and be still. According to the Mayo Clinic, meditation is considered a type of mind-body alternative medicine. I am so glad to see the medical community embrace this. Some studies show that it can also reduce high blood pressure, relieve pain and reduce the habit of emotional eating. Meditation reduces negative feelings and helps you handle stress. It has benefits similar to those resulting from practicing gratitude.

A 2014 article in the journal *Eating Behaviors* reported that practicing meditation may reduce anxiety, depression, insomnia, duration of illness and more. As it applies to emotional eating, meditation can reduce the emotional response to stress and the need to search for comfort, which is sometimes found with food. Studies suggest that mindfulness meditation effectively decreases binge eating and emotional eating in populations that engage in these behaviors, although the evidence for its effect on weight is mixed.[43]

We know that meditation is shown to reduce stress, and when an emotional eater reduces stress, he is less likely to respond to emotional triggers to overeat.

Don't get hung up on whether you'll be able to clear your mind long enough to practice meditation. That is exactly the reason you want start: the practice of meditation quiets your mind. Can you carve out 10 minutes to sit in peace and quiet?

Sit and listen. Clear your mind or do your best to focus on what you WANT. Often, my meditation time is when I focus on what I want to attract in my life, which always includes peacefulness. You can sit quietly with a clear mind, or you can focus on an image of what you want for yourself. It can be as big, farfetched and compelling as you can make it! It's Not All About the Food.

Breathing techniques are also calming. Breathe in through your nose deeply and through to your gut, hold it for a few seconds, and then blow it out with a whoosh sound through your mouth. This will have an instantaneous relaxing effect. Do that a few times in a row, and see how you feel. It does exactly the opposite of what stress does to your mind and body. Breathing techniques lower your blood pressure, slow your heart rate and calm you down, helping you think more clearly. You can practice deep breathing techniques at home or at your desk at work. This is free and easy, you can do it anywhere and it benefits your health.

I love a good mantra. As a child, I was not the best basketball player, but while practicing free throws in my driveway, my dad told me to me say, "I can, I can, I can, I can," before every shot. I made more shots than I missed when I did that, and that was quite the improvement! More so, it encouraged me to practice more and get better. Success breeds success. "I can" is powerful. Tell yourself that you can, you will and you are. You want to state everything you want as if it were already happening in the present tense. Then, make it happen. Tell yourself that you are amazing! Chant it and scream it and make it true. It is true if you believe that it is.

Mindfulness techniques such as practicing gratitude, meditating and repeating mantras are present moment practices. Other present moment practices (and stress reducers) include exercising regularly, enjoying your favorite hobby, socializing with friends, using breathing techniques and practicing yoga. When you engage in such activities consistently, they have a calming, peaceful effect that helps us make better choices in the present moment: choices to think more positive thoughts and take more constructive actions.

Hope for the Future

The third piece of positive emotions is hope for the future. When we have something to look forward to we feel happy! Planning a vacation can actually be a better experience than the vacation itself. The anticipation of the future vacation promotes positive emotions. It is the action of working toward what you are hoping for that brings joy; yet, recognize that it starts with a thought and a vision. Creating, learning and accomplishing bring positive emotions. When you envision your slim self, wearing your new cute and sexy clothes, seeing yourself with that bounce in your step, or being called sexy, or whatever it is for you—you will focus on that excitement and hope for the future. It feels good to take steps in the direction of our dreams.

"Whatever you can do or dream you can, begin it. Boldness has genius, power and magic in it!" - Johann Wolfgang von Goethe

Another positive psychology model of transformational change explains the connection between happiness in the present and hope for the future. We know when we put our attention to the present moment, we can create the future that we want for ourselves. It is the small successes you achieve in the present moment that energizes your hope for the future.

You must imagine and pursue personal goals to create the life you imagine. Just like Goethe said, there is "power and magic" in chasing your dreams. Pursuing goals boosts your wellbeing and positive emotions.

Dayne

My son Dayne is an amazing young man. One of his many strengths is persistence. I sometimes joke with him and tell him what a beautiful gift his persistence is… while I am asking him not to use that gift with me! When he thinks he wants or needs something, he uses that strength relentlessly to get it, in a nice way of course.

One summer, Dayne had a special request. He likes to BMX bike and often watches videos of professional BMX bikers who practice jumps and tricks on giant dirt mounds. So he asked me, "Mom, can you buy dirt so I can have bike ramps in our backyard?" He was dead serious, envisioning what he has seen in these videos. I am talking giant mounds of dirt! I answered, "No, I am not spending my money on dirt." But that didn't stop him from asking me a million times each day for about a week. That is only a slight exaggeration! By the second day, I was walking away from him every time he started to ask.

What I saw transform the following weekend was amazing. Dayne recruited a friend to help him rake a dirt path in the greenbelt behind our house. Then I saw them create two bike ramps by propping up some old plywood they found in our garage with rocks and sticks. I was a proud parent as I watched this transformation of greenbelt into BMX course.

Dayne had a vision for himself to get better at BMX, and part of that vision was to build giant bike ramps from truckloads of dirt. As he discovered, there is often a huge gap between what we envision for ourselves and where we are today. Instead of giving up, though, he chose to take one small, achievable step in the direction of his vision. He was resourceful. He didn't blame me for not buying dirt; he didn't make excuses about not having the right tools to get started on his vision; and he didn't get mad or resentful. He simply took one step in the direction of his dream. One small step to imagine, pursue and create.

That is why I say he is amazing…and…SO ARE YOU.

Sometimes we forget, because life does that to us.

You have gifts, talents and strengths that are perfectly unique to you. You can also be resourceful. You have everything you need right now to take one step in the direction you want to go and begin closing the gap between where you are today and your vision. That gap can be overwhelming unless you break it down into achievable parts. Those achievements are energizing. That is *hope for the future.*

So what this means when you are in this to lose weight is that you enjoy and focus on the bike ride, not the weight loss. Enjoy the moment. One small step at a time, until eventually, you are where you want be. What happens, then, is that your horizons expand and you see more opportunities and you continue to grow and dream and achieve. This is a journey, and you should have some fun along the way.

When we process our emotions in the most positive way, we find contentment with the past, happiness in the present and hope for the future.

We will cover the second precept of Positive Psychology—positive individual traits—in the next chapter, as well as in Part 2. The third precept is positive institutions, which are what result when individuals' personal qualities combine to make communities and institutions thrive. Communities grow and thrive when qualities like good leadership, a sense of tolerance and justice are in abundance. I suggest this precept is strengthened when we care for ourselves and master our wellbeing, because then our contributions to the greater good can be stronger.

4

Authenticity: Your True Self

Authenticity is the degree to which you are true to your own personality, spirit or character, DESPITE what the world is telling you to be.

– DEFINITION

Authenticity is your mind, body, spirit connection. It is when you know who you are at your very core and are acting on that truth in a kind and loving way. It is when you are at peace with yourself and the world around you.

If you get anything out of this book at all, I want you to understand what it means to know and be your authentic self. Ironically then, this chapter on Authenticity: Your True Self, is the shortest chapter in this book. Another way to think about finding your authentic self can be found in Maslow's concept of self-actualization.

From Maslow's perspective, being self-actualized means that you are at your best; know yourself well; handle problems as they are; love deeply and are content; know your strengths, gifts and talents; and grow and learn through life. He believed that a young person cannot be self-actualized because he has not yet had the life experiences from which older people learn. Our experiences reinforce how we process our world through our thoughts and, therefore, influence how we handle problems (stress). Maslow said that when a self-actualized person has a problem, for example, he handles the problem like it is a task to be dealt with and then checks it off his list.[44] It is peaceful to deal with the things within our control and not concern ourselves with the things that are not. A person who is not self-actualized will take a more ego-centric approach to the problem and make it much larger than it is.[45] This person might say, "Oh my gosh! I have this problem! It is one more thing that I have to do. Why does this always happen to me?!"

I would like to add that we know that not everybody grows wise with age, and not everybody becomes self-actualized. I would also argue that young people, even if not yet capable of self-actualization, have amazing moments of genius and wisdom. I learn from my children every day and from many people younger than I am. Children tend to have a simple and authentic perspective. If you have children, then you know exactly what I mean.

Identifying your strengths, talents and gifts will help you know yourself better and become aware of your authentic self.

Pay attention to the things that give you energy and what your natural inclinations are. What gets you into "flow"?

This term *flow* was coined by Hungarian psychologist Mihaly Csikszentmihalyi. He describes flow as a state of energized focus, when you are fully engaged and immersed in an activity or process. It is when you are in complete enjoyment of the activity. In essence, flow is characterized by complete absorption in what what you are doing, and when your skill set is matched with the right amount of challenge that keeps you engaged. It is what some of us call "being in the zone."

Journal Exercise: (download your free *Healthy Weight Success Journal* at healthinspires.com)

1) **What energizes you? What are the activities that get you into flow, or a state of energized focus, so much that time passes very quickly when you are engaged in them? (These activities are likely to involve the use of your strengths, gifts, talents, and interests; they are likely to point to what you most value.)**

Find your flow in order to keep taking steps toward knowing yourself. If a task matches your strengths and your skill, you will do well with it. However, if it is too easy, you will get bored and if it is too challenging, you may get frustrated, stuck or overwhelmed.

Your strengths then, are tied to your authentic self. How could they not be? Your strengths are your God-given talents, and your authenticity is who you came into this world to be. These are what make us unique, so it makes sense that they are tied together. In positive psychology parlance, our strengths are our natural capacities for certain thoughts, feelings and behaviors. We all possess multiple character strengths in various degrees, but a few will be predominant for each of us. Character strengths are associated with the six virtues of wisdom, courage, humanity, justice, temperance, and transcendence. We naturally gravitate toward things that allow us to use or natural abilities and these allow us to persevere and overcome adversity and contribute to our communities.

If each of us is doing what she is meant to do, then everyone is better for it. It truly is for the greater good that you find your purpose and be yourself; and you will be happier, healthier and more productive too. Taking time to be your best self is not selfish: It is a selfless act and a way to show love for others. Self-care includes all things related to your wellbeing such as finding your purpose and taking care of your health. Taking 30 minutes each day to exercise is just as important as brushing your teeth. So that means making sure you get seven or eight hours of sleep each night is your contribution to society! Eating right is good for you and for all of us. We have a health crisis in our nation, and that's not good for any of us.

When you are focusing on what you want and listening to who you are at your very core as your authentic self, then you will lose weight and keep it off for life. When you are trying to figure out what you will do to lose weight, do not get stuck despairing over the gap between where you are now and your vision. Simply start. If in the past you joined a gym and you didn't like it, then do not join a gym. If you dislike salad, then don't punish yourself by starting with salad for lunch. Instead start with an outside walk, and add vegetables that you find palatable to your lunch. Baby steps. Start by knowing and listening to your true self.

A 2015 Gallup survey found that 32 percent of U.S. workers were engaged in their jobs, the highest the engagement score has been since the annual survey's start in 2000. But the same survey found that 50.8 percent of employees were not engaged, and 17.2 percent were actively disengaged. That is alarming! That is 68 percent of us who are not engaged in our work! I should add that engagement scores are higher among executives and those in leadership positions and lower among manufacturing workers.[46]

The Gallup survey bolsters my opinion that we need to dream bigger and take steps toward those dreams in a daily discipline of learning and growing. If you feel stuck in your job, recognize that you only *think* you are stuck and, therefore, *feel* you are stuck. You are not actually stuck. Is somebody making you stay in your position? You can change. Take the first step and tell yourself the truth, assess your situation for what it is, explore your options, and then make a plan to change. Learning more about who you are and what your gifts, strengths and talents are will help you get there.

Part 2 will clarify this strategy for making any change, including weight loss. It's Not All About the Food.

A friend recently told me she is going to make it her job to say "yes" to helping people! She said the good keeps coming back to her (as in karma) when she helps people. She has a great talent and she knows what it is, and when people ask her to share her talent in small ways, she does it gladly. Because of her generosity, people often recommend her for large projects. I congratulated her and told her she had figured out the secret to life. That, my friend, is *purpose*. That is *knowingness*. That is *love and kindness*. That is *authenticity*. She is peaceful.

We can call it knowingness, authenticity or self-actualization—its achievement has been a core tenet of great thinkers across the world, both secular and spiritual, for thousands of years.

Do not be conformed to this world, but be transformed by the renewing of your mind. Then you will be able to discern what is the good, pleasing, and perfect will of God. -Romans 12:2, *Berean Study Bible*

Discover your true self, and you will be transformed.

5

Relationships: Your True Heart

"Seek first to understand, then to be understood."

- STEPHEN R. COVEY

There is nothing more important than your relationships and human connectedness. Life is enhanced when you have others to share in your life experiences, and you will find that very little in life is conquered alone. We need each other. The relationships you have feed your heart and soul. When you are communicating with love and kindness, regardless of subject matter, and listening with the intent to understand what the other person is sharing, you will connect at the potential depths of that relationship. This is the peaceful and principled approach to healthy relationships, and it starts with yourself.

We have to first be kind and loving to ourselves before we can nurture our relationships with others. You cannot give away what you do not have: You must have self-love first. You must process your thoughts properly, take care of your physical and emotional health through healthy lifestyle habits, proper diet, regular exercise, the practice of gratitude, and take time each week to turn your dreams into reality and fill your inner needs and desires.

This means that you must first keep your commitments to yourself. When you have scheduled for something important to you, and then allow a seemingly urgent matter to have priority over your bigger picture, this is a form of self-sabotage. This is making impulsive decisions in the moment rather than principled decisions. If you plan on waking up as soon as your alarm goes off to fit in 30 minutes of exercise, and then instead, you push snooze when commitment time comes, that hurts your personal integrity and your commitment to yourself. You lose out on the opportunity to strengthen your mind, body and spirit. It is also easier to cave in the next time. Honoring your commitment to yourself is empowering and strengthening and builds momentum toward your new normal.

LIVING BY PRINCIPLES

This concept applies to all important relationships in your life—with your spouse or life partner, your children, parents, siblings, colleagues, and anyone you want to connect with. Living by principles tells the story of who you are; feeds your emotional, intellectual and spiritual needs; and positively affects your relationships. You know you are living by principles when you are peaceful and have a certain knowingness, good energy and more easily find time for the important things in your life.

This idea of keeping your commitments to yourself, focusing on big picture items in your life and making decisions based on correct principles cultivates wisdom, integrity, trust, sincerity, honesty, confidence, perseverance and dependability. We are all busy, and have life demands, circumstances and situations that test us. Reacting to difficult situations isn't peaceful. Living and practicing a principle-centered life is essentially "doing the right thing." And we all know that is sometimes the hardest thing to do. People come first. When living by principles, your relationships with yourself and with others will evolve peacefully:

- You will have increased self awareness.
- You will have increased confidence.
- Your life and experiences will validate your decisions, so there will be no need for validation by others.
- Others' attitudes and behaviors will not affect you.
- You will listen and act on what you may call your intuition, your gut instinct, conscience or the holy spirit. (How many times have you said "if I had just listened to myself...")
- You will view change as an opportunity to contribute.
- You will serve, encourage and build others up.
- You will interpret life experiences as opportunities for learning.

- Emotions and circumstances will be less likely to drive your decisions.
- You will have clarity and consider the big picture, outcomes and long-term results of your actions, decisions and choices.

CONNECTING THROUGH THE LIMBIC BRAIN

Our relationships are built on the way we communicate and connect with one another through the limbic system, which is the emotional center of the brain where feelings and emotions originate. The limbic system is involved in motivation, emotion, learning, arousal and memory. By definition, the limbic system is *a complex system of nerves and networks in the brain, involving several areas near the edge of the cortex concerned with instinct and mood. It controls the basic emotions (fear, pleasure, anger) and drives (hunger, sex, dominance, care of offspring).*

The limbic system includes the hippocampus, hypothalamus, amygdala and the thalamus, which also encompasses autonomic, endocrine and hormone regulation. It functions to connect us deeply with other human beings whom we love and want to be with, and to help us relate even with strangers when we take a moment to slow down and listen. It is through the limbic brain that we begin to take on traits of those who we spend time with such as spouses and best friends. The limbic brain generates the connection and is the reason that your life partner, in a sense, is half of your brain. It's the reason that you have this knowing about each other that you could have never had early in your relationship.[47]

IN YOUR MARRIAGE

We all need love, and it is healthy to keep passion alive in your marriage. You can have hot and heavy, crazy and fun moments in your mature and long-term relationship. Yet if crazy thoughts fill your mind all the time, you might never get anything done and never have the opportunity to enjoy the depths of mature love. It is a choice you make to keep love fun, passionate, caring, adventurous, fulfilling and kind—or whatever YOU NEED IT TO BE. Think about how you greet your spouse at the end of the day when he or she walks through the door after work. You may be in the middle of cooking dinner or paying bills, perhaps heading out to pick up the kids or racing off to an evening meeting. But that doesn't mean you can't acknowledge your spouse with affection. When life gets busy, I have playfully told my husband that I could have anybody as a roommate, but I'm in this for the perks too! You can keep the passion alive. Have those deeper conversations and find what works for you.

You will always get more of what you focus on. Focus on what you love in your partner and not on what annoys you. A good question to ask yourself if and when you ever have a negative thought about your partner is, "I wonder if he/she ever thinks that way about me?" Reality check! Negativity needs to go away, and it is healthy for your relationship to focus on the amazing and beautiful qualities of your partner. What you focus on expands. What and who we appreciate, appreciates.

Should you choose and are able to hang in there and stay connected to your partner through child rearing, the financial ups and downs, and your search for meaning, your relationship comes full circle and can be even better than before. Treat your spouse as you would like to be treated. I have learned that when I relate to others from a state of love and kindness, empathy, compassion, support, respect, non-blame, non-judgment and forgiveness, the person on the receiving end responds in kind. Funny how it works that way.

In your relationships, you have a choice to connect or not. When you spend time together, you connect. When you don't, you disconnect. Life gets busy. Knowing that relationships are the most important things in our lives, ask yourself if the time you are giving to them is equal to the amount of value you place on them. This is a choice as much as anything else. Taking a purposeful 10 minutes each night to reengage and know your partner—to listen, to share and reconnect—will keep the feelings alive. You can kill 10 birds with one stone and make this a 10-minute walk.

A 10-minute walk with your partner or friend will:

1) Nurture your relationship
2) Provide physical activity
3) Promote blood flow to the brain
4) Provide stress relief
5) Help you sleep better
6) Burn calories
7) Increase muscle mass
8) Enhance weight loss or weight maintenance
9) Act as an antidepressant/positive mood boost

10) Make you less likely to seek less healthy mood boost-
ing alternatives.
BOOM!

This brings me to your health. Your self-care and self-love
includes your healthy weight, regular exercise, healthy diet,
sense of purpose and passion. All of these matter to your partner relationship and the attractiveness you feel for each other.
Getting healthy together is best, and at the very least, you
simply can start modeling healthy behaviors. Communicate,
encourage and inspire. Never criticize.

WITH YOUR CHILDREN

When you are at your wits' end with your children and you
lose your patience, you lose peacefulness, your leadership position and your positive connection. You know as well as I do
that you get back when you give. If I take an unkind tone or
raise my voice to my children, or to anybody, for that matter,
then I get it right back or it becomes a power struggle. If I ask
or speak in a kind and loving tone, then everybody wins. Love
and kindness wins every time. Seek first to understand. Your
children need to be heard, and they need to know that you are
listening.

Maslow said that young people cannot be self-actualized
because they have not yet had enough life experiences.[48] I cannot tell you how many times my very own young children have
shared their thoughts with me that have changed my perspective, or have taken positive action in their own lives beyond

what one might expect from their years. I see that they are processing things brilliantly with moments of "self- actualization" and genius. They are geniuses—and your children are too—and so are you.

I have twin teenage boys whom I adore and who test me at every mile, and I love them for that. They teach me, I learn from them and they are the loves of my life. I have their best interests at heart and everything I do for them is because I love them. That doesn't mean that I always make the right decisions or that I do everything for them, and they know that. As their parent, I do my best to nurture and inspire their growth into healthy and happy adults and as productive and contributing members of society. But I have shared with them it is not my job to make them happy in the moments that warrant such a comment. Happiness comes from within.

The importance of patience, love and kindness with your children is worth an additional mention. They need to connect with you at a deeper level with both quantity and quality of time. Evidence suggests the amount of time you spend with your young children correlates to them growing up as healthy, emotionally stable, resilient adults. Rest assured for the working parent that this evidence includes the good and loving care that your children receive from their primary caregiver while you are at work. Choose a good one.

From babies to adolescents, our children learn early to connect with us through their limbic brain processes. They read our emotions and our reactions, and these connections reflect how they grow into adulthood. Some studies suggest that this influences their choice of whom they fall in love with.[49] With 50 percent of American children in a single family home by the time they are 18 years old, it is important for you to choose your partner wisely, and go into your marriage and partnership with forever on your mind.[50] Stay connected and give it your all.

WITH ALL PEOPLE

There are many ways to nurture healthy relationships. It starts with clear communication and with love and kindness. We all have a human need for emotional connection. We can find it in a marriage, a club, an organization and even over the Internet. The social components of our lives feed our souls. Social engagement is free, uplifting and energizing "therapy." Connecting with others keeps you busy and healthy, is worth every bit of time and is the gift that keeps on giving.

You may have heard that 80 percent of our conversations are misunderstood or misinterpreted. These misinterpretations occur because as we are listening, we are projecting our own life experiences and perceptions into what we are hearing.[51] This happens even in the most intimate of relationships.

After 22 years of marriage and 26 years together, I like to joke with my husband, "You don't even know me!" I actually think he knows me better than I know myself, yet sometimes we miscommunicate because our own life experiences and perceptions cloud our communications. We are not the same people we were a year ago, and depending on the day, we may not be the same people with the same views we had even a day ago.

To achieve healthy and happy relationships in all parts of your life, here are five communication principles to follow that will bring you peace and strengthen those relationships.

PRINCIPLE 1: CLARIFY, CLARIFY, CLARIFY

Stephen Covey said, "We typically first seek to be understood. Most people do not listen with the intent to understand; they listen with the intent to reply."[52] Slow down long enough to listen to what other people are sharing with you.

One summer, a friend, who lives in a neighborhood past ours, offered to pick up our son from a lacrosse clinic. That was great news in a three-day whirlwind of organized carpooling for 10 kids in a far-away sporting activity. We had been meeting at the shopping mall by our house to group the kids, pick up and drop off. What her offer meant to me was that we needed to meet her at the mall as I had been doing the past few days. My husband interpreted her offer to mean she would bring our son all the way home because she had to drive past our neighborhood to get to her house.

Well, long story short…my husband was right. But instead of us taking time to clarify, we ended up wasting a whole lot of time and energy. I urgently sent my husband to the mall to meet our friend there to pick up our son. My husband didn't question me, and I didn't ask what he was thinking. To make matters worse, in his rush out the door, he forgot his cell phone. While my husband was at the mall waiting for our son, our friend dropped our son off at home. Oops! About an hour later, my husband finally showed up. He hadn't wanted to leave the mall and miss the drop-off in case that they were running late or by chance something had happened; and we had no way to be in touch because his cell phone was at home. Had he listened to himself, he would have been waiting comfortably at home for our son to be dropped off. However, since I was the one organizing the carpool, my mind was stuck on meeting at the mall. It was a complete disaster that could have been avoided by clarifying. Each of us drew our own conclusions based on our perceptions and experiences.

Many times a miscommunication is innocuous. You and a friend might walk away from an exchange with different images in mind about what was just said, each layering your own perceptions and experiences onto the conversation. The miscommunication can be completely harmless. In the carpool situation, however, it was a huge energy and time taker. No matter what the situation, a well-defined problem or task is more than half of the solution.

To completely understand what someone is saying, always repeat back what you think you heard him say.

"If I understand you correctly, I heard you saying_____."

Then hear what he says.

Clarify more than once to make sure there is understanding.

If you are on the delivering end of the request, you can ask the other person to please repeat back to you what he heard you saying. I do this with my children. To make sure I am understood, I ask them to repeat back what I just said. It is the best energy saver in the world. It also prevents the "I forgot" syndrome.

PRINCIPLE 2: EMPATHIZE

Empathy and compassion are the moral and gold standards for any communication and relationship. To simply say, "I understand how you must be feeling," is better than sharing a personal story to match theirs, or to one up it. Empathy means you are able to connect and identify with another's feelings, attitudes and emotions. It acknowledges and validates them in their experience, and it raises them up. Being empathetic is an act of acknowledgement and validation. Practice this. Empathy is love and kindness.

PRINCIPLE 3: APPRECIATE

I have never met a person in the world who doesn't like to feel appreciated, valued and respected. Saying, "thank you" is powerful…especially when you mean it. When you appreciate others, you are appreciated in return. When you give love, you get love. But the opposite is also true—when you give anger or detachment, you get it right back. What energy are you sending out? People mean well—at least most people do most of the time. With this in mind, appreciation comes easier.

PRINCIPLE 4: WITHHOLD JUDGMENT

Judging does not make a person who you judge him to be. Instead, it just makes you a person who judges. When you point your index finger at somebody, three fingers are left pointing back at you: This is a vivid reminder that each of us has plenty of things to personally improve on. Judgment is a negative emotion and actually short-changes you of an opportunity to learn and grow.

You may sometimes cross paths with a person who has bad energy and puts off bad vibes, or who is always negative or judging. You can steer clear of those people or politely excuse yourself. This point deserves a safety message: There is a difference between politely excusing yourself from the company of those who are unpleasant and responding to an imminent threat. We have a built-in safety mechanism called fight or flight that automatically kicks in when we sense danger. It prepares us to flee from or face imminent threat. Listening to your intuition is not judgment. When your intuition tells you something is really not right, remove yourself immediately.

PRINCIPLE 5: WITHHOLD BLAME

Rid yourself of blame. Blame is the best way to keep yourself stuck where you are and to make excuses for why you can't change or take responsibility for your own actions. For example, it is easy to blame your spouse or children for the junk in the house that you eat. You might complain, "If I didn't have to be in the kitchen cooking, I wouldn't be snacking" or, "If I didn't have to buy ice cream for the kids, then I wouldn't be eating ice cream at night" or, "If they would quit bringing junk into the house, then I wouldn't eat it." Can you hear how silly this sounds and how damaging that way of thinking is to your cherished relationships?

I agree staying away from the kitchen outside of mealtime is helpful in any weight loss strategy. Blaming somebody else for your behavior is something you might want to rethink. It is harmful to you and your relationships and promotes anger and resentment. Blame is negative and keeps you right where you are. Take responsibility. You can apply this to any area of your life, and not just the food antics. You must look inside yourself for love, peacefulness and happiness. Looking inside gives you contentment with the past, happiness in the present, and hope for the future. Looking outside fuels blame, negativity and discontent.

Journal Exercise: (download your free *Healthy Weight Success Journal* at healthinspires.com)

1) **Relationships are important and so are the principles that we live by. Focus on strengthening important relationships in your life and how you will apply these principles. Write a committment to practice each principle in the way that you want to apply them.**

FINAL THOUGHTS

Our life experiences change us. Be open to new possibilities and opportunities, and to learning, accepting, appreciating and communicating in healthy and constructive ways.

Choose your friends and partners wisely. They fuel your soul. Work in a place whose culture matches your values and values you. Change if you are not happy. Do that with love and kindness too. Withhold judgment and appreciate more. Blame will keep you stuck. Speak your truth with love and kindness; listen with empathy and compassion; and clarify, clarify, clarify.

I had the privilege of hearing Vice Admiral Vivek H. Murthy, our 19th U.S. Surgeon General, speak in 2016 in Austin, Texas. He said, "kindness is healing" and that in order to have good health, we need to address and take care of more than just the body. He said we need to address our emotional and spiritual needs, as well, by practicing the healing that comes with kindness.

Finally, in their brilliant book, *A General Theory of Love*, Drs. Lewis, Amini and Lannon remind us, "Who we are and who we become depends, in part, on whom we love."[53]

Choose wisely.

Part 2: Plan on It

Having a plan provides a necessary directional force for all that you desire in your life. Setting goals, developing strategies and creating your vision will help you stay on your path and move in the direction of your dreams. When you focus on what you want and have a plan to get there, you will live on purpose and will feel energized and inspired as you take steps in the direction of your vision.

If you stay focused, give your best in all ways every day, and approach others with love and kindness, your life will be significantly better, even if it doesn't end up following your specific plan. This is what it means to be detached from the outcome, and maintaining detachment is as important as having a plan. Detachment from the outcome enables inner peace. You may have heard the phrase, "Let go and let God." That means to enjoy the journey, and where your plan leads you will be better than you could have ever imagined.

You will learn the importance of, and how to create and reach, your behavioral goals in Chapter 6. Chapter 7 will show you how to use your strengths and your motivators to overcome obstacles and stay on track. Finally, in Chapter 8, you will learn the components of writing a compelling and energizing vision statement that helps you create the life you have imagined. I want to share how to create your reality processes first, and then using this information, how to write a powerful and focused vision statement. Carl Jung said, "Your vision will become clear only when you can look into your own heart. Who looks outside, dreams; who looks inside, awakes." These chapters fulfill this awakening.

6

Goals: Know Where You Are Going

"Stop setting goals. Goals are pure fantasy unless you have a specific plan to achieve them."

\- Stephen Covey

The difference between wishful thinking and having a plan that includes steps to reach your goals is the difference between fantasy and reality. Simply saying you want to lose 30 pounds does not get the weight off. Deciding that you are going to lose weight and planning your approach are necessary steps. As you plan your weight loss, you will want to have strategies in place that help you through obstacles and challenges and keep you on track and making the right choices every day. You will find more on that in the next chapters.

Dwight D. Eisenhower was a five-star general in the United States Army during World War II and the 34th President of the United States from 1953-1961. He once wisely said, "In preparing for battle, I have always found that plans are useless, but planning is indispensable."[54] This is true for anything in life. Preparation is everything. If you are always taking steps in the direction of your vision, you may not arrive exactly at what you thought was the preferred outcome, but you will nonetheless be happy with yourself.

The general guideline for goal setting is that when the right amount of challenge is matched with your ability, you succeed. In a work setting, Hans Selye, MD, the researcher who coined the term *stress*, said that he chose work that matched his skill (ability), and didn't take on work that exceeded the good stress that helped him be productive.[55] If your goals are difficult and cause stress, they will be too challenging or too overwhelming to pursue. On the other end of the spectrum, if you set goals that are too easy, you will not feel a sense of accomplishment when you achieve them. Such low-level goals provide no energizing function. Your vision is the far-reaching dream. Your goals and plans will get you there.

OUTCOME VS. BEHAVIORAL GOALS

Each year on January 1st, nearly half of all Americans undertake a behavior change program. The most common News Year's resolutions are to lose weight, quit smoking and exercise regularly. The good news is that those who make a resolution are 10 times more likely to change the behaviors they are seeking to change than those who do not make a resolution. A review of studies shows that it's at the six-month mark where people fall off the wagon and revert back to old habits.[56] Knowing this will help you recognize when your energy around goals starts to wane. At that point, you need to look at your motivators and take steps to reenergize. Time to change it up!

The ultimate reason New Year's resolutions fail for many is because when people make those resolutions, they haven't really thought through an action plan; they only have "outcome goals." Outcome goals are the end result without a strategy to get there. You say, "I want to lose 10 pounds," but you don't talk about the behavioral piece that includes the necessary plan, action steps and strategies to help you succeed, especially when you experience obstacles that derail you. Having a plan is the way to success.

Positive affirmations alone do not make the weight go away. Having absolute willingness to change and taking action steps to make healthier choices does. Action comes right after getting your thoughts and your story straight. You know as well as I do that once you start rolling, it gets easier as momentum and success take over.

Behavioral goals are different from outcome goals. Setting behavioral goals will make it possible for you to achieve the outcomes you desire. To help you create positive change, set up reward systems for new behaviors you will undertake when you inevitably hit recognized triggers for unhealthy behaviors. Behavioral goals help you take action and hardwire new neuropathways.

You currently have some strong rituals and triggers that keep you in patterns that might make your goals difficult to achieve. This idea of rewiring your pathways is how cognitive behavioral therapy works for something like smoking cessation. If the person planning to quit smoking typically has a cigarette with her morning cup of coffee, she will need to make changes in her morning routine to avoid the cigarette trigger. She may need to wake up and get in the shower first, get dressed and then pour the coffee in her to-go cup to drink it during her drive to work. Eventually the craving will dissipate while she stays focused on creating new patterns and routines, being in control of her choices, saving money, feeling good, and gaining the confidence and strength that comes with kicking an addiction.

It is not a good feeling when something has more control over us than we wish it did. If your morning ritual includes stopping at Starbucks for a 400-calorie pastry and a 400-calorie grande frappuccino on the way to work, then you may need to take another roadway, or drive in the lane that insures you cannot get over in time to stop. You could plan to take a to-go cup of black coffee from your home instead. Or you could make healthier homemade muffins that have fewer than 200 calories. Start making behavioral goals related to changes you are willing to make.

THREE-MONTH GOALS

Three-month goals are important because they are medium-term, action-oriented, and give us a way to start, learn and maintain a new set of behaviors. A three-month time frame is both long enough to help you create new behaviors and habits, and short enough to create a sense of urgency around creating those habits. This timeframe keeps you engaged and motivated to continue healthy habits and achieve success.

All goals should be structured using the S.M.A.R.T. goal technique. This acronym stands for:

S: Specific
M: Measurable
A: Achievable
R: Realistic
T: Time-bound

You should create three-month goals that lead to the behaviors you want to be doing consistently three months from now and in the direction of your best possible self, as you will set out in your vision statement.

You want to make sure your actions are resulting in your desired outcomes. It is very easy to take actions all day long and not get the results you are looking for. You can busy yourself to death with to-do lists, wasting precious time and energy. You must make time for your bigger goals—the behavior-changing goals—or the day-to-day busy-ness will steal all of your time.

Keep your mind focused on what you value and why it is important to you. You will find time for the important things in your life. Once you have retold your story and realize only you are standing in your way, you will find time for your health.

I will use the infamous New Year's resolution to lose 10 pounds as a three-month goal example. Let's say it is December, and as you are enjoying the holiday festivities, you say to yourself, "I am going to enjoy the holidays, and starting on January 2nd, I am going to lose 10 pounds." Sounds good. That is an outcome goal without a plan. To make this a reality and a lasting change, you will start by asking yourself these questions:

Journal Exercises: (download your free *Healthy Weight Success Journal* at healthinspires.com)

1) **What behaviors do I want to be doing consistently in three months that will enable me to lose 10 pounds?**
2) **What is my desired outcome?**

Taking time to answer these questions will help you determine the actions you are willing to take that will produce the outcome you want. This is a large piece of the puzzle. You can have a great idea, yet without the right plan and strategy to accomplish it, you will not get very far down your path.

Think in terms of "Do *This* in order to *Be* That."

Here are some examples of behaviors that you can build into your goals: Plan meals, exercise five times a week, drink eight glasses of water each day, read inspirational words every day, practice gratitude before going to bed each night, have a girls' night once a month (or twice), speak only kind words to all, prepare two meals in one night to save time, go to the store once a week, pack fruit for a snack every day.

Here are some examples of outcomes: Lose weight, look good, feel good, strengthen my heart, have more energy, fit into smaller-sized clothing, be stronger, have better habits, have healthier relationships, have confidence, be more social.

Here are examples of what your three-month behavioral goals and desired outcomes might look like:

Behavioral Goal #1: I will walk three times per week for 30 minutes with my friend Kim, at a fast pace that pushes my limits.

Desired Outcomes: Increase my cardiovascular health so that I live a longer and healthier life and to help me lose weight.

Behavioral Goal #2: I will purchase fresh fruits and vegetables every week from the farmer's market on my way home from work on Monday, and will eat at least three servings of vegetables and one or two servings of fruit every day.

Desired Outcomes: Lose weight so that I have more energy and feel more youthful.

Behavioral Goal #3: I will lift weights for 20 minutes on Monday and Wednesday mornings before work.

Outcomes: Increase my bone density so that I reduce my risk of osteoporosis, sculpt and shape my body and increase my metabolism.

Behavioral Goal #4: I will write about three things that happened each day that I am grateful for in my journal every evening before I go to bed.

Desired Outcome: Reduce my stress level and increase peace of mind.

Journal Exercise

3) Write Three-Month Goals (3-5 goals):

Behavioral Goal:

Desired Outcome:

Behavioral Goal:

Desired Outcome:

Behavioral Goal:

Desired Outcome:

Behavioral Goal:

Desired Outcome:

Behavioral Goal:

Desired Outcome:

In order to achieve your three-month goals and create your desired habits, you are going to set weekly S.M.A.R.T. goals so you know exactly how you are going to get there. It is important to remember that you need to carve out time to accomplish your bigger goals; otherwise, the busy-ness of life wins. Setting weekly goals keeps you on task.

WEEKLY GOALS:
The structure for weekly goals also follows S.M.A.R.T.

S: Specific
M: Measurable
A: Attainable
R: Realistic
T: Time-bound

These weekly goals enable you to take small steps toward your three-month goals and toward lasting change. Achieving small successes opens your mind to see beyond your current perceived limits. The adage that success breeds success is absolutely true. Weekly goals and achievements are energizing, they enhance belief and provide hope.

Having said this, you need to set goals that you are confident you can achieve. Make them challenging enough so you realize what you are capable of (remember there is a right amount of healthy stress). You should be able to achieve about 80 percent of your goals. If you are achieving 100 percent of your weekly goals, that tells me you can accomplish more. If you are achieving less than 60 percent, then take a look at your goals and ask yourself what is it that you are not willing to do to meet them? Make necessary changes, find new motivators, and/or break down your goals into achievable steps.

The R in S.M.A.R.T. Goals stands for Realistic. It is important to be realistic because you want quick victories to gain your momentum. If they are not realistic, you will not be able to reach them, and you might lose momentum. Make them realistic and be resourceful.

I love to tell my MS 150 story to illustrate how we achieve things in small steps. The MS 150 is a two-day, 150-mile bike ride that is a fundraiser for the Muscular Sclerosis Foundation, and it is staged in many cities across the nation each year. A cycling enthusiast friend encouraged me to participate and helped me by making sure I had the right equipment for the ride and that I had somebody to train and ride with (support). I bought the bike I had talked about buying for a year (contemplation), and I started training in preparation for the race, but probably not far enough in advance. Regardless of training, I believed I was capable (mental strength) and I was physically ready *enough* (physical strength).

Race day came, and I learned that the MS 150 is set up in approximately 10-mile increments where there are rest stops for participants to eat, hydrate, use the restroom and so forth. The 10-mile increments made the ride safe and achievable. There were mile marker signs all along the way to encourage every cyclist, marked, "10 miles to the next rest stop;" and then, "5 miles to the next rest stop;" then, "You are almost there, 2 more miles;" and finally, "Rest stop here." There was also community support along the way, with many people lining the route cheering for us.

The organizers set up people to succeed. We know that small successes lead to greater successes. Small wins lead to bigger wins because you build momentum, motivation and confidence as you accumulate those small wins. You build your mental and emotional strength once you start experiencing small wins. In this way, you build self-efficacy, or the belief that you can.

This example shows how breaking down your vision into achievable steps is the way to get there. I could not have ridden 150 miles all at once.

Another great example of setting realistic goals comes from my friend, Jeremiah, who I mentioned in Chapter 2. He asked himself what he was willing and unwilling to do, and that is where he started. All of his goals were realistic. He was willing to take the cream and sugar out of his coffee. He was willing to give up dessert, but not his occasional alcoholic beverage.

Jeremiah still spends most Saturday mornings planning the week's meals with his wife. It keeps his entire family healthier. What is good for him is good for his family. He said for seven months he lost weight, and at about that point, he started maintaining and sustaining. The small changes he made equaled lasting changes. He decided to lose weight, made a plan, knew his motivators, understood his obstacles and challenges and figured out how to achieve his goal in small increments.

To write your weekly goals, choose two or three topics from the following categories: fitness, nutrition, weight loss, stress management, purpose, learning, and anything that involves your mind, body and spirit. Then, decide on three to five weekly goals that you are willing to achieve within these categories.

This may sound like a lot of goals, especially since I have been saying to take baby steps and to change one thing at a time. No worries. I can show you what this looks like, and it is not as overwhelming as you might initially think.

Examples:

- I will pack an apple every day for a snack and eat it when I am hungry.
- I will substitute one tablespoon of avocado on my toast instead of butter for breakfast every morning.
- I will drink two more glasses of water each day at work by filling my blue cup two extra times, once in the morning and once in the afternoon.

What about thinking and feeling goals? Yes!

- I will write three things I am grateful for each night before I go to bed in my gratitude journal.
- Every time I think a negative thought about myself, I will immediately turn it into a positive thought.

Examples of three-month goals and weekly goals in the S.M.A.R.T. goal format:

- Three-month goal: I will walk three times a week for 30 minutes.

- First week: I will walk 15 minutes on Tuesday and Thursday this week.
- Three-month goal: I will eat five servings of fruits and vegetables five days a week
- First week: I will eat a salad with my lunch three days (M-W-F) this week.

As you think, so shall you be.

Journal Exercise:

4) **Write your weekly goals. Choose two or three categories to focus on, and write three to five weekly goals in total.**

Week 1:

Category
Goal

Category
Goal

Category
Goal

Category
Goal

Category
Goal

To stay on track, it is important to know what is going to get you through your obstacles—and that is covered in the next chapter!

7

Strategies: Finding Meaningful Motivators and Strengths to Overcome Obstacles

"The more we do, the more we can do."

- WILLIAM HAZLITT

FINDING MEANINGFUL MOTIVATORS

The more you connect your goals with your values and motivators, the more successful you will be. Your emotions and your physiology are truly inseparable. It could be that you want to have more energy, feel more confident or have more mental focus and be more productive. You may want to feel peaceful, more balanced, more in control, more relaxed, look better in your clothes and feel more attractive. It could be that you want to delay aging, or that you want to set a good example for your children. You may want to sleep better, improve your mood and reduce depression, or reduce your cholesterol or high blood pressure. The list of motivators goes on and on, and the variations are endless. Ultimately though, motivators all lead to peace of mind.

We are motivated by things that cause pain (fear causes pain) or pleasure. I suggest to you, and even plead with you, don't wait for the crisis. If you are overweight, you have an increased risk for disease, period. Motivators can be anything that inspires you to make positive change. Your motivators give you a reason for doing something that satisfies you and are what make you enthusiastic to change behaviors. You may have a reunion coming up and you want to look good, for example.

A word about fear as a motivator:

Fear is a motivator. Using fear as a motivator in the present moment to diminish the likelihood of a future health crisis is better than waiting to use fear as a motivator after the crisis has happened. You know that smoking causes cancer, so plan to quit now. You know that being overweight contributes to your disease risk. You many know that heart disease is the number one killer of men and women in the world. You also may know that these diseases are mostly preventable. There is scientific evidence that 60 to 80 percent of disease is preventable through eating a proper diet, maintaining a healthy weight, managing stress and getting regular exercise. What you can't prevent are your genetics and bad luck.

I once asked a highly respected cardiothoracic surgeon whether a health crisis, like needing to have open heart surgery, makes his patients change their diets for good. He said in his experience, the crisis and accompanying fear promote diet change for a while; but eventually, many of his patients revert to their normal routines. He added compassionately, "Change is difficult." The prevailing belief is that change is difficult, but I don't think it has to be. It can be easy. Find someone to consult with on a regular basis who believes in you and your ability to change; support helps you change. That is what this entire book is about.

In the behavioral model of change, fear of health consequences is supposed to fuel change. The question is, does it fuel lasting change? Just like anything else, it only does if the consequences remain important to you. That is why you need to know why losing weight is meaningful to you, and why you need to create more meaning along your weight loss journey. Recognize that your motivators will change, and finding new ways to stay inspired is important.

Values are principles that you build your life on and live by. What you value is deeply meaningful to you. Having integrity and being compassionate are values, for example. Your actions to follow through on your commitments signify your integrity, and if this is one of your core values, fulfilling it makes you feel good—that's your motivation. Your values will guide your decisions, desires and actions. For instance, you wouldn't take a job with significant travel if you value time with family over other things.

Here are some common motivators: confidence, self-esteem, knowledge, feeling good, energy, peacefulness, self-satisfaction, life satisfaction, having choices, better vacations, good health, progress, security, certainty, looking good in clothes (or without clothes), attention. A goal like running a

5k or participating in a biking event can also be a short-term motivator.

For inspiration, it might help you to know that many studies show that if you have a BMI of 25 or greater and you lose five to 10 percent of your body weight, then it is likely you'll be able to reduce or completely get off your medications, lower your blood pressure and/or cholesterol level and, therefore, reduce your disease risk. So, if you weigh 220 pounds now, and you lose 11 to 22 pounds, you will reap those benefits. Does that motivate you? Eleven pounds may sound more easily achievable than whatever your bigger goal is, and that may help you get started.

Do you like the idea of not taking medicine, feeling better, stronger and healthier; not to mention looking better? Decide that you will take your first walk today or on Saturday for 15 minutes. You might decide to exchange a fatty or sugary snack for a healthier snack. You may substitute one meal that includes fried food or a heavy sauce for a lighter meal with lots of vegetables. Small changes will make a huge difference. We need to dial back the all or nothing approach. This is exactly one of the premises of cognitive psychology. All or nothing, most of the time, will be self-defeating. Slow and steady wins the race. The slow and steady race is comprised of daily healthy choices that add up to your meaningful lifetime.

You want to nail down why losing weight is so important to you and know what your motivators are and what you value. Pleasure is a strong emotion and motivator, and attaching meaning to what you want for yourself is pleasurable. Pleasure affects your mental, emotional and physical states. To discover your true motivators, ask yourself cascading questions starting with:

"Why is losing weight important to me?":

You might say: "I want to look good."

Then ask:

"Why is looking good important to me?":

You might say: "I want to look good because it makes me feel good."

Then ask:

"Why is feeling good important to me"?:

And you might end up with: "When I feel good, I can do anything I put my mind to and I have confidence and peace in every area of my life."

In the cascading questions example, you would arrive at a prime motivator: that you want confidence and peace. That is powerful.

Ask yourself cascading questions several times and you may find other motivators and values related to courage, self-reliance, conviction or resilience. Really knowing what is important to you will help you find time for the important things in your life outside of the day-to-day tasks. That knowingness and the actions you take to reach these goals on a consistent basis, while being detached from the outcome, gives you peace: the ultimate life satisfaction.

Take the time to ask yourself cascading questions about why losing weight is important to you. You will get to the real reason(s) - your values - and you will find your motivator(s) to inspire you to get there. You can have any number of motivators, as long as they resonate with you.

Journal Exercise: (download your free *Healthy Weight Success Journal* at healthinspires.com)

1) **You want to nail down why losing weight is important to you and know what your motivators are. Ask yourself this question three to five times.**

Why is losing weight important to me?

Why is (what you answered above) important to me?

Then, ask yourself, at least one more time, why is (what you answered the second time) important to me?

One more word on motivators. Think of the times when you were at your best and feeling good and feeling healthy and strong. Ask yourself what was going on in your life at that time. What made it easy to take care of yourself? Know that you can recreate those conditions (or create new, different conditions that are equally enabling) and realize you can do this. Believing that you can is the key to your success.

OVERCOMING OBSTACLES

Obstacles are part of life. Remember what Dr. Hans Selye said about stress: "The only people who do not have stress are the people in the ground." The same is true about people who have no obstacles to face. It is best to recognize what stands in your way, handle it as a task to be dealt with, and check it off the list. Don't make a problem bigger than it is.

Know that you simply have a choice to make; that is all. Peace of mind comes from making the right choices. When we are not being controlled by unhealthy cravings or desires, we are free. When our needs are being met, we make good choices. When they are not being met, our emotions, feelings and choices are not always healthy.

You know, from our earlier discussion, that the subconscious mind is always there, ready to resort to patterns created through a lifetime of repetition, as well as to take over your current thoughts. To clear the subconscious mind obstacle, you have to make choices every day that create new neuropathways, and then you must repeat, repeat, repeat and continue to repeat to create new habits. To do this, you must know your triggers and substitute a new trigger behavior that ties to a reward. The reward reinforces your new response (behavior) to the trigger. The rewards provide the meaning and motivation that reinforce new behaviors. Creating a positive and meaningful association will help you continue these new behaviors.

So, when you face an obstacle, see it for what it is, and decide what to do. Determine what you will do to get over this obstacle, and one way is to ask yourself *"If this (happens) then what (I will___)."* If your plan was to exercise with Kim on Monday night and now Kim can't walk with you...what will you do? Only you can decide. Look at your options: You can go for a walk by yourself or ask another friend to walk with you. If the obstacle is that you couldn't get home in time from work to walk with Kim, your options might be to walk later that evening, go first thing in the morning or plan for tomorrow night instead. Communication with Kim is the first step.

To make sure your strategies are in place, practice the "if this, then what" game. For example, say to yourself, "If Kim cannot walk tonight then I will walk by myself or find somebody else to walk with." Or, "If life throws me a curve, and I cannot walk at my committed time tonight, I will take my work-out clothes to the office and walk during lunch tomorrow." Draw upon your strengths to overcome obstacles until it becomes habit. You know that you will go tomorrow at lunch if tonight does not work out as planned. See the problem for what it is, decide how to handle it, be positive and move on. Peace!

Studies show that positive emotions not only make people more resilient and able to cope with life's occasional adversities, but positive emotions also increase people's open mindedness, and their creativity and capacity to take creative action.[57]

Journal Exercise:

2) **Fine-tune your workable strategies for each of your goals this week to help you achieve them even in the face of obstacles. What obstacles do you anticipate?**

Week 1: If this, then what?
Using Your Strengths to Overcome Your Obstacles

Selye's work related to stress and fulfillment was further developed by a positive psychologist and pioneer, Mihaly

Csikszentmihalyi, who you learned earlier coined the term "flow." Flow is when you are in a state of energized focus where time passes quickly, and it feels almost euphoric while you are focused on the task at hand.

I'm sure you have experienced this state of flow in your life. When you are in this state of energized focus, you make significant progress, and your work is amazing. I call that being inspired, which means you are "in spirit." Being in spirit is when you know that what you are doing comes from something deep within you—from your authentic self. Flow happens when you are creating and discovering something new. Flow is where the right amount of challenge meets your skills and abilities—you are using your strengths at their fullest potential. Flow is magical. It is also momentary.

Pay attention and recognize the thoughts and actions that give you energy. Those are your gifts, strengths and interests that will contribute to your joy, happiness and life satisfaction, which can last and last.

Journal Exercise:

3) **Think of a time when you have felt flow. What were you doing? What did you like about it? Why did it make you so peaceful and energized at the same time?**

Each of us has a few predominant strengths as well as some level of capacity for each of the 24 positive psychology character strengths, which fall under six core virtues, as I mentioned earlier. These six virtues were identified by Dr. Marty Seligman (a pioneer in Positive Psychology), with the help of Dr. Christopher Peterson. Through research, they discovered these same six core virtues were valued in almost every culture.

Those 24 character strengths are:

Wisdom and Knowledge	Courage
1. Creativity	1. Bravery
2. Curiosity	2. Perseverance
3. Judgement	3. Honesty
4. Love of learning	4. Zest
5. Perspective	
Humanity	**Justice**
1. Love	1. Teamwork
2. Kindness	2. Fairness
3. Social Intelligence	3. Leadership
Temperance	**Transcendence**
1. Forgiveness	1. Appreciation of beauty and excellence
2. Humility	2. Gratitude
3. Prudence	3. Hope
4. Self-regulation	4. Humor
	5. Spirituality[58]

It is a fun exercise to take the Authentic Happiness assessment at the University of Pennsylvania's website (www.authentichappiness.com) to find your predominant strengths. Most likely the results won't surprise you, but they may give you more mental strength to plow ahead, as well as help you figure out how to overcome obstacles. The site was developed from Seligman's work. He is author of a book by the same name, *Authentic Happiness.*

I also have an appreciation for StrengthsFinder 2.0, an online strengths assessment tool. Partnering on the StrengthsFinder book were Tom Rath, scientists at Gallup and the late Dr. Daniel Clifton, a leader in strengths-based psychology. StrengthsFinder identifies 34 strengths, called "themes and ideas for action." When you take the assessment, you will learn your top five predominant strengths as well as how you might apply them, based on your personality. Here are the StrengthsFinder themes and ideas for action:

Achiever, Activator, Adaptability, Analytical, Arranger, Belief, Command, Communication, Competition, Connectedness, Consistency, Context, Deliberative, Developer, Discipline, Empathy, Focus, Futuristic, Harmony, Ideation, Includer, Individualization, Input, Intellection, Learner, Maximizer, Positivity, Relator, Responsibility, Restorative, Self-Assurance, Significance, Strategic, Woo.[59]

Your strengths are what make you special and reflect your spirit. Your strengths tie directly to your authentic self. When you are playing to your strengths, things are easier, they feel right and natural. So, you want to use your strengths to overcome challenges. You can sharpen your strengths through effort and focus.

I recently coached a new mother who wanted to lose her baby weight. She told me she would use her strength in creative thinking to help her lose weight. She listed several enjoyable things that she could do to keep herself active, like taking an online yoga class that she could invite friends to join. She said she also enjoys painting and would spend more time painting, because when she's involved in purposeful work, not only does it distract from thinking about food, it increases her self-satisfaction. Sometimes it is as simple as that.

8

Vision: Dream Big!

In order to carry a positive action we must develop here a positive vision.

- DALAI LAMA

VISUALIZATION:

Emily Cook, a member of the United States freestyle ski team, visualizes each aerial jump as part of her training for the Olympics. With her eyes closed, she imagines and feels every physical movement and motion of the jump. She uses the term *imagery* to explain how she replicates the physical motions, feels her muscles tighten when they should, feels the wind on her neck, and even hears the crowd roaring. Using imagery, she practices her jumps, and it has helped her consistency and performance. She is in her jump before she is in her jump.

While imagining her jumps, Emily thinks about distractions that might arise and practices stopping negative thoughts and blocking the distractions so that she can get back to where she needs to be mentally in order to perform.[60]

Nicole Detling, a sports psychologist with the United States Olympic team, says, "People are recognizing that training the mind is just as important, if not more important, than training the body." She says that the athletes who use imagery—in addition, of course, to physical training and skill-building—tend to have better and more consistent performances than those athletes who don't. This information is not surprising at all.

There are many exceptional athletes with the capability to win in whatever sport they compete; but what sets apart the actual winners is the mental game. This is true in life. Visualization is not new to elite athletes; it can help get you to any goal you may set for yourself.

Visualization is not new to weight loss either, and there are many amazing ways that technology is taking this concept and running with it. At the 2016 SXSW in Austin, Texas, Dr. Daniel Kraft gave a presentation, "The Future of Medicine: How Far Can Tech Take Us?" One of the most innovative health promotion tools he talked about was a mirror that actually provides a reflection of your skinny self, or your buff self—however you want to look. Then you can press a button and see a vision of the opposite—you, after eating too many Duncan Donuts®—the way you really don't want to look! This technologically enabled mirror harnesses the power of visualization to motivate people to achieve their health goals.

So you must take time to visualize what you want for yourself. You can do this when you pray, walk or meditate. Picture what you want, see yourself in action, in the scenario that you desire for yourself. Hear, feel, sense and picture yourself going through the motions just as it will be, and practice it as if it were already true. Visualizing is a present moment practice. Reinforce visualization by writing it down in a vision statement.

CREATING YOUR VISION STATEMENT:

A vision is a compelling statement about who you are and what health-promoting, life-giving behaviors you want to be a consistent part of your life. A vision is a picture that you have developed and tailored to reflect your deepest desires for what you want in your life. Your vision can be as big as you want it to be, and you do not need to limit it to weight loss. It's not all about the food—creating a vision helps you see where you want to be and provides energy and direction that will lead to life satisfaction, and that's about way more than food!

Start brainstorming and picturing yourself as the very best you. Know that your vision is possible and it starts with your thoughts and beliefs. Here is some related wisdom from throughout the ages for your inspiration:

"For as he thinks in his heart, so is he."

- PROVERBS 23:7

"A man is but the product of his thoughts what he thinks, he becomes."

- MAHATMA GANDHI

"As a single footstep will not make a path on the earth, so a single thought will not make a pathway in the mind. To make a deep physical path, we walk again and again. To make a deep mental path, we must think over and over the kind of thoughts we wish to dominate our lives."

– HENRY DAVID THOREAU

Therefore I tell you, whatever you ask for in prayer, believe that you have received it, and it will be yours.

– MARK 11:24

Your vision statement provides an energizing push that helps you move through the five stages of change that we talked about in Chapter 2: pre-contemplation, contemplation, preparation, action and maintenance. It provides focus. Your vision is best when written in the present tense, in your voice, and as if what you want is already happening and already true.

In the present tense, as if it is already happening:
Believe that it is already happening, and it will happen. Athletes, celebrities and people who have lost weight practice visualization and recognize this as a winning strategy. Close your eyes and see yourself exactly as you want to be, look and feel, and see it as if it is true in this very moment. You have what it takes.

In your voice:
Write it in your voice and hear yourself saying it. As matter of fact, read it aloud as much as you'd like. Believe it and live it.

Attach meaning:
Your vision statement includes your motivators, how you feel, the obstacles you are likely to face and the strengths you will use to overcome those obstacles.

Examples of what your vision statement might look like:

1) I am 120 pounds and feel amazing. I am strong and confident and know I can do whatever it takes to achieve all of my desires. I have a bounce in my step and have energy all day long to accomplish tasks at work and enjoy my evenings with my family. People notice my energy and make comments, and I am attracting nice people. I have increased my value at work and my boss promoted me and gave me a raise. I am treating myself right with daily exercise, and I like the way it makes me feel. Feeling good and looking good are my motivators. I know that life gets busy and if I miss an exercise commitment to myself, I simply resume the next day. Now, when life gets busy, I take time to pause and take a few deep breaths to refocus, and I keep my commitments to myself. I approach people and problems with love and kindness.

2) I am hot and sexy. I am 50 pounds lighter, strong, lean, and I feel good! I am shopping for clothing that makes me feel pretty and boosts my confidence. I have complete control of what goes in my mouth. I plan meals for the week each Sunday before I go to the store to make sure I am leading my family by my healthy example. Planning meals leads to healthier eating. I know that modeled behavior is the best thing for my children to see. I have an afternoon snack at work so that I do not go home really hungry, and then I make better choices. People make comments about how good I look and ask me how I lost so much weight. I tell them I decided to take care of myself. I have a better relationship with my spouse, my children and my colleagues. It must be because of my newfound confidence and self-love. I have created a new habit of getting up from my desk when I feel stressed and taking a walk outside to clear my head, think through how to tackle whatever is stressing me and get my positive frame of mind back. I ask for help when I need it, which also relieves stress.

3) I am maintaining a 40-pound weight loss, and I am happy and have so much energy that people notice. I like it when people notice, and that makes me feel good. My motivators are feeling good and having confidence. I am in control of my weight, and I know I have control in each present moment. I make healthy choices 80 percent of the time. I allow myself two of my favorite meals in the right portions each week. This keeps me

strong and satisfied. At work, when I go out to eat with coworkers, I decide in advance that I will order a salad topped with a lean protein, no matter what everybody else orders around me. Sometimes I order something less healthy, and when I do that, I apply the 80/20 rule and make sure my next meal is healthy. I am now Director of Operations with a $25,000 raise, and work with the dream team. My energy is contagious and my leadership comes from my passion for the work that I do because it is matched with my skill set. I go to work every day to serve and give my best, which makes me feel strong in all areas of my life. I recognize that stress will come, and I will take time to process it the best way possible, take a walk to think and clear my head, and get back to doing my best as soon as I can. I have complete life satisfaction. I am in control of what I can control. I feel amazing!

Notice that the motivators, strengths and obstacles are in these statements. For example, the motivators are feeling good and looking good, setting a good example for family, having confidence. The obstacles are feeling stressed and ordering less healthy food when you might intend otherwise. The strengths are tenacity, courage, leadership, decisiveness or perseverance.

Write your vision framing what you want, rather than what you don't want. Do not analyze where your obstacles come from or why. Your past is what you leave behind. You must have contentment with the past. It is good to know what your triggers are and what your obstacles are, so you can have a planned distraction such as a walk. You must immediately engage in your planned distraction at the moment you recognize your trigger. Otherwise, it is way too easy to rationalize and make excuses for yourself as humans do.

We can get stuck wondering "why" we do something instead of simply recognizing the action and then quickly deciding to substitute a different action. We don't need to focus on fixing what is wrong. Focus on what is good and working in your life and expand on those things. It was Carl Jung who said we outgrow our problems, not because we don't have them, but because they become less important and they lose their urgency when we are focusing on what is working in our lives.

If you decide to take the "traditional diet approach" and tell yourself, "I will not eat any sugar today," you immediately set yourself up for mental resistance. What will you focus on? Sugar. What will you think about? Sugar. When you focus on something, that's all you want. That is how people are wired.

If you know this is how people respond to resistance, then you will believe how powerful it is to write your vision statement the right way. Keep your eye on the prize. Do not think about what you are "missing." You are not missing anything. Instead, you are gaining everything healthy for your mind, body and spirit and ridding yourself of the thoughts and habits that have led you to an unhealthy and undesirable weight. So, rather than focusing on not having soda with your lunch, for instance, you would write and say and think, "I will drink water with my lunch today." Focus all of your attention on what it is that you desire.

My husband's mom told him when he was nine years old, "Somebody has to be the best in the world at something, and it might as well be you." Know that you are and can be the best at something—you have a purpose and you are ready to fulfill it. You want your vision statement to be palpable. Be bold!

Journal Exercise: (download your free *Healthy Weight Success Journal* at healthinspires.com)

1) **Ask yourself the following questions. Knowing the answers will help you write a better vision statement and create a better and stronger plan to achieve your dreams. This exercise will also help you know yourself better and know what it is that you really want. You can have multiple answers under each question.**

Values:
What do I value?

Why do I value that?

For example: Why do I want to lose weight?

Why does this vision really matter to me?

Outcomes:
What results do I want to achieve?

Who is the ideal person I want to be?

Behaviors:
What behaviors do I want to do consistently?

Motivators:
Why is (are) this (these) meaningful to me?

Strengths:
What strengths, talents and abilities will I draw upon?

Challenges:
What challenges will I overcome?

Strategies and support systems:
What are workable strategies for overcoming the obstacle, and what strengths will I apply?

What support team do I already have?

What support team and structures will I put in place?

GAP ANALYSIS

What is the gap between where I am today and my vision?

Think about all these questions as you pray, meditate, go for walks, energetically voice your mantra and spend some quiet time. Start thinking and keep thinking about what you want for yourself. You will need to be very specific as you create your vision. Remember the funny Geico commercial where a man asks the Genie for a million bucks, and a million male deer appear? You understand the significance of being clear and specific when making a request! Asking to be happy, for more money or for a better relationship isn't specific enough. A vision is a clear picture. It is an image of EXACTLY what you want.

This is a psychological game and you can win. Once you have written your vision, place it where you can look at it every single day. Focus on it and take action. I have one, and it is right in front of me. I have tweaked my vision on several occasions through the years, but it remains much the same as when I first wrote it. My vision gets more real as I work toward it. Your goals help you measure your success toward this vision. Your goals fill the gap between where you are now and reaching your vision.

Remember my son's bike ramp story? Like there was for him, there is a gap between where you are today and where you want to be. Do not get overwhelmed. You simply start taking one step at a time, consistently, as a daily discipline. Weeks go by, then months, and before you know it, one year will have passed. You might as well start taking steps in the direction of your dream today.

Outside of believing that you can, your willingness to take the necessary steps to achieve your vision is the most important factor. Make no mistake: There is no amount of hoping, wishing, dreaming and visualizing that will make your dreams come true. It is your focus on your vision, and its connection to your heartfelt purpose, that directs you to take the necessary steps to achieve your grandest dreams. The only person who can ever get in your way is you. Take what you have control over and make it yours. Your willingness and decision to do what it takes is what creates the changes in your life, and those achievements will inspire you to continue.

You must believe that you can and:

- Decide and be willing to make changes
- Have a plan
- Create goals
- Take action steps
- Prepare strategies for those obstacles that you WILL experience
- Change and update your motivators as needed
- Visualize your best possible self

Journal Exercise:

2) **Write your vision statement about what you want to be and who you know you are. Remember to include your strengths, challenges and motivators. Use the space provided in the workbook. Keep it close so you can focus on the prize anytime you need reinforcement. Spend some time with this. Write down what comes to mind and you can fine-tune it as you go.**

My Vision Statement:

Putting it all together:
Ask yourself what you want in your life (create a vision), and think about what significant positive impacts on your life you want to see in three months, six months, one year, two years and three years (goals). Figure out what motivates you, know your strengths and play to them, start in the present moment and take daily and consistent actions that create new habits that change the direction of your life. Make corrections as needed, stand back up if you have a setback, and keep driving toward your vision.

If you have dieted off and on for years, have lost weight and gained it back, now is the time to view it differently. Setbacks will come, but you will go easy on yourself and simply resume with a good next choice. Maintain your vision and focus on what you can do in this very moment to get you to where you want to be. Consistent, actionable steps, taken over time, will help you reach your goals and propel you toward your vision. That doesn't mean every day will be perfect. Life is trial and correction; enjoy the journey, be detached from the outcome and have some fun along the way.

> *"Yesterday is gone. Tomorrow has not yet come. We have only today. Let us begin."*
>
> — MOTHER TERESA

Part 3: Complete Awareness

Having self-awareness means you know yourself deeply and know why you do the things that you do. Only then are you able to make necessary changes to meet your needs and support your values. Self-help author Debbie Ford once said, "Self-awareness is the ability to take an honest look at your life without any attachment to it being right or wrong, good or bad."

In Part 3, I provide a more complete view of American public health, food industry tactics and politics. Becoming more aware of the games played by food producers, industry groups and government agencies will help eliminate health claim confusion and inspire your positive health change. Everybody is selling something, and often, your best interests are not the concern. After reading this section, you will no longer fall prey to marketing gimmicks or dieting trends that may have caught your attention in the past. It's one thing to be self-aware, but you also need to understand how all these groups could potentially railroad you.

Part 3 facilitates your *Complete Awareness.*

9

State of the Union: We Can Do Better

*"Every man is a builder of a Temple called his body,
nor can he get off by hammering marble instead."*

- HENRY DAVID THOREAU

OVERWEIGHT AND OBESE

According to the current U.S. Surgeon General, Vice Admiral Vivek H. Murthy, "Obesity is the fastest growing cause of disease and death in America."[61] The crisis is not unique to the United States. The World Health Organization (2003) reports that the obesity epidemic is a major contributor to the global burden of chronic disease and disability; it "affects virtually all age and socioeconomic groups and threatens to overwhelm both developed and developing countries."[62]

The trend is especially disturbing among young people. Over the past 30 years, childhood obesity has more than doubled, and obesity among adolescents has quadrupled.[63]

PERCENTAGE OF OBESE AMERICANS[64,65]

	1976-1980 Data	2011-2012 Data	2013-2014 Data
Adults 20 to 74	15.0%	35.1%	37.9%
Adolescents 12 to 19	5.0%	20.5%	20.6%
Children 6 to 11	6.5%	17.7%	17.4%
Children 2 to 5	5.0%	8.4%	9.4%

The more recent 2013-2014 obesity report updates the adult obesity rate to 37.9 percent and obesity and overweight combined to 70.7 percent. These numbers are heading the wrong direction.[66] Another alarming statistic is that children and adolescents ages two to 19 are 17.2 percent obese and an additional 16.2 percent are overweight.[67]

The obesity crisis not only affects the health of individuals, it affects the nation and the world. Because obesity negatively affects wellbeing in every way, it impacts military strength; workplace productivity; family dynamics; the healthcare system; rates of depression; the incidence of cancer, diabetes, heart disease, stroke, and disability; quality of sleep; quality of life; the ability to cope with stress; and the body's natural ability to regulate itself.

The research shows that if you are overweight as a child, then you are more likely to be overweight as an adult. I want you to know that research provides statistics and averages, but you don't have to be a statistic. The outcome for any one individual is self-determined: Anyone can be an outlier and you can buck the trend. Being fatalistic about your weight is damaging to you. You can lose weight and keep it off. That doesn't mean it is going to be easy—at first—but it can be, once momentum takes over. You make choices every day to become and be healthy. You take it one day at a time.

You have everything you need right now to create change, and it starts with one small step. You can override your less healthy ingrained habits and tendencies with healthier ones. It takes a decision, then effort, planning, and repetition, repetition, repetition.

THE PUBLIC HEALTH PICTURE

The CDC's latest Vital and Health Statistics summary report for U.S. Adults (age 18+) was published in February 2014 (using 2012 data). I reviewed this national health survey and calculated the statistics for 100 U.S. adults. It is not an exact science, yet it makes for easy math and paints a vivid picture. So, for every 100 adults in America over the age of 20, we look like this:

- 9 have diabetes
- 3 have pre-diabetes
- 35 are overweight
- 28 are obese
- 52 regularly drink alcohol
- 10 are depressed
- 8 have some form of cancer

- 11 have heart disease
- 24 have hypertension
- 6 have coronary artery disease
- 3 have had a stroke[68]

Heart disease is the number one killer of both men and women in the United States and the world today. It kills more people every year than all cancers combined. It is interesting to note that diabetes is closely linked to heart disease. A person with diabetes is two times more likely to have a heart attack than somebody without diabetes; and two out of three people with diabetes ultimately die from heart disease or a stroke.[69]

Health experts agree that, not counting smoking, weight is the largest predictor of all disease risk. We know that obesity-related conditions including heart disease, stroke, type II diabetes and certain types of cancer are some of the leading causes of *preventable* death; and more than one-third (34.9 percent) of all U.S. adults are obese (that's 78.6 million people!).[70] To pile on, the estimated annual medical cost of obesity in the U.S. was $147 billion in 2008; the annual medical costs for those who are obese were $1,429 higher than for those of normal weight.[71] Not to mention, obese people frequently do not feel well, and their quality of life is affected.

The most recent data provided by the CDC and the American Diabetes Association indicate that 9.3 percent of our population has diabetes (29.1 million people), with 21 million having been diagnosed via the HgA1c blood test, and the remaining 8.1 million undiagnosed. The diabetes disease burden is projected to increase through 2050.

During an annual lecture series in Austin in 2015, I heard obesity expert Dr. Barry Popkin present his latest data showing that most of our extra calories come from extra snacks and beverages that once upon a time were not available in the marketplace, with the bulk of them coming from snacks. We have shifted from eating three balanced meals a day, with perhaps one whole food snack, to eating multiple snacks between meals that are mostly high in sugar and fat and come packed with all sorts of artificial ingredients.

Michael Moss, author of the #1 New York Times bestselling book, *Salt Sugar Fat*, says that we consume 22 teaspoons of added sugar every day.[72] The CDC reports that 15 percent of our calories come from added sugar each day, which equates to about 18 teaspoons of sugar per person per day. Their data also show that 25 percent of the population consumes some sweetened beverages each day (more than one 12 oz. can of soda), 5 percent consumes four or more 12 oz. cans of soda each day, while half the population says they have none.[73] There is a discrepancy between the CDC estimated 18 teaspoons of sugar per day and Michael Moss's estimate of 22 teaspoons, but either way—that is a lot of added sugar! For perspective, we know there are 65 grams of sugar in one 20 oz. Coca-Cola®, and that is 15 teaspoons of sugar. There are four teaspoons of sugar in one Pop-Tarts®, for another example.

People tend to underreport the "bad" stuff and embellish the "good" stuff when they self-report, and the CDC sugar stats are self-reported, so it's likely people are eating more sugar than they admit. People also tend to underreport their weight, and older people tend to over-report their height. Taken together, we have very skewed perceptions of our weight and health. One study estimated that nearly three in 10 overweight adolescents do not consider themselves overweight.[74]

The misperception of weight status has been documented repeatedly among overweight and obese adults. This misperception is thought to lower weight loss motivation and healthier behaviors.[75] Last, many parents think their children are normal weight when they may not be.[76]

With 69 percent of Americans overweight or obese, it is easy to understand how and why our perceptions of normal weight are skewed. For example, a body-mass index (or BMI—a measure of body fat based on one's height and weight) of 25 is considered "overweight" and may not appear to look heavy by today's norms.

Being honest with ourselves about our bodies helps us take steps to better health. Do not make your weight a bigger issue than it is, but tell the real story and take the first step.

DEPRESSION
In 2014, a CDC study found that 7.6 percent of those 12 and older reported depression (survey period 2009-2012).[77] While many people get the blues due to regular life stressors and feel unmotivated for short periods of time, clinical depression lasts for more than two weeks and interferes with functionality, the ability to work, eat, sleep, and care for those whom you love.

Crisis situations can truly test us; and true sadness, such as over the loss of a loved one, is real. But the false reality we create by telling ourselves we are not worthy is a different game altogether.

Depression is real. You can make yourself more depressed by falling into a pattern of negative thinking that creates your reality. Negative thoughts can become your truth, and you cannot escape the depression until you can see things differently.

Women and people between 45 and 64 years of age are more likely to be depressed, as are people with less than a high school education, those previously married, individuals unable to work and unemployed people without health coverage. Young adults, ages 18 to 24, can also be prone to depression.

The Anxiety and Depression Association of America reports that at any given time, 3 to 5 percent of the population is depressed, and that Americans have a 17 percent chance of becoming depressed at some point in their lives. I must add that the counselors and health care providers that I talk to consistently say these numbers seem low, based on their experience.

So what does depression have to do with weight? Depression is highly correlated with obesity and other disease states caused by obesity: One report found that 43 percent of adults with depression were also obese.[78] Repeatedly trying to diet and failing is a depressant. All or nothing approaches to dieting eventually fail, and can leave you in despair.

Unfortunately, we are treating our depression with antidepressants. A CDC data brief confirmed, "Antidepressants were the third most common prescription drug taken by Americans of all ages in 2005–2008 and the most frequently used by persons aged 18–44 years. From 1988 through 2008, the rate of antidepressant use in the United States among all ages increased nearly 400 percent."[79] The third place ranking continues per the latest CDC 2013 data.

There are two schools of thought related to the use of antidepressants, each championed by experts. Some believe these drugs provide insignificant results and increase mortality. Others say that they decrease mortality and help boost mood. There is concern about overuse of these medications such as Paxil, Zoloft and Prozac. Medications as powerful as these should not be taken lightly. In a recent article, comedian Sarah Silverman talks about her past depression and its reoccurrence. Knowing that she is susceptible, she says she has developed strategies to prevent depression before it hits. She says that she always makes sure to have antidepressants with her, but she doesn't take them. Having them with her gives her a sense of peace and makes it less likely that she will need them. It is a game she plays, and it results in mental wellbeing.

I am certain there is misuse of antidepressants. I am also certain they can be used to help truly depressed individuals get over the hump. Perhaps for those struggling with major depression, these drugs can make a significant difference while they make behavioral changes and learn healthier responses to triggers. The healthiest way to deal with depression is to learn coping mechanisms and develop support systems to lean on when we face inevitable low points in our lives.

Learning coping mechanisms throughout our lives is key, and passing those on to our children is also key—especially if you are more susceptible to becoming depressed. The theory that "chemical imbalances" cause depression is being disproven. The bigger picture view, as explained in Part 1, is that ALL EMOTIONAL RESPONSES HAVE A CHEMICAL CONSEQUENCE. When we laugh, for example, endorphins are released, and these chemicals make us feel good. When we allow life situations to get us down, and we have feelings of depression, stress hormones such as cortisol are released. This *could* potentially turn into clinical depression for someone. So once again, how we respond to stress creates chemical patterns, for better or for worse. To be clear, certain health issues and illnesses can certainly lead to feelings of depression due to hormone changes, and this is why I believe there is a place for antidepressants—just not at the rate they are being prescribed.

In addition to taking prescribed medicines that dull the senses, depressed and troubled people often turn to alcohol and other legal and illegal drugs to numb their pain. Alcohol is the most commonly used controlled and addictive substance in the United States: 17.6 million people, or one in every 12 adults, suffer from alcohol abuse or dependence (National Council on Alcoholism and Drug Dependence (NCADD)).

Approximately 120 people die each day in the United States of a drug overdose.[80] Opioids are powerful painkillers that are highly addictive, and opioid dependence affects nearly five million people in the United States and leads to approximately 17,000 deaths annually.[81] Heroin use is on the rise and jumped by 63 percent between 2002 and 2013. Addiction to this dangerous drug is now seen in both men and women, in all age groups, and its use is becoming more prevalent in higher income brackets, correlating highly to those also addicted to opioids.

Some people are more prone to depression than others, and it's important for them to take preventive strategies and avoid drugs—legal or otherwise—if at all possible. Know that help is available. If you are someone who is prone to depression, there are many things you can do that help to keep episodes at bay—and the list looks a lot like the steps to take toward good health as presented in this book:

- Practice positive psychology techniques, which are proven to boost your mood and increase resilience.
- Be honest and accurate with yourself.
- Do not take an all or nothing approach to your fitness and diet.
- Focus on all of the good things in your life, practicing gratitude every day.
- Nurture your relationships.
- Engage in purposeful work.
- Maintain a healthy diet rich in fruits and vegetables.
- Exercise. Clinical evidence shows that exercise is a natural antidepressant.

TAKE CARE OF YOURSELF

The best thing you can possibly do is to take your health into your own hands, take responsibility for yourself and your children, and take care of yourself to the best of your ability.

American writer Henry Miller once said, "Our own physical body possesses wisdom which we who inhabit the body lack. We give it orders which make no sense." It is easier to take care of yourself than it is to continue engaging in unhealthy behaviors.

The more you learn about food and nutrition and the games the food industry plays, the better prepared you will be to make the right choices. Knowledge is power.

Recognize that healthcare is a big business, and incentives are not always in the right place: you are the only one who has ONLY your best interests in mind. In our changing world of healthcare reform, healthcare systems and insurance companies dictate more and more of the care you will receive. Shared cost savings is the motivator, and "value-based medicine" is the buzz phrase. Value-based medicine is when health care providers use health claims data to identify those at risk for chronic disease or acute episodes and refer them to low-cost specialists whose care statistically results in good outcomes. In theory, this sounds like a good process to reduce healthcare spending, yet it is also questionable: There are provider bonuses at stake dependent on cost savings. Whenever profit is the motivator, there is potential risk for poor judgment, manipulation or abuse.

Taking care of yourself includes choosing a good doctor to see for your preventive screenings, and getting to know your important health-related numbers (see below). Then if you need medical care, you will already have an established relationship with a physician whom you trust as well as some established baselines. Choose a doctor who is state licensed and board-certified. You can check the credentials of physicians on many different websites, as well as see their affiliated hospitals, review any malpractice suits, and check whether they accept your insurance plan on websites such as www.medicare.gov or on your own health plan's website. Word of mouth is also a great reference.

So what are the baselines? Let's go through them—and remember that the majority of these measures are within your control. What is not in your control is called genetics and, sometimes, bad luck. Knowing your health-related numbers will aid in self-awareness and help lead you to make positive change. Let's get down to business.

What your numbers should look like:

Nutrition (your daily diet): How healthy is your diet? Your daily diet should consist mostly of plant-based foods such as leafy greens, cruciferous veggies, brightly colored veggies and fruits, as well as some grains. Those should be enhanced and flavored with oils and good fats such as olive oil, canola oil, avocado, nuts and seeds, in moderation. You need lean proteins, preferably in the form of fish and then chicken, as well as plant-based proteins. You should keep refined carbs to a minimum (white breads, white rice, white flour, cookies or crackers, for example) and go for the whole grains such as oats and barley and the ancient grains such as quinoa and kamut. Those refined flours leave you craving more.

The fats you consume should come from olive oil, canola oil, avocados, nuts and seeds. If you often eat out of a box, or consume a lot of refined carbs, sugar or sodium, then you need to cut back.

Finally, anything you are eating that is highly processed or has a list of ingredients that you cannot pronounce is not healthy. Nutrition comes from real and whole foods. That is what I mean by nutrition. There is more about these real foods and portions in Chapter 12—but here is a sample menu to give you a sense of what I'm talking about:

Breakfast: 1 slice of whole wheat toast (or not), 1 egg plus 1 egg white, avocado and tomato slices, ½-1 cup of blueberries

Morning snack: Small piece of fruit or 6 oz. low fat or nonfat yogurt (only if you are hungry—It is always good to ask yourself before you eat: "Am I hungry?")

Lunch: Bean chili, 2 cups of greens for a salad, small whole wheat roll

Afternoon snack: 1/4 cup of hummus and 6 baby carrots

Dinner: 3-4 oz. grilled chicken or salmon (3 oz. looks like a deck of cards), 3/4 cup of quinoa or brown rice, 1/2 cup of asparagus, 2 cups salad that includes mixed greens and sliced fresh veggies

There is not a lot of room for unhealthy foods in our diet. One cookie is okay, or one small piece of chocolate…but if having just one is not your thing, then wait until you gain momentum with making healthy choices your new normal, and you won't crave these foods like you used to.

Health: Is your overall health excellent, average or poor? This measure takes into account mental and physical health, injury and illness. Health is impacted by the social and economic environment, the physical environment, and individual characteristics and behaviors. Some of these factors are in our control, and some are not. You want to do everything within your control to eliminate and reduce your risk factors for disease and illness and enhance your health.

Weight: A reasonable measure of a healthy and ideal weight is body mass index (BMI), although it's going to be a little different for each of us. Body shapes, muscle mass and where people carry weight all differ. Your healthy ideal weight will be one that you are comfortable with and that you can maintain. Use a weight range as your goal rather than an absolute number, so you are not focused on one number. Weight fluctuates slightly over the course of the day and month. Use the BMI tables to see what your ideal weight range is, and pick a healthy weight range from there that you can reach and maintain.

BMI: Body mass index (BMI) is a measure of body fat based on height and weight that applies to adult men and women. It is divided into three categories. Commonly accepted BMI ranges are:

Under 18.5 = underweight
18.5 to 24.9 = normal weight
25 to 30 = overweight
Over 30 = obese

There is some debate about where the BMI category lines should be drawn, as well as whether the BMI is an effective measure of healthy weights. For example, a man could be extremely muscular and fit and have a BMI of 25. So the BMI does not tell the whole story— but for now, it is still the best clinical measure of a healthy weight.

Studies show that if those who have a BMI of 25 or above lose even five to 10 percent of their body weight, many health benefits ensue: lower blood pressure, reduced risk of diabetes and reduced dependence on medications.[82]

Blood pressure:
Here are blood pressure ranges and what they signify:

≤120/80	Normal
120-139/80-89	Prehypertension
140-159/90-99	Hypertension Stage 1
≥160/100	High Blood Pressure/Hypertension Stage 2

If your BP is higher than 160/100, you need emergency care! Keeping your blood pressure under control is a large part of maintaining good health. Every time your heart beats under high pressure, you are causing significant damage to your artery walls, straining them, chipping away at the lining, and increasing your chances of suffering a heart attack. Take steps to have your blood pressure under control.

Waist circumference: A healthy waist circumference for women is 32 inches, and for men it is 35 inches. If you are a woman and your waist circumference is 35 inches or greater, then you are at risk for cardiovascular disease, diabetes and hypertension. For a man, that number is 40.

Life satisfaction: Are you engaged in purposeful work and satisfying past-times? Are you happy and peaceful? Do you have meaningful relationships and support systems in your work and your personal life, and hobbies that you enjoy to meet your needs? If you are not living the life you imagined, refocus on what you want and take steps to get there. The more steps you take, the easier it gets and the happier you will be.

How do you feel most days of the week: Are you energetic and able, or tired and grouchy? Feeling good makes it easy to wake up, get to work and handle your daily tasks. Know what your motivators are and what gets you out of bed each morning—then make sure to get more of whatever that is into your life!

Sleep: Studies show that we need seven to eight hours of sleep each night to gain its restorative benefits: regulating our hormones, sharpening cognitive function, improving mood, reducing stress levels and more. Less than that takes its toll on all those things mentioned. Studies show that people who get less than six hours of sleep each night show signs of cognitive impairment.[83] More on sleep in Chapter 14.

Energy: Are you high-energy or lethargic? You can have more energy throughout the day with a few tweaks. Physical activity, pursuing a great idea and socializing all boost your energy. The exercise of writing your vision is energizing in itself!

Work: Do you look forward to hitting it on Monday, or do you keep Friday in your sights all week? It is important that you enjoy your work. It should be matched with your skills, abilities, strengths and interests. If you feel stuck, understand that you likely have more choices than you think you do. You have all the power to make a change. Ask yourself is your dissatisfaction related to your attitude or to the actual work? If it is the work, then you need to look at making a change. If it is your attitude and disengagement, then work to reengage, start a new project, learn more about your company or work or set more appointments to gain positive momentum. You can take classes online, and maybe your company will help pay for some continuing education if it's related to your work and will improve your skill set. You must be proactive. It starts with you. You must make the change.

Journal Exercise: (download your free *Healthy Weight Success Journal* at healthinspires.com)

1) Now, take stock of your current reality:

Nutrition (diet):

Health:

Weight:

BMI:

Cholesterol:

Blood Pressure:

Waist Circumference:

Life satisfaction: (Are you happy? Content? Fulfilled?)

How do you feel most days of the week? (Is it easy to wake up and get to work or handle your tasks?)

Are you sleeping well? How many hours?

How is your overall energy throughout the day?

Do you enjoy your work?

> *"Take care of your body. It's the only place you have to live."*
>
> – JIM ROHN

10

The Food Industry: Making Sense Out of Nonsense

"No one chooses wishful things, but only that things might be brought about by his efforts; choice relates to things that are in our power and involve a rational principle."

- ARISTOTLE

As obesity rates continue to rise, there are more people "trying" to lose weight. The weight loss gimmicks are too numerous to count, and the food industry is continually changing and refining marketing tactics. The food industry includes grocery stores, food manufacturers, restaurants, lobbyists, and even politicians and government agencies. The paid marketers latch on to one line of a study and lead us down rabbit holes and to extremes, creating confusion that helps us dig ourselves into a deeper hole. Anyone can cherry-pick from the literature to find studies to support almost any food or nutrition belief. Studies of varying validity are conducted by the food industry, the medical research community and many players in between.

It is no wonder we are confused. We are confronted by a $5.32 trillion U.S. retail food market with a lot of power, spending millions on advertising.

I am skeptical of the food industry! That includes all players listed above. I know better than to speak in generalizations, but that's what I'm doing! I am guessing that the CEO of Kellogg's, for example, does not have his hand in a box of CHEEZ-IT®, and the CEO of Nestle does not dine on Lean Cuisine®. They know better. Food manufacturers are in business to sell products, grow market share, generate revenues and then report that information to shareholders.

I am all for free markets and capitalism. But I am also for integrity, truth, honesty, passion, goodness and purpose. We should be able to create wealth for ourselves within these parameters and live amazing lives. I am also all for informing you so you can make healthy choices, buy the right foods, eat well and be well. This chapter, by exposing the sheer nonsense of the industry, will inspire you to make healthy food changes. We can change industry offerings with our personal buying power. You get to choose whether you buy what somebody is advertising. If you are unsure what is true, sit quietly and consider what you know to be true for you and your health. You will find the truth.

THE GROCERY STORE

I am forever grateful for grocery stores and what they bring to our community. I am especially fortunate to have four grocery stores within five-miles of my home. I do not have to prepare the land, till the soil, plant the seeds, nurture, grow, and harvest the crops or be a rancher, milk my cows and slaughter my animals. Instead, I can walk in, buy what I need and walk out; at least in theory.

Grocery stores are a service business providing us with convenience and many choices to meet our demands. They also want to sell goods that generate revenues.

The $5.32 trillion dollar U.S. retail food market includes $606.3 billion in sales from 38,015 supermarkets. On average, U.S. households spend $4,015 for at-home food and $3,008 for away-from-home food annually.[84] The number of products, on average, on the shelves in the average supermarket expanded from 8,948 to 39,500 from 1975 to 2015.[85,86] It bears repeating that the industry wields great wealth and power, and deploys a massive amount of strategic marketing and advertising to persuade you to buy what's on the shelves.

When you walk into a grocery store, the smells of the bakery, strategically located, seduce you. Everything is strategically placed to make you cover more ground and buy more—with a lot of the products people consider necessities at the back so that consumers need to travel every aisle to get there.

The music being played, the location of the goods and the specials being offered are all the result of reams of research related to purchasing psychology, making you more likely to buy. The brightly colored produce section creates a good mood for shopping the moment you walk in. Ads offering items "10 for $10" or "Buy one, get one 50 percent off" are alluring. Most of the time, you can buy just one of those 10 items for the sale price, but we don't know that, so we buy more than we need.[87] Shopping carts are bigger than they used to be, allowing room for larger items and impulse buys.

Many grocery stores offer organically and locally grown fresh produce among the conventionally grown offerings, and a whole lot of food "products." Ironically, the "healthy living" section often features packaged and processed supplemental products including things such as protein bars, protein mix and supplements—instead of the produce section, which is the REAL healthy living section. The fewer processed foods you buy, the better off you will be.

Don't fall for the claims: low-fat, heart healthy, "now made with real fruit juice," gluten-free, or "now with whole grain." Read the ingredients. Marketing departments are paid to know what you want to hear, what is trending and what makes you more likely to buy.

Make a list and stick to it! I am sure you know from personal experience that shopping while you are hungry is not a good idea. You are more likely to make impulse purchases. Stick to your list, and eat one of your apples on the way home if you are hungry. You do not need that extra 250-calorie "bar" of junk anyway. Real food tastes so much better.

I saw a snack item advertised as a "healthier junk food." That's transparency! There are healthier choices in junk foods than others. So if you are going to choose some type of *bar* to eat, then at least go for the healthier junk—choose something without food coloring, preservatives and high fructose corn syrup that contains real ingredients like nuts, oats and honey. When you are buying what you think is a whole food like brown rice or frozen broccoli, check the ingredients to make sure the "food" you are buying is the only ingredient. Whole grain brown rice should be "whole grain brown rice" and frozen broccoli should be "broccoli." You have seasonings at home.

GLUTEN-FREE

Gluten is a naturally occurring protein found in grains such as wheat, barley and rye that gives elasticity to dough and stability to the shape of baked goods. It is also used as an additive in many processed foods for texture. Approximately one in 100 Americans (one percent) have Celiac disease, an autoimmune disorder that causes the body to attack the small intestine when gluten is ingested. Celiac can lead to other debilitating medical problems if not diagnosed and treated. An additional 18 million people, or about six percent of the population, are believed to have gluten sensitivity, a less severe problem with this protein.

Nielsen reported that 11 percent of households bought gluten-free products in 2011 and that 30 percent of Americans surveyed said they would like to cut back on gluten.[88] Oh boy. When a poll is showing that 30 percent of Americans want more gluten-free foods, a marketing opportunity is born. As a matter of fact, Mintel estimated that sales of gluten-free products would reach $8.8 billion in 2014, representing an increase of 63 percent from 2012 to 2014 and 136 percent from 2013 to 2015.[89,90] All gluten-free food segments are growing, and the gluten-free snack segment is growing the fastest. There was a 163 percent increase in gluten-free snack food sales from 2012 to 2014: to $2.8 billion in sales.[91] That tells me more junk is coming our way, and it is labeled gluten-free.

The food industry and grocery stores are loving this gluten-free fad! Even the Girl Scouts piloted a gluten-free cookie during the 2013-2014 cookie sale season. The gluten-free aisle now at your grocery store is full of junk, and stores are experiencing increased sales from Americans' increased demand. Snacks that are naturally gluten-free like potato chips are now advertising this fact on the packaging. That does not make potato chips healthy! However, this labeling is working to the manufacturers' benefit. Food analysts say the 456 percent increase in potato chips sales from 2012-2014 was the largest contributing factor to the 163 percent increase in overall gluten-free snack sales. Popcorn is also now being labeled gluten-free. Popcorn in the natural kernel form and air popped at home, or popped in a little canola oil and lightly salted is good. Microwave popcorn with all its chemical additives is an easy thumbs down.

The gluten-free food market will continue to thrive, especially with 41 percent of adults saying they agree that gluten-free is beneficial for everyone,[92] not just for those who have issues with gluten. The number of people who recognize that gluten-free is a fad increased from 33 percent in 2013 to 44 percent in 2014, but understanding it's just a fad hasn't slowed the buy-in. The number of Americans following a gluten-free diet nearly doubled from 2013 to 2014, from 15 percent to 22 percent.[93] Those who market gluten-free as a healthier, more natural option have been very successful. Of course, there are those people who must maintain a gluten-free diet for medical reasons, but the uptick in the market for gluten-free is mostly due to the public perception—built by clever marketers.

But there are plenty of naturally gluten-free foods, and they are found in the produce, meat, seafood and dairy sections of the grocery store. Beans, nuts and many grains are also naturally gluten-free. Foods *labeled* gluten-free, on the other hand, are almost always processed food products that we should not be eating. With the exception of those people who have a true gluten intolerance, our health issues are more likely due to the consumption of processed foods, in general, and not necessarily only because of the gluten. Processed foods have all sorts of additives, including gluten, and ingredients made in the lab.

Consider going back to the basics. A *real* gluten-free diet is made up of mostly fruits and vegetables, lean meats, fish and the naturally gluten-free grains. Gluten-free grains/starches to cook at home are: rice, cassava, corn, soy, potato, tapioca, beans, sorghum, quinoa, millet, buckwheat, groats, arrowroot, amaranth, teff, flax, chia, yucca, gluten-free oats and nut flours.[94]

The real gluten-free diet includes preparing and cooking meals at home, staying away from packaged processed foods and having treats only sometimes. Like anything else, start by simply choosing one thing to change. Recognize the hype and marketing around processed gluten-free foods and decide to buy cleaner and real foods.

Together, we have the power to change the food industry offerings by what we demand and what we buy.

ORGANICS

October 2012 marked the 10th anniversary of the USDA Organic seal. Our government has been strengthening oversight of the organic food industry, including establishing processes, refining applications and hiring inspectors. USDA Secretary Tom Vilsack has every intention of helping organic agriculture grow and thrive and increasing the number of certified organic operations.

What we love about organic agriculture is that it avoids most synthetic materials, such as pesticides and antibiotics, and follows standards related to how farmers grow crops and raise livestock. The USDA organic standards cover the product from farm to table, including soil and water quality, pest control, livestock practices and rules for food additives. Crops can only be grown in fields that have been free of fertilizers and pesticides for three years. There can be no genetically modified ingredients, no watering with sewer sludge treated water, no irradiation and no pesticides. Animals can only be fed grains that have been grown organically, and they are given no antibiotics unless they are sick, and no growth hormones. Animals must have access to the outdoors so they are free to roam and engage in their natural behaviors. Organic farms and processors must also separate organic food from non-organic and submit to an annual onsite inspection.[95]

What we don't love about organic agriculture is the price we have to pay to get it. All operations that grow, handle, or process organic products—if they want to call their products organic—must be certified. They receive the organic seal of approval once certified. More than 25,000 farmers, ranchers and other businesses receive premium prices for their products through the growing $35 billion U.S. organic retail market.[96]

The USDA Organic seal tells you that a packaged food product is at least 95 percent organic. It also tells you that it will not contain artificial ingredients or preservatives such as food colorings, hydrogenated oils or BHT (preservative). At the very least, it is a better choice of processed junk food as compared to other choices that have added artificial and synthetic ingredients.

While the USDA does not claim that organic foods are more nutritious than conventionally grown foods, what you get when you buy organic is knowing that you will not have pesticide residue on your produce, or foods made from genetically modified seeds, or meat that has been loaded up with hormones to help the animal grow for market. I suggest that if you can buy organic, then do that. [As an aside: the term *natural* on food labels does not mean organic, yet it should mean that you are buying something that at the very least does not include artificial or synthetic ingredients including color additives or a food product that would not normally be expected to be in that food.]

It is easy to get caught up in the marketing and "science" and food industry hype. Recognize that your primary food issue might not be whether you buy organically grown produce. It could be the consumption of processed or fast foods. No amount of organic apples can make up for the fact that you are also consuming chips or crackers, refined foods, large portions or fast food too often.

If you are interested in knowing what produce you might consider buying organic, there is an annual dirty dozen list ranking the top 12 fruits and vegetables in order of pesticide residues. Most of the fruits and veggies on the most contaminated list are those with edible outsides.

The 12 most contaminated:	The 12 Least Contaminated:
<ul><li>Peaches</li><li>Apples</li><li>Sweet Bell Peppers</li><li>Celery</li><li>Nectarines</li><li>Strawberries</li><li>Cherries</li><li>Pears</li><li>Grapes (Imported)</li><li>Spinach</li><li>Lettuce</li><li>Potatoes</li></ul>	<ul><li>Onions</li><li>Avocado</li><li>Sweet Corn (Frozen)</li><li>Pineapples</li><li>Mango</li><li>Asparagus</li><li>Sweet Peas (Frozen)</li><li>Kiwi Fruit</li><li>Bananas</li><li>Cabbage</li><li>Broccoli</li><li>Papaya[97]</li></ul>

GENETICALLY MODIFIED/ENGINEERED ORGANISMS

GMOs, or Genetically Modified Organisms, are seeds and foods that were developed, starting in the 1980s, to be pest-resistant and heat-tolerant. The term GMO is used inter-changeably with GE, or Genetically Engineered. Proponents are the farmers that use the seed as well as big businesses like Monsanto, ConAgra and the food companies that use their fin-ished products in their processed foods such as Sara Lee and Coca-Cola and Kellogg's, to name a few. These businesses also partner in lobbying against the labeling of foods and products that contain GMO. Their concern is that their business will be hurt because consumers may see products containing GMO as harmful, since the seeds have been manipulated through biotechnology. On the other hand, consumers may see GMO produce as a good value because it's cheaper: It can be grown with fewer pesticides and less frequent land tilling, making it more economic. In 2013, 169 million acres, or half of the U.S. land used for crops, were genetically engineered.

After much lobbying, the GMO labeling dispute has been resolved. On July 29, 2016, President Barack Obama signed a bill into law requiring the labeling of genetically engineered ingredients. Within the next two years, the legislation requires most food packages to carry a text label, a symbol or an elec-tronic code readable by smartphone that indicates whether the food contains GMOs. The food industry reports that GMOs from corn and soybeans are found in 75 percent to 80 percent of our foods.

Herbicide tolerant (HT) crops are GE crops developed to survive application of herbicides that previously would have destroyed the crop along with the targeted weeds. Here are some facts:

- Acreage of HT soybeans grew from 17 percent of all U.S. soybean acreage in 1997 to 93 percent in 2013
- Acreage of HT corn reached 85 percent of all U.S. corn acreage in 2013
- Insect-resistant corn and cotton have been available since 1996, and the bacteria (bacillus thuringiensis (Bt)) used on these crops protects the plant from certain insects over its entire life
- Plantings of Bt corn grew from about 8 percent of U.S. corn acreage in 1997 to 76 percent in 2013
- GE corn accounted for 90 percent of all corn acreage in 2013
- The five crops that are most genetically engineered are soy, canola, corn, cotton and sugar beets[98]

Even though the Food and Drug Administration says GMOs are safe to eat, I am skeptical. Genetic engineering sounds unnatural to me. I wonder if we are getting what we need from these foods and whether the nutrients in them can be absorbed in the same way organically grown foods are. The skeptics wonder about how GMOs affect our DNA. A review of several studies conducted by GMO opponents reports that the modified genes in plant and animal RNA, specifically microRNA, have been associated with diseases such as cancer, Alzheimer's and diabetes. They believe that evidence exists that GMOs cause harm to humans.[99] One study shows that once GMO genes are absorbed and enter the blood stream, the genetically modified DNA can actually be identified in the blood, muscle tissue and liver. And the study suggests that rats being fed a GMO diet eat more and grow fatter than those on a non-GMO diet.[100] To be fair, the scientists doing this research are opposed to GMO.

We have decades of assurances from biotechnology firms, food processors, federal regulators, and even a substantial share of scientists, that foods containing GMOs are safe. But there are studies, as mentioned above, that give me pause. And there is plenty of evidence indicating that there is reason for concern regarding the institutions involved in ensuring the safety of our food and water supplies. Think about lead in the water in Flint Michigan, or wood shavings in parmesan cheese or fish fraud in restaurants. In one investigation, 674 fish samples were collected from supermarkets, restaurants and sushi counters in 21 states. Eighty-seven percent of the snapper samples were not snapper, for one example.[101] According to the *New York Daily News*, in another investigation, Walmart's Great Value brand parmesan cheese contained about 8 percent cellulose (wood) and another brand's 100 percent parmesan cheese manufactured by Castle Cheese contained no parmesan at all and instead was made of swiss, mozzarella and cheddar.[102] There was also an awful olive oil scam not too long ago, where producers were adding chlorophyll to other kinds of oil to make it look the color of olive oil to deceive buyers and make larger profits.[103] All of this is disturbing, and especially when you pay a small fortune at the grocery store to have the health benefits of olive oil. Unfortunately, there is plenty of fraud out there—and our food safety agencies may or may not detect it—or may not detect it before it harms us!

You can identify produce that is genetically modified, organic or conventionally grown by looking at the PLU stickers and codes on produce; that is, if your grocery store chooses to use them. Not all of them do. In general, the PLUs are four- or five-digit codes that differentiate the produce. A five-digit code beginning with an 8 signifies a genetically modified product, a five-digit code beginning with a 9 identifies an organically grown product, and a five-digit code beginning with a 0 (or a four-digit code) marks a non-qualified (i.e., conventionally grown) product. In two more years, we will have electronic codes as part of the recently signed bill.

How our food is grown matters. The health of the soil, how crops are rotated and whether the seeds have been genetically modified are important variables, among many, that affect the nutrition in our food. You can read conflicting studies that provide support for conventionally grown, genetically modified and organics. I do not have the answers here, but I do think organic is clearly the winner, most importantly because organic produce is held to higher standards. We want fresh, nutrient-rich foods, delivered in a timely manner. We want them to be safe. The best case scenario is that you are able to buy locally and organically farmed produce right after it's harvested. There are many farm-to-table and farm-to-work enterprises contributing to a healthier society, and if you can patronize them, you'll be doing yourself a huge favor.

However, this discussion takes our focus away from what really matters first. If deciding between a genetically modified or an organic apple was our real issue today, we would not be an overweight and unhealthy population. It is easy to get caught up in the marketing and "science" and food industry hype. Again, do not let this hype distract you from the larger issues.

U.S. FOOD REGULATION AGENCIES

Our government, like all governments, is large and slow moving, administratively heavy, with many moving parts, rules and procedures.

The Federal Trade Commission (FTC) is an independent agency of the United States government comprised of three bureaus related to consumer protection, competition and economics. The FTC's charge is to protect consumers from unfair, fraudulent or deceptive business practices; to make sure our markets are free and open for competition; and to provide sound data analysis that informs antitrust, consumer protection and business regulation.

In response to the childhood obesity epidemic and following a mandate from Congress, in 2005, the FTC subpoenaed 44 food and beverage companies in the course of examining their practices of marketing to children and adolescents. The FTC found that in 2006, the food industry spent more than $2.1 billion marketing food to children and adolescents and $116 million marketing carbonated beverages to students in schools.[104] The report described product types (cereals, fast food, candy, etc.) and marketing methods (television, internet, prizes, event sponsorships, etc.) used by the industry to market to children and adolescents. Television was still the main source of advertising back then—now digital media and other very insidious forms of advertising plague the platforms where children congregate such as games, social media and a multitude of mobile applications.

While a 2012 FTC follow-up study found that food industry expenditures in marketing to children actually decreased by 19.5 percent to $1.79 billion, marketing to all age groups was a whopping $9.65 billion (2009 data[105])! Three quarters of that $1.79 billion youth directed marketing was from fast service restaurant foods, sweetened carbonated beverages and breakfast cereals to the tune of $1.29 billion.[106] How much was spent marketing fruits and veggies to teens that same year? That would be four-tenths of one percent.[107]

Marketing works. Studies looking at correlations between food advertising and food consumption show that we eat more because of marketing techniques. One study showed that children consumed 45 percent more snacks when exposed to food advertising and that adults consumed more of both healthy and unhealthy snack foods following exposure to snack food advertising. In both studies, food advertising increased consumption of products not even in the advertisements, and these effects were not related to reported hunger or other conscious influences.[108] Food advertising has the power to prime automatic eating behaviors and, thus, influence far more than brand preference.

But the more you know about these tactics, the less likely you will be influenced.

Food industry trade groups like the National Dairy Council, the Federation of State Beef Councils and Cattleman to

Cattleman are big and influential. Agricultural producers who are part of these groups pay into programs called "checkoffs," where a percentage of the profits from products sold is dedicated to generic marketing campaigns without reference to a particular brand. A dairy farmer might contribute $.15 cents to the dairy checkoff fund for every 100 pounds per milk sold, which pays for the familiar celebrity milk mustaches ads.[109] Another example is the "Beef; It's what's for dinner" campaign, which is funded by the beef checkoff fund. These checkoff programs are regulated by the USDA, but they are not government agencies.

It is up to us to change our food choices. Our government will never make the food industry stop producing junk. Also, because of food industry politics, you will not find "eat less" in our USDA healthy guidelines, there are only admonitions to eat more. Can you imagine the backlash from the National Dairy Council if the USDA advised: "Drink less milk" or "Eat less beef"? That would not go over so well. The USDA's key recommendations from the 2010 American Dietary guidelines look something like this:

- Increase vegetable and fruit intake
- Increase whole-grain intake by replacing refined grains with whole grains
- Increase intake of fat free or low fat milk and milk products, such as milk, yogurt cheese, or fortified soy beverages.
- Increase the amount and variety of seafood consumed by choosing seafood in place of some meat and poultry

The newer 2015-2020 American Dietary Guidelines promote healthy foods similarly, with an added focus on reducing added sugar, saturated fat and sodium consumption. This is the first edition to recommend a quantitative limit on added sugar consumption.[110]

It is nice to see recommendations for foods that provide more potassium, dietary fiber, calcium and vitamin D, which are nutrients of concern in American diets. These foods include vegetables, fruits, whole grains, milk and milk products. But even too much real food is damaging. Choose real food in moderation.

SCHOOLS, KIDS, PARENTS AND CONSUMPTION

In his book *Fast Food Nation*, Eric Schlosser exposes how the food industry and community institutions compromise our children's health for money. In 1993, a nationwide junk food and junk beverage advertising trend started in our public schools. That year, the Colorado Springs School District negotiated the first contract of its kind with Burger King. That first deal allowed Burger King to place ads in the school hallways and on the sides of school buses for $37,500 a year. Disappointed with the $37,500, school administrators hired a marketing professional, Dan DeRose, who renegotiated the contract and tripled the school district's revenues within the year. By 1997, DeRose negotiated a 10-year contract that made Coca-Cola the school's exclusive beverage supplier. That contract brought in $11 million over 10 years and paid for everything from football stadiums to field trips and school supplies.[111] In exchange, soda companies had access to their present and future loyal customers and the opportunity to create tastes, habits and loyalty for their products with the potential to last a lifetime. It only cost the health and nutrition habits of the city's children.

Author Michael Moss writes in his book *Salt Sugar Fat*, that soda companies target established soda drinkers to increase beverage sales. It is easier for them to sell more soda to the person who already drinks soda, than to get somebody who doesn't drink soda to start. They like to create "heavy users." Beverage companies sell their soda as loss leaders in grocery stores to get you hooked on more. Keep in mind that a 20 oz. soda has about 65 grams of sugar, which is 15 teaspoons! I may not find soda machines in my children's public school, but I do find equally artificial and sugar-laden Powerade®, made by The Coca-Cola Company. And this may be even worse for our kids than soda, because so many people THINK these "performance" beverages are better for them and may consume more.

We really need to see through the marketing and make the right choices. I would much rather see milk in school vending machines than sweetened beverages. In 2013, chocolate milk was advertised as a great after-workout beverage. My view is that chocolate milk is a better and much healthier option than a sweetened, artificially colored sports drink. Chocolate milk has protein and nutrients that refuel our bodies. The sugar and the chocolate may be an issue; however, organic chocolate milk (no HFCS, no food coloring, no artificial ingredients) after your child's soccer game is a healthier choice than blue Gatorade®.

The FTC report I mentioned earlier also found that those companies promoting food and beverage products to children or teens reported in-school marketing expenditures of $149 million, representing 8.3 percent of all youth expenditures.[112] Junk food is still prevalent in our public schools. The fryers may be out and the soda vending machines are gone, yet Chick-fil-A and pizza contracts are negotiated as well as a selection of less than healthy snacks, and Powerade® has replaced soda. The administrators at my sons' high school found that students were coming to school with Starbucks, so they filled the demand by opening up an onsite coffee shop.

It is a good habit to look at the nutritional labels on the food you are purchasing for your children. The USDA mandated that chain restaurants with more than 100 stores must make their nutrition content public. This transparency is supposed to make you think twice about what you and your children consume. However, despite the fact that McDonald's Chicken McNuggets® contain ingredients such as chicken ground with chicken skin, water, food starch-modified, sodium phosphates, baking soda, sodium acid pyrophosphate, sodium aluminum phosphate, mono calcium phosphate, calcium lactate and more—whenever I drive by our local McDonald's, the drive-thru line is wrapped around the building. I think people are still not paying attention or are not planning meals appropriately.

If you must have fast food for whatever reason, at least use the available nutritional information to choose the lesser of two evils. Chick-fil-A is not good for you, I'm not advocating it: The eight-count chicken nuggets contains 1,060 mg sodium and 13 grams of fat (this is two-thirds of the American Heart Association's recommendation of 1,500 mg of sodium per day).[113] But because it claims to be made of "real chicken," Chick-fil-A nuggets have more protein and less fat than McDonald's nuggets.

*Chick-fil-A® Nuggets - 4-piece	**McDonald's Chicken McNuggets® - 4-piece
Calories 135 Total Fat 6.5g Saturated Fat 1.25g Sodium 530mg Cholesterol 35mg Carbs 5g Protein 14g	Calories 190 Total Fat 12g Saturated Fat 2g Sodium 360mg Cholesterol 25mg Carbs 12g Protein 9g
Ingredients: nuggets (whole chicken breast, seasoning [salt, monosodium glutamate, sugar, spices, paprika], seasoned coater [enriched bleached wheat flour {with malted barley flour, niacin, iron, thiamine mononitrate, riboflavin, folic acid}, sugar, salt, monosodium glutamate, nonfat milk, leavening {baking soda, sodium aluminum phosphate, monocalcium phosphate}, spice, soybean oil, color {paprika}], milk wash [water, nonfat milk, egg], peanut oil [fully refined peanut oil, with Dimethylpolysiloxane, an anti-foam agent added]).	Ingredients (Before the July 2016 revamp): chicken ground with a bit of chicken skin, water, food starch-modified, sodium phosphates, baking soda, sodium acid pyrophosphate, sodium aluminum phosphate, mono calcium phosphate, calcium lactate, enriched flour, yellow corn flour, bleached wheat flour, food starch - modified, wheat starch, dextrose, salt, spices, corn starch, canola, corn, hydrogenated soy bean oil, citric acid, dimethylpolysiloxane, TBHQ. (McDonald's is revamping the ingredients summer 2016).

*Nutrition content taken from the 8-piece nuggets nutrition information from the Chick-fil-A® website and divided in half. Chick-fil-A® does not have a 4-piece option outside of a kid's meal. The nuggets come in 8- or 12-piece options. (6/11/2016)

**Ingredients and nutrition information is taken from a poster on the McDonald's website developed to sugarcoat the ingredients; therefore, these ingredients may or may not be in the order of abundance in the recipe. They are listed in order of the Chicken McNugget®-making process (6/11/2016).

To be fair, with the revamp of the McDonald's nugget recipe, here are the new ingredients and numbers: white boneless chicken, water, vegetable oil (canola oil, corn oil, soybean oil, hydrogenated soybean oil), enriched flour (bleached wheat flour, niacin, reduced iron, thiamine mononitrate, riboflavin, folic acid), bleached wheat flour, yellow corn flour, vegetable starch (modified corn, wheat rice, pea, corn), salt, leavening (baking soda, sodium aluminum phosphate, sodium acid pyrophosphate, calcium lactate, monocalcium phosphate), spices, yeast extract, lemon juice solids, natural flavors.[114]

And the small print, pulled at the same time the new ingredient list was made public, says, "Our fried menu items are cooked in a vegetable oil blend with citric acid added as a processing aid and dimethylopolysiloxane to reduce oil splatter when cooking. We are no longer adding TBHQ to our restaurant cooking oil, but as we transition to our new oil supply, some restaurants may have trace amounts of TBHQ in their cooking oil for a period of time. This information is correct as of July 2016 unless otherwise stated."[115]

McDonald's Chicken McNuggets® – 4-piece (new recipe)

Calories	180
Total Fat	11g
Saturated fat	2g
Sodium	340mg
Cholesterol	30mg
Carbs	11g
Protein	10g[116]

I am not a fan of any fast food. I have been able to bypass the drive-through and get home to a healthier meal by packing water and healthy snacks or by knowing it is worth the wait to get home. Recognize that there are healthier fast foods than others. Taco Bell will offer you a bean burrito as a healthier option, or you could find a sandwich shop and purchase a turkey sandwich loaded with veggies on whole wheat bread. The best option when you're pressed for time is to make a sandwich at home and load it with veggies.

It is up to us, as parents, to lead our children into a lifetime of good habits. Pack a healthy lunch for your children that includes water and fresh produce. Frustratingly, having the healthy lunch doesn't mean your children will eat it, but at least you are showing them what to eat and creating healthy habits. Kids are kids: most of the time, when given the choice, junk reigns—so as much as possible, don't give the choice!

There is a time and a place for treats, and morning is not the time. At a swim team event when my kids were in elementary school, a friend of mine complained that her daughter was eating Skittles at 7 a.m. I playfully asked, "Who gave her the money?" Thank goodness she acknowledged the question with an agreeable laugh. The real question is, "Why are we selling these types of concessions, especially at an early morning swim meet?!" You know why. Because it raises money for the team, and the team leaders know these types of concessions will sell. Another obstacle is finding the volunteers willing to buy and sell fresh produce that they feel won't sell to begin with. You know the rule…*he who first complains must volunteer.*

And who among us hasn't done the exact same thing? I teach about healthy eating for a living, and even I have been guilty of enabling some poor food choices. When my twin boys were 13 years old, we went on a family vacation to a Florida beach. Because we were on vacation, when I went to the store to stock the rental house for the week, I intentionally bought many snacks that I typically don't buy, thinking that decadent treats would make the vacation even more special. By the second day, all of the snacks were open, and at least half were eaten.

The kids were eating too much junk, and I was the one who bought it! I really didn't want to say anything—after all, I wanted the boys to have a good time—but finally, I couldn't help myself! I asked Luke and Dayne in a slightly elevated and alarmist tone, "How much junk are you going to eat?!" Without hesitation, Luke looked at me, shrugged, and politely said, as literally as you can imagine, "I don't know…as much as we have?"

I died laughing at his response! He nailed it! If you buy it, they will eat it, period!

For those of you who are parents, your job is to provide healthy choices for your children for a lifetime of good health. Do not listen to the marketing! Don't keep soda at home. Don't have junk readily available. Child nutrition studies show that we must not only have healthy foods available but also prepare and offer those foods to them. They will reach for foods that are convenient, so make sure those convenience foods are fresh fruits and veggies.

I find the marketing aspect of our food industry incredibly disturbing. However, there are things you can do to curb its influence. You can turn off media, you can eat more mindfully, and you can get a new hobby to stay busy and active. You do not have to buy or eat these foods. Use your purchasing power to change food industry practices, tactics and ingredients. You have to decide what goes into your grocery basket and into your home and into your body and the bodies of your family members.

> *"Perceptual reality is different for different species. In certain species it is a mode of observation so what we call scientific fact is usually not ultimate truth, it is perceptual experience, and it's a mode of observation."*
>
> — Deepak Chopra

11

Clinical Evidence: Scientific Miracle or Marketing?

"Modern medicine, for all its advances, knows less than 10 percent of what your body knows instinctively."

\- DEEPAK CHOPRA

Doctor's offices are selling diets. Insurance pays for bariatric surgery. Overweight people are getting liposuction and other body-shaping treatments. We are bombarded with advertisements for some miracle something or other such as coconut oil, testosterone, pharmaceutical weight loss therapies, quick fix diets and weight loss programs or products.

You might agree that your state of mind on any given day determines what you buy into. Staying true to your principles is a much better approach to decision making than relying on a mood. Look to yourself for answers instead of outside of yourself. How do you know if a study finding is credible? You can almost always find the qualifying verbiage, "evidence suggests" attached to stories about study results because there are always caveats. There are holes in every study. I suggest that when it comes to health and disease, read the science, but apply common sense.

For instance, when we learn that broccoli is good for us, it should come as no surprise. When we hear that naturally occurring stanols and sterols in plant foods can reduce cholesterol, that also should come as no surprise. When we hear that chocolate with added sterols proves to reduce cholesterol…I hope you're raising an eyebrow rather than opening your wallet at the candy counter.

The media magnifies study results, and we take the ball and run with it. I happen to like the studies like one that I read at one time, that show eating a small apple before dinner reduces calorie consumption by 160 calories each day. I like the meta-analysis that reviews 22 studies and finds for every seven grams of dietary fiber eaten, the risks of CVD (Cardiovascular Disease) and CHD (Coronary Heart Disease) are each lowered by nine percent.[117] Studies like these confirm what we already know about whole and nutritional foods.

It is okay to question nutrition or health studies supported by the food industry and to question new health claims. Even if a study isn't funded by the food industry, it can be misinterpreted by the press or poorly communicated such that readers don't understand the statistics cited, or twisted by a clever marketer. For example, I remember an insert in the

Austin American-Statesman a couple of years ago regarding the health benefits of nitric oxide, as found in beets. That is great information supporting why you might consider incorporating beets into your healthy diet. However, the promotion was for a crystalized packet of "all natural" something made from beets…OH, COME ON! That is not a beet! As I write this, I have a beet salad in my fridge as my go-to food this week. Eat real food.

Studies that proclaim the magical benefits of one food promote extremes. For example, there are claims that oranges help prevent cancer and other diseases. This anti-cancer activity is determined by testing the actions of phytochemicals, the non-nutritive plant chemicals that fight disease. Laboratory tests may determine that a plant food displays anti-cancer activity, or slows the growth rate of cancer cells, or helps regulate hormones or shows anti-inflammatory activity. We can see these results in the lab using petri dishes, but you cannot say that eating one particular food will save us from cancer. There is not one magic bullet. What you *can* say is that a diet rich in plant foods helps reduce disease risk.

I agree, just like you would, that an orange is a nutritionally dense food and an exceptional and healthy choice. However, it is not the orange alone that makes you healthy. All of your health and lifestyle habits matter. Nutrient absorption may be affected by drinking too much caffeine or alcohol, or you may have other health issues related to smoking, exercise, stress or even age. But maybe you heard about how great oranges are, so the orange might replace a less healthy food that you were eating before, and may help you eat less overall because you are more satisfied. Maybe eating oranges instead of what you used to eat has helped you drop a few pounds—and now that you feel better, you start exercising. So, eating oranges is a good thing—but not because of the sensational claim.

I want you to believe that eating a healthy diet rich in plant foods is the easiest, least-expensive way to reduce your disease risk, and it reduces your healthcare budget and make you feel good! Most experts agree that a diet rich in antioxidants, phytochemicals, fiber, lean proteins, plant-based foods and omega 3 fatty acids is a heart-healthy diet, a diabetes-preventing diet, and a healthy weight management diet. Such a diet simply reduces disease risk. These are your naturally gluten-free foods, your superfoods and your high fiber foods. There is not one specific vegetable that will prevent all disease—instead, it is your overall diet and lifestyle habits that matter.

CHOLESTEROL-LOWERING FOOD PRODUCTS
Plant sterols and stanols are substances that occur naturally in small amounts in many grains, vegetables, fruits, legumes, nuts and seeds. They work by blocking the absorption of cholesterol in the small intestine and, thereby, prevent it from being absorbed into the bloodstream. They look a lot like cholesterol on a molecular level, so essentially, they get in the way. A healthy diet rich in stanols includes leafy greens and some whole grains, but manufacturers have started adding stanols to foods as well. Many doctors recommend the fortified juices

and spreads containing stanols and sterols, but this is not an invitation to consume too much of anything.

Mars, Inc. came out with a line of sterol-laced chocolates called CocoaVia in 2005. Scientific evidence tells us that eating about two grams of plant sterols every day lowers cholesterol by about 10 percent in people with high cholesterol. The study, published in the *Journal of Nutrition* in April, 2008, showed that "the regular consumption of a heart-healthy chocolate bar (CocoaVia, Mars, Inc.) can lower total and LDL-cholesterol levels as well as reduce systolic blood pressure, a new study has shown. The benefits of eating the chocolate, a dark chocolate product supplemented with plant sterols, occurred without any weight gain, suggesting the cocoa-flavanols-rich treat might be helpful in the dietary management of cardiovascular risk, say investigators."

You have to eat this EVERY DAY to get the benefits? It might make sense, if you have high cholesterol, and if you replace a less healthy daily treat with this treat. But not all of us question studies like this. For example, a gentlemen attending one of my nutrition presentations half-jokingly asked, "Where can I buy that chocolate!?"

The New England Journal of Medicine reported on the cholesterol-lowering benefits of consuming Benecol branded margarine, which has added plant sterols. Apparently, you have to consume it every day in order to receive the benefits—but Benecol has hydrogenated oil in it as well. Hydrogenated oil is trans fat, and the worst artery-clogging fat we can consume. Trans fats every day! What do I think about this? Uh…NO.

The only way this would make sense is if you were a person who was already consuming cookies or crackers with high trans fat content every day, and you replaced those with this product that has less trans fat. Okay, so you would come out ahead in that context, but it is a clearly another "lesser of two evils" scenario.

Even Minute Maid® jumped on this bandwagon, coming out with "heart-wise" orange juice packed with a solid dose of phytosterols. Sterols in pill form are also widely available. You can find sterols in granola bars and more. All I can say is, nutritionist and food politics expert Marion Nestle, Ph.D., once commented that even she gets confused about what to believe anymore. My belief is that if we simply started eating real foods, all of this would be a non-issue. Choosing an apple every day instead of a granola bar would be to your health benefit.

COCONUT OIL

I did not ride the coconut oil wave either. Coconut oil is a saturated fat, which means it's an artery-clogging fat. Studies looking at how coconut oil consumption affects heart disease risk are scarce because most studies have evaluated long chain fatty acid saturated fats, and coconut oil has a medium chain fatty acid structure. The claim is that the medium chain fatty acids of coconut oil "burn" faster. This claim does not help the fact that it is a saturated fat. Saturated fats can be either short chain, medium chain or long chain fats, differentiated by the number of carbon atoms. Short chain fatty acids are considered to have six or fewer carbon atoms, medium chain fatty acids have eight to 10 carbon atoms, and long chain fatty acids generally have 12 or more carbon atoms. The healthier, unsaturated fats—both mono and polyunsaturated—are all long chain fatty acids. Most saturated fats are short chain fatty acids and then some are medium chain, like coconut oil.

There is just one study on this subject completed in the last 17 years. Malaysian researchers found that when they fed young men and women 20 percent of their calories from coconut oil for five weeks, LDL ("bad") cholesterol was eight percent higher and HDL ("good") cholesterol was seven percent higher than when the participants were fed 20 percent of their calories from olive oil.[118] Raising LDL is not a good thing.

Frank Sacks, a professor who studies cardiovascular disease prevention at the Harvard School of Public Health in Boston, said, "We know that raising LDL (lousy cholesterol) levels increases the risk of heart disease, [however] we can't say that raising HDL (healthy cholesterol) with diet or drugs can lower the risk of cardiovascular disease." Sacks' bottom line: "Since polyunsaturated oils lower LDLs and coconut oil raises LDLs, we can't recommend that people replace olive, canola, or other liquid oils with coconut oil."[119]

There is one large study that concludes it is the medium chain fatty acids of coconut oil saturated fat that helped one group lose four pounds over another group that consumed olive oil while on a restricted 1,500-1,800 calorie diet. This is one study. On the other hand, multiple studies have shown, and cardiologists agree, that olive oil has health and heart health benefits.

You can find many claims about the benefits of coconut oil, yet the Malaysian study supports my beliefs about it. I again contend that you cannot say that one food is the reason why someone is healthy. It may be that eating the one food encourages the elimination of other poor choices, and that is a benefit. If consuming coconut oil somehow encourages consumption of more vegetables and less saturated fats overall, then that might be a winning argument. Coconut oil, alone, as an addition to one's diet (which may include too much saturated fat already), or as a replacement for olive oil, is not the best choice. Olive oil has shown to reduce LDL, raise HDL and have heart healthy benefits.[120]

The best way to lower your risk for heart disease, Alzheimer's and other diseases is to consume a diet rich in dark and colorful vegetables, whole grains and lean meats—and to exercise. Sound familiar? Diet and exercise reduce risk factors for just about every disease…and…I am sticking with my extra virgin olive oil and canola oil.

PROBIOTICS

Probiotics are microorganisms that have a beneficial effect on the host. The claims are that these beneficial forms of gut bacteria reduce harmful bacteria and may relieve intestinal discomfort and aid in digestion. This claim is good for the yogurt manufacturers and the sellers of cleanses. My thought is that if choosing yogurt eliminates something less healthy that you were eating, then this is a good choice. But your body is an amazing machine that can take care of your gut just fine when you are making healthy choices.

It may be that probiotics aren't something magical, but simply that they can or should be part of a healthy diet. It is more likely that we are not eating healthy to begin with. In 2001, the World Health Organization convened an expert group of scientists and industry representatives to review the science and make recommendations for the evaluation and validation of probiotic health claims. Some studies show benefits and some have conflicting results. Since not every health claim could be substantiated with sufficient evidence for the claim being made for that specific microorganism, the WHO researchers declined to endorse some health claims of probiotics.[121]

RESVERATROL

Resveratrol in red wine has gotten a lot of attention. Resveratrol is a phytochemical that is shown to be good for our brains, our hearts and our health. However, red wine contains alcohol. Alcohol is a toxin and a human carcinogen.

So you tell me: If I have one glass of wine every now and then, is that healthy? Probably. If I have two glasses, and I feel bad the next day, do you think that is a good thing? Probably not. Too much of a good thing is not good. Yes, resveratrol is good, and yes, wine sometimes in small amounts is also good. But alcohol depletes nutrients and deteriorates memory. Resveratrol is good for memory, your heart and muscle strength, but you can also get the health benefits of resveratrol from other foods such as grapes and blueberries.

The CDC recommends if you do not drink alcohol, then do not start. If you do drink alcohol, the recommendation for women is to have no more than one alcohol serving per day and, for men, no more than two per day. One alcohol serving/drink is the equivalent of a 12 oz. beer, a 5 oz. glass of wine or 1.5 oz of hard liquor.

pH AND ACIDITY

Oh please stop. Your body has powerful mechanisms in place to maintain homeostasis and a normal pH of 7.4. The pH of your body is regulated in three ways: through your kidneys, through your lungs and through chemical buffers within your cells and body fluids. Having said that, if you are not able to clear carbon dioxide through normal breathing, or you have kidney disease or your kidneys cannot remove enough acid from the body, then you may have a problem.

Acidosis, a pH of below 7.35, can occur if you're a heavy drinker, your liver doesn't function properly, you are on certain medications, have diabetes, have cancer or just had surgery, for a few examples. Acidosis is typically found in unhealthy individuals or in those undergoing intensive medical care. A study published in *Diabetes Care* reviewed the incidence of acidosis in hospitalized patients who were on metformin. They found that nine patients out of 100,000 may experience acidosis.[122] Metformin is a medication used to control high blood sugar and is taken by people with diabetes. I have learned that some physicians are prescribing it for physician-supervised weight loss.

If you are otherwise healthy, your body will regulate itself beautifully. The appropriate diet to prevent acidosis is the one I have been sharing with you all along. If you are buying a product or specific food or drink to prevent acidosis, then I would say you have been had. I should add that it probably doesn't hurt, yet it is *completely* unnecessary. The principle of moderation in all things remains. Eat your fruits and vegetables and portion control your meals.

LOW TESTOSTERONE

Testosterone levels typically decline with age. Hormone replacement for Low T seems to be a newer fad; and many doctors support it, but not all of them. I raise my eyebrows when I see testosterone clinics popping up all over Austin, especially since we do not know the long-term effects of testosterone replacement.

While the marketing for Low T treatments promises a man that he will lose weight and have more muscle mass, a better sex drive, more alertness and energy, I believe these results are really unlikely. A recent study of 800 men, 65 years and older, being treated at 12 centers nationwide indicated there was only modest improvement in their sex lives, walking strength and mood. More than half of the men reported no change in sexual desire.[123]

In 2014, after the U.S. Food and Drug Administration (FDA) investigated the risk of stroke, heart attack and death in men taking FDA-approved testosterone products, the agency began requiring manufacturers to add to their warning labels the increased risk of heart attack and stroke with testosterone use. Two studies, in particular, sparked this action—each suggested an increased risk of cardiovascular events among men prescribed testosterone therapy. Other studies reported an increased risk of heart attack, stroke or death associated with testosterone treatment. Still others found no such risks.[124]

The more body fat a man has, the more estrogen he has. If the muscle mass increases and the body fat decreases, then more testosterone and less estrogen is the result. If you haven't exercised for years at a time, then you have been losing muscle mass at a faster rate than if you had been exercising. So, once again, exercise is the solution.

OTHER "SCIENCE" FACTS OR FICTION

Stress

How does stress relate to being overweight? If you are eating processed, refined foods that wreak havoc on your blood sugar levels, affecting every organ in your body—your liver, brain, skin and heart—then, it would make sense that you do not feel your best and won't handle stress as well as a person who has a healthy diet and exercises daily. Stress releases the hormones cortisol and norepinephrine, and those hormones run through your bloodstream, enabling arteries to clog with cholesterol more easily than if you had coped better with stress. Hans Selye, MD, reminded us that stress plays a role in all disease.

Some studies show that there is a relationship between stress hormones and obesity; yet others suggest that being overweight in the first place is what messes up your hormones. So while there's no clear cause and effect, there is the suggestion that stress potentially contributes to the development of obesity.[125]

In our fast-paced society, where we overeat, have a sedentary lifestyle and don't get enough sleep, it stands to reason that the resulting stress will trigger hormone imbalances and food cravings. When you are stressed, you are more likely to eat for comfort, and typically, comfort foods are high in salt, sugar and fat. Knowing that your hunger hormone regulators, leptin (suppresses appetite with low values during the day and rises at night, leptin is tied to circadian rhythms) and ghrelin (regulates food intake), are out of whack when you are tired might help you prioritize sleep, and therefore, handle stress better.

Sleep helps you naturally regulate your hormones and deal with stress better. How stress, sleep and food affect weight is iterative and additive. You may not be sleeping well because you are overweight, and not the other way around. You may not be sleeping well because you are stressed; and then, you are stressed because you're not getting enough sleep. To make matters worse, if you are tired, you may snack more for energy to stay awake; and you are less likely to exercise because you are tired.

Stress affects everyone. The best way to manage your stress is to process your thoughts in a healthy and positive way. Eating is not a solution to stress, it just offers a distraction and adds to the problem. Cut the words "emotional eater" out of your vocabulary. You are a healthy eater, and you have a strategy for when those moments of stress tempt you to fall into old habits. You will change your patterns to healthier ones.

SUGAR CRAVINGS

Some recent studies have compared sugar's effect on the brain to that of heroin, nicotine or alcohol. Some scientists are saying sugar has addictive qualities due to a dopamine response, which is similar, but much less volatile, to that released with the use of such drugs. Dopamine is the happy neurotransmitter in your brain associated with the reward and pleasure centers of the brain.

From a clinical perspective, labeling our actions as "diseases" or "addictions" *supposedly* helps to alleviate the stigma surrounding the condition. However, using the word "addiction" to describe sugar cravings is alarming to me. I prefer to use the softer and more descriptive word "habit." The word "habit" implies we can change. I worry that calling a sugar habit an addiction allows for a sense of defeat and suggests that sugar cravings have control over us. But that is preposterous! I acknowledge that cravings are real, and I am not denying that you may feel out of control sometimes…but you can regain control.

We need to understand what keeps those sugar cravings alive. First, we need to know where the sugar is. Sugar is in the obvious foods such as in breakfast cereal, soda, candy, cakes and cookies. But it is also in much less obvious places and in most processed foods such as spaghetti sauce, crackers, flavored yogurts, trail mix, dried fruits and granola bars. What's more, starches such as white bread and pasta break down into sugar. The list goes on. Check your food labels and review ingredients before you buy anything.

When you consume sugar in the form of these empty calorie, processed foods, your taste receptors activate the brain's reward system, and you get the dopamine response. Consuming healthy foods elicits a dopamine response, too, and we feel satiated. But consuming processed foods results in a decrease of the receptors in charge of satiety, so you will crave more and never feel satisfied.

If you rarely eat sugar or do not eat much at any one time, you will get the dopamine reward but not the cravings for more and more. However, if you consume sugar often or in large quantities, your dopamine levels do not balance out, and the cravings continue. Because sugar is in so many processed foods, you may be consuming more sugar than you think, and that keeps the vicious sugar craving cycle alive and well.

When you consume sugar, your brain asks, "Do I want to do that again?" The answer is a resounding YES! Reward! It is good to know that dopamine is also released during sex and when socializing with people we like. It is released during all activities that make us feel good and bring us pleasure. This is why making plans with friends is rewarding and energizing. Having a planned distraction, like going for a walk with your spouse, when you feel a craving coming on will be a nice reward to hardwire as your new natural response to the sugar craving.

OBESITY—A DISEASE?

At the American Medical Association (AMA) 2013 Annual Meeting, physicians voted overwhelmingly to label obesity as a disease. It is no surprise there was opposition to this decision.

Proponents say that obesity is a pathophysiologic disease that requires a range of interventions to advance treatment and prevention including behavioral modifications (therapy), medications and surgery. Opponents say that although obesity is an epidemic, it does not meet the criteria for disease. One physician likened obesity to smoking. Smoking isn't a disease, although it can "cause disease such as lung cancer and emphysema in the same way that obesity can lead to diabetes and hypertension."[126]

Both proponents and opponents of the decision say that combating obesity requires behavioral modifications. I agree. Behavioral modification programs such as those that deal with smoking cessation or weight loss only work when participants are willing to make changes, and such programs require self-discipline and perseverance. I understand that some think saying that obese people need to practice self-discipline comes across as lacking compassion. I propose that denying self-discipline has to be a large part of the solution is more harmful. You have to be willing to change and willing to put in the effort. I didn't say it was easy. Nothing worthwhile is.

The "obesity is a disease" proponents say that losing weight is more than a self-discipline issue. Sure it is. I didn't say that self-discipline is THE ONLY solution. Consider that in obese people, hormones have changed, the endocrine system has changed and neuro pathways are hardwired to respond to triggers in certain ways—thus, having support to make changes is an essential part of the solution. But if you believe that weight loss and healthy weight maintenance are out of your control, that allows you to never be held responsible for your ability to overcome life's hardest challenges. The problem with calling obesity a disease, from my perspective, is that it allows people to say: "I have a disease, so I cannot change and it is not my fault." This is dangerous thinking.

The person who decides to quit smoking uses every strategy and resource available to overcome his addiction. Quitting the habit takes self-discipline, a deep desire for change, strength, strategy, courage and support and a completely new way of thinking. Then, to continue not smoking, the ex-smoker has to make a choice every day—in moments of stress, when others are smoking around him, when he pours his cup of coffee that used to be accompanied by a morning cigarette for 15 years—to not reach for a cigarette. Smoking is a tough addiction to break. The American Cancer Society has a whole list of guidelines to help people quit smoking. It is intense.

The American Cancer Society reports that four out of 10 smokers made a quit attempt last year (meaning they quit for at least one day) and that 100,000 smokers will quit for good this year.[127] The CDC reports that, "Most former smokers quit without using one of the treatments that scientific research has shown can work."[128] This suggests that most people do just DECIDE to quit and accomplish cessation on their own (like my father—one day he just said, "Mind over matter" and was finished); but many reach for treatments that have proven effective such as counseling, medications, behavioral therapies, hotlines and more.[129] Such approaches and resources are similar to those available for those seeking to lose weight.

It would make sense, then, that the National Weight Control Registry (NWCR) reports findings on weight loss similar to those related to smoking cessation. The NWCR is the largest prospective investigation of long-term weight loss maintenance and currently tracks more than 10,000 individuals who have lost significant amounts of weight and have kept it off for long periods of time. Of the people registered who have kept the weight off for at least 5.5 years, 45 percent lost weight on their own, and 55 percent lost weight with some type of program.

Ridding ourselves of the triggered behaviors that seem to control us is a matter of practicing every day until we can replace the unhealthy behavior with a healthy one. This is true for issues related to food, or smoking, or alcohol or drug addiction, anger, depression or whatever the destructive or debilitating behavior may be. Having support and resources helps, yet deciding you are ready to change, believing that you can and taking action is how you succeed.

Unfortunately, behavioral modification therapy as part of the weight loss game is not a quick fix. It takes time and multiple sessions, and health plans typically do not cover therapy, or at least not long-term therapy. Doctors do not have time to counsel these patients to the degree it would take to modify their behavior; and although some doctors may have weight loss programs, they are expensive or not comprehensive enough. This is a health spending issue. The obesity "support groups" I found online are sponsored by the proponents for bariatric surgery. That is a one-sided push for medical obesity solutions. I believe it is a nasty trend.

It is certain that coding obesity as a disease will result in more bariatric surgeries being covered by insurance, more drugs used, more weight loss/control pharmaceutical drug research and more physician-managed weight loss programs. Even in the wake of healthcare reform, we are continuing to spend time and resources on treating the problem rather than preventing it—even though it is so clear how to prevent obesity in the first place. It is a fact that our diet has changed significantly in the past 30 years, contributing to one-third of Americans being obese and a 400 percent increase in morbid obesity since 1986. It is also a fact that the annual medical cost of obesity in America is $147 billion, and that obese people pay an average of $1,429 more annually for medical care than people of average weight.[130] This is all preventable.

Bariatrics is the study and treatment of obesity and includes gastric bypass surgery, gastric band or sleeve gastrectomy. In gastric bypass surgery, the stomach is cut to form a smaller stomach pouch, and then the small intestine is cut and reattached to the smaller stomach pouch. The gastric sleeve is a stomach stapling surgery that drastically reduces the size of the stomach. And the gastric band (lap-band) is a surgery that restricts the amount of food you can eat. The band is attached to the top portion of the stomach and slows the consumption of food, and it has not been as "successful" in supporting long term weight loss. All of these surgical procedures reduce the amount of food one can eat. But like all weight loss strategies, these measure also require behavior modification in order to result in successful weight loss and improved health. You can't have surgery and then eat the same things you have always eaten and expect good results; just as you can't go on a diet, hit your goal and then start eating the things you ate before and expect to maintain.

Hospital-based bariatric programs partner with health plans and board certified surgeons with experience in bariatric surgery to create "centers of excellence," and then arrange a fee or rate with the insurance carrier. For insurance companies, it costs less in administrative effort to negotiate a $5,000 rate for bariatric surgery than it does to process claims for chronic disease therapy over time. Insurance companies save money paying for surgery rather than paying for the chronic disease healthcare expenses caused by obesity. There are more and more of these bariatric centers popping up all over the country. It is most alarming that these include specific centers for pediatric bariatric programs. Something is terribly wrong with this picture.

You will hear more and more advertising for bariatric surgery because, in the long run, it costs the health plan payers less, and it generates revenues for those participating. The ads will make people believe this is their *only* solution, offering justifications for surgical solutions, acknowledging the suffering that comes with weight struggles and making people feel good about that decision.

There is more information promoting these surgeries than opposing them, and this is the trend that will continue into the unforeseen future. Studies in support of these surgeries are often sponsored by the companies that make the medical devices used in them. For instance, *The New England Journal of Medicine* recently published a study supporting bariatrics, sponsored in part by Ethicon (a Johnson & Johnson device company). The science behind the bariatric push is that it "cures" type 2 diabetes. No kidding: Any significant weight loss will reduce the risk of diabetes. We are a quick-fix society, and the co-morbidities associated with obesity are the justifications for these extreme solutions.

The latest support for bariatrics is coming from the study of our microbiota—what we used to call "gut flora," or the micro-organisms living in our intestines. Evidence suggests that the gut microbiota plays a significant role in how we process, store and expend energy from our diet. The microbiota presents differently in lean and normal weight people as compared to obese people. The argument, then, is that the gastric bypass surgery in obese people actually changes the gut microbiota to that of a normal weight person, even though the obese person is not (yet) a normal weight. This is the justification for the bariatric push from a clinical perspective—not to mention, it is big business.

What we know about bariatrics and microbiota is that it is NOT completely understood. The accumulating evidence suggests that the microbes are different in obese people and normal weight people, yet not every study has similar results. We know that diet affects the pathogenesis of obesity, and is a key contributor to overweight. We are not clear on how the gut microbiota structure changes. But we also know *for sure* that diet, calorie restriction and physical activity change gut micro-biota. One Mayo Clinic study published in 2012 shows that gut microbiota structures can be drastically altered by variations in calorie intake. Another study of microbiome transplantation in mice also showed that by shifting from a low-fat plant-based diet to a high-fat, high-sugar diet altered the gut community structure and metabolic functions within one day.[131]

In 2013, there were an estimated 179,000 bariatric surgeries performed in the United States, up from 158,000 in 2008. This is good news, according to the American Society for Metabolic and Bariatric Surgery (ASMBS). In the May 2014 issue of the ASMBS news magazine, the organization's past president said, "The good news is cases are growing again… The bad news is this still represents less than one percent of the eligible patient population surgery."[132] I recognize that proponents of this trend might actually *believe* this is the solution. But *I believe* this is a quick fix that doesn't address the root causes of the problem, and it's a profit-driven surgery targeted at people who have "tried everything else."

There is little debate that diet is the key contributing factor to obesity. We change for the worse the body's amazing natural ability to regulate itself when we make poor food choices. Overweight changes our endocrine system, our brain, our guts, our feelings and our emotions. It is destructive, but it is preventable and reversible—and the bariatric solution is a nasty trend.

A better approach is to widely disseminate resources related to prevention, and to provide counseling and nutritional advice to those who are struggling with weight. This book is one of those resources! The approach I advocate builds solid, strong, resilient and courageous individuals and communities. People who believe that they "cannot" help themselves lose hope and make no progress. The other "solutions" put forth for this health problem only contribute to the degradation of our society. I am not saying bariatric surgery is not useful for some morbidly obese people. But I'd like to see the bariatric surgery trend slow down, and I'd like to see more spending on weight gain prevention and health promotion and education.

The solution, as I see it, is more health education for all, especially for young children and for those with few resources. We know that socioeconomic status plays a significant role in obesity. Those living in poverty, or near-poverty, are likely to live in food deserts, where the only source of food is a convenience store that stocks highly processed and packaged goods. They have very little disposable income to spend on exercise facilities, equipment or clothing and may be unaware of the long-term effects of poor diet and lack of exercise—or simply, they must focus on more immediate challenges related to meeting their basic needs.

There are many good health education programs that support people at all income levels. Some of those resources are the American Diabetes Association, WeViva (a newer nonprofit that brings free Zumba and cooking classes to apartment-dwellers), the Department of Health and Human Services (HHS) and the YMCA, to name a few. The Surgeon General recently commended the YMCA for its good work to strengthen spirits, minds and bodies. I am a big fan of the YMCA because of its community programs, outreach and work in schools—and it provides financial assistance for those who need help. The Y's laudable value platform is Healthy Living, Social Responsibility and Youth Development. The earlier and the more affordable (i.e., free) outreach, the better. There are obstacles to overcome, including access to transportation, availability of fresh fruits and vegetables and cultural barriers.

I believe that school systems should mandate a modern day home economics course that focuses on self-care, nutrition, food prep and awareness of food marketing techniques. Sprinkle in the promotion and practice of positive psychology, the power of choice, purpose and gratitude, and we just might raise a healthy generation. That would be empowering.

> *"By abstaining from pleasures we become temperate and once temperate we are more able to abstain from them. Likewise, once habituated to despise what is terrible we become courageous."*

> - ARISTOTLE

FINAL THOUGHTS

The U.S. weight loss market totaled $64 billion in 2014.[133] There is an unbelievable amount of noise out there: slick marketing campaigns, industry-sponsored studies and profit-motivated medicine. But you already know how to take care of yourself, and only you know what you are truly capable of. Make certain you are telling yourself the right story. Do not let anyone convince you that you need something you don't. You have everything you need right now to start. The solutions are inside of you and not outside of you.

> *"The journey of a thousand miles begins with one step."*

> - LAO TZU

12

Real Foods: What and the Why

"Our bodies are our gardens to which our wills are gardeners."

The greatest philosophers recognized that we are what we eat, and that everything we put into our bodies affects every part of our being (spirit), our physical body and mind. Aristotle believed that which nourishes the body also nourishes the soul, and Hippocrates said, "Let food be thy medicine and medicine be thy food."

Food is meant to nourish our bodies. It is not to fill emotional voids. Keep your focus on what you want. If you are unclear of what you desire, keep practicing everything in Part 1, and it will reveal itself to you and put you on your path.

If you have looked to food to fill emotional needs, reaching for products that are high in sugar, fat and salt, it's time to change the way you eat. And you can do it by taking just one step at a time; you do not have to completely change your diet overnight. Take your food preferences into consideration when you are making healthy changes, as those will play a role in your success. If you do not like to drink your food, then a fruit smoothie with blueberries and spinach might not satisfy you. But, a spinach salad with blueberries might do the trick. Remember Jeremiah's story. He changed what he was willing to change first, and lost 50 pounds in seven months and is maintaining. You will get healthier by making one healthy choice at a time, and one day at a time, and then the years start to pass by and your new preferences become a way of life. You will know when it is time to enjoy a favorite food in the right amount and then get back to your normal diet routine.

We know for scientific fact that people who eat a diet rich in plant foods have lower disease risk than those who don't. We also know that evidence suggests that the main predictors of disease risk are weight and waist circumference. Plant foods taste amazing, and the truth is that you will crave them more and more as you go down this path. Less healthy foods will not taste as good, they will taste artificial.

REAL FOODS
Real foods have many fun names. You may have heard them called:

Superfoods
High fiber foods

Cancer fighting foods
Rich in phytochemical foods
Gluten-free foods
Rich in antioxidants foods
Plant foods
Flatten your belly foods
Low-fat foods
Low glycemic foods
Fat burning foods
Energizing foods
Rich in vitamins and minerals foods
"Drop pounds fast" foods
Eat for your skin foods
Colors of the rainbow foods

In general, these are your plant foods.

In this chapter, I am going to arm you with food lists for your consideration and information. These are healthy food lists from each macronutrient group (carbohydrates, proteins, fats) to choose from. Much of the general information such as this is from our USDA Dietary Guidelines. I am not telling you what to do. That will never work. I have never met a person in all of my life who likes to be told what to do.

So, start with what you are willing to do—go back to Part 2 and revisit your vision, your plan and your personalized approach to your weight loss and better health. The more you learn, the more you do, the stronger you get, and the cycle continues. This is an upward spiral that you create for yourself, and much better than any alternative.

Let's start with a basic framework and a healthy structure to follow. The Mediterranean diet is a good foundation because it focuses on plant foods. When following these guidelines, taking into account your food preferences and eating the right portions, you will be on the right track.

THE MEDITERRANEAN DIET

The Mediterranean diet is associated with a reduced risk of heart disease and cancer, as well as a reduced incidence of Parkinson's and Alzheimer's diseases in a clinical analysis of more than 1.5 million healthy adults who followed this diet. A vegetarian diet results in the same reduced risks, as does one rich in fruits and veggies and omega-3 fatty acids. These are just different ways to say the Mediterranean diet, or a superfoods or an anti-cancer diet...you get the picture.

The Mediterranean diet recognizes the importance of being physically active and enjoying meals as a social celebration with friends and family. The most significant part of this diet is plant-based foods such as fruits and vegetables, whole grains, legumes and nuts, olive oil, herbs and spices, and heart-healthy oils such as olive

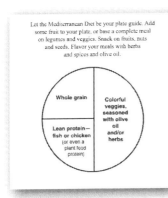

Let the Mediterranean Diet be your plate guide. Add some fruit to your plate, or base a complete meal on legumes and veggies. Snack on fruits, nuts and seeds. Flavor your meals with herbs and spices and olive oil.

Whole grain

Colorful veggies, seasoned with olive oil and/or herbs

Lean protein— fish or chicken (or even a plant food protein)

oil in place of saturated fats such as butter. Easy on the salt, and use herbs and spices to flavor foods instead.

The diet suggests eating fish and seafood often, at least two times per week. Poultry, eggs, cheese and yogurt should be consumed only in moderate portions daily to weekly. And finally, a very little red meat and sweets may be consumed—and red meat no more than a few times a month. Oh, and there is the option of drinking red wine in moderation, too!

It's good for me that the Mediterranean diet includes bread. In the Mediterranean culture, people eat bread, but they dip it in olive oil rather than spread butter on it. One tablespoon of butter has seven grams of artery-clogging saturated fat. Butter is one of those foods that is meant to be consumed very sparingly. So you really can eat bread in a healthy way. Another healthy way to enjoy bread is to make bruschetta topped with fresh tomatoes and basil, olive oil, balsamic vinegar, and a little garlic and salt and pepper. I have included my favorite bruschetta recipe in the Appendix.

And as with everything, moderation is the key! Too much of anything is not good!

The nutrient-dense food list below matches the Mediterranean diet, and these are the foods that should make up most of your diet. There is room in your diet for other favorite foods sometimes and in moderation. You get to decide what those "sometimes" options look like for you. You will know what is worth it to you as you become more aware, as you see results, and as your taste preferences change.

The Best-in-Class foods:

VEGETABLES:
Any leafy green vegetable:
Arugula, Collard Greens, Endive, Escarole, Kale, Mustard Greens, Romaine lettuce Spinach, Swiss Chard, Turnip Greens, Watercress

Any cruciferous vegetable: (This class of vegetables is especially known for cancer-fighting properties)
Broccoli, Brussels Sprouts, Cabbage, Bok Choy, Cauliflower

All other vegetables:
Asparagus, Artichokes, Bean Sprouts, Beets, Carrots, Celery, Cucumbers, Eggplant, Garlic, Onions, Leeks, Mushrooms, Okra, Parsley, Peppers, Radishes, Squash (yellow, zucchini, spaghetti, butternut, acorn), Sweet Potatoes or Yams, String Beans, Turnips

Fruits:
Apples, Apricots, Avocados, Bananas, Blackberries, Blueberries, Cantaloupe, Cherries, Grapefruit, Grapes, Guavas, Honeydew, Kiwi, Kumquats, Lemons, Limes, Mangos, Nectarines, Oranges, Papayas, Peaches, Pears, Pineapple, Plums, Pomegranates, Raspberries, Rhubarb, Strawberries, Tangerines, Tomatoes

Starches and whole grains:
Wild Rice, any Ancient Grain (Quinoa, Farro, Kamut, Amaranth, Chia Seed), Brown Rice, Sweet Potato, Lentils, any Bean such as Garbanzo, Black or Kidney

Oils and fats:
Only Unprocessed and Unrefined oils such as 100% Virgin or Extra Virgin Olive Oil (organic if you can), Unrefined Cold Pressed Canola Oil (organic if you can), Flax Oil, Grape Seed Oil, Sesame Oil

Dairy:
Nonfat Greek Yogurt, Nonfat Milk (skim), Unsweetened Milk Alternatives if dairy is an issue for you (all in moderation)

Protein:
Fish (Salmon, Tuna, Trout, Mackerel, Sardines), Eggs, Chicken, Turkey

Nuts and seeds:
Almonds, Walnuts, Flaxseeds, Chia Seeds, Nut Butters

This real food diet will make you feel amazing. You don't know how good you can feel until you feel this good.

The Macronutrients: Fats, Carbohydrates and Proteins
Now, I'll go into a little more detail about these macronutrient groups, what they do for our bodies, and why they're important. I'll also provide some guidance on what is considered the right amount of each, and what that looks like in terms of portions.

FATS
Monounsaturated and Polyunsaturated Fats
The right fats, monounsaturated fatty acids and polyunsaturated fatty acids (including the omega-3 fatty acids) are essential

to help our bodies transport and absorb the fat-soluble vitamins A, D, E and K in our bloodstream. These vitamins maintain healthy tissues, hormones, skin, brain and individual cells throughout the body. Essential fatty acids are, well, essential for many body functions. We need these in the right amounts for growth, brain and hormone functions. Fat is a macronutrient just like carbohydrates and proteins. Fat provides energy, but just like anything else, if we eat too much, it is stored as fat. So, you will want to replace saturated fats with the heart healthier fats.

Monounsaturated fats are fat molecules that have one unsaturated carbon bond in the molecule, called a double bond. Polyunsaturated fats are fat molecules that have more than one unsaturated carbon bond in the molecule. Oils that contain mono and polyunsaturated fats are typically liquid at room temperature but start to turn solid when chilled. Monounsaturated fats and polyunsaturated fats can help reduce your LDL (lousy) cholesterol levels in your blood, which, in turn, can lower your risk of heart disease and stroke. Monounsaturated fats are also known to increase your HDL (healthy) cholesterol levels.

Foods and oils high in monounsaturated fats are plant-based olive oil, canola oil, peanut oil, safflower oil and sesame oil. Other sources include avocados, peanut butter and many nuts and seeds.

Oils rich in polyunsaturated fats also provide essential fats that your body needs but can't produce itself—such as omega-6 and omega-3 fatty acids. You can get the omega-3 fatty acids by eating cold water fish such as salmon or mackerel, herring or trout.

Most foods contain a combination of unsaturated fats. When it comes to the fats and oils, I would focus on knowing which ones to reach for and why: some are good for your arteries, brain function, maintaining a healthy weight or increasing energy; others raise your good cholesterol and lower the bad, and therefore, are good for overall heart health. Do your best to use the ones listed here instead of others. The USDA's recommended daily allowance for oil for women is five to six teaspoons and for men, six to seven teaspoons.

Oils, walnuts and flaxseed are the best way to get these essential fatty acids if you are not a fan of fish. If you do not enjoy fish now, try to like it grilled, broiled or baked and not fried. Mind your portions and load your plate with leafy greens because your healthy fats are still "fat." Use olive oil instead of butter on your veggies and bread. You are much better off eating half an avocado flavored with some fresh-squeezed lemon and a little salt and pepper than a "protein bar" or a muffin or a cookie.

Saturated Fats

Diets heavy in saturated fat correlate with premature death. One in every four men and women in the world (and in the U.S.) die of heart disease each year. This is a global issue that is mostly preventable. Too much saturated fat consumption is a risk factor for heart disease.

Fat Source	Serving Size
Cold pressed organic canola oil (because the canola crop is one of the most highly genetically modified, and refined oils are not healthy, you want to buy organic if you can)	1 tsp = 40 calories = 5 g fat
Extra Virgin Olive Oil	1 tsp = 40 calories = 4.5 g fat
Avocado	1 oz. = 3 small slices = 50 calories = 4.5 g fat
Almonds	1 oz. = 23 almonds = 14 g unsaturated fat
Walnuts	1 oz. = 12-14 halves or 1/4 cup = 18 g fat
Flaxseed	2 Tablespoons = 75 calories = 5 g fat
Cold water fish—salmon, mackerel, herring	1 oz. = 58 calories = 3.5 g fat (a portion is typically 3- 4 oz.)

A saturated fat is one that contains only saturated fatty acids, is solid at room temperature and comes mainly from animal food products. Examples of saturated fat are butter, lard, meat fat, solid shortening, palm oil and coconut oil. Saturated fat tends to raise the level of cholesterol in the blood. High cholesterol is a risk factor for heart disease.

I mentioned my views on coconut oil in Chapter 11. Coconut oil is 92 percent saturated fat. More specifically, one tablespoon of coconut oil has more saturated fat than found in steak or bacon in equal portions. It is used for commercial frying and in candies and margarines, as well as in non-edible products such as soaps and cosmetics. I am not a fan of this coconut oil trend. You can find studies to support whatever side of the fence you are on. I am on the "it's a saturated fat" side. Research has shown that olive oil increases HDL and lowers LDL and reduces your cardiovascular disease risks.

Our bodies do not require saturated fat for nourishment. Higher intake of saturated fats is associated with high levels of LDL, which is the bad cholesterol that lines your arteries. Higher total and LDL cholesterol levels are risk factors for cardiovascular disease.

The American Heart Association now recommends that between 25 and 35 percent of your total daily calories should come from fats from foods like fish, vegetable oils and nuts, with the aim that no more than five to six percent of total calories come from saturated fat. The USDA says no more than 10 percent of total daily calories should come from saturated fat. Even if you limit your intake of saturated fat to seven percent, you are reducing your cardiovascular disease risk.

For perspective, if you are eating a 1,600 calorie/day diet, six to 10 percent of those calories would be 96 to 160 calories or 10.7 to 17.8 grams of saturated fat, respectively. There are nine calories in a gram of fat.

Servings and portions are confusing and often different. A portion can be larger or smaller than a serving and is how much food you decide to eat at one time. A serving is the amount of food that is listed on the nutrition facts label package or the guide given to us by authorities (such as a "serving" of rice should be the size of your fist). A correct serving size of steak may be 3-4 oz., but a restaurant is likely to serve a portion around 5 oz. or even 8 oz. You may have heard of "portion distortion" because of our oversized American meals. These extra-large "servings" (portions) helped us forget what a meal should look like proportionally, and portion distortion can sabotage your diet.

If you were to look at the food label on a package of chips for the "serving size," you will see that the serving size is 11 chips, or 1 oz. Then you will see that 1 oz. of chips has 120 calories, so many grams of fat and so on. The issue is that we are not always choosing to have 11 chips, and the portions add up quickly. Managing portions is a great first step. With this in mind, you can see how having 11 chips with your sandwich sometimes is not a terrible thing. Crunchy red bell pepper strips are clearly the healthier choice—but 1 oz. of chips is not going to do you in, unless that leads to more. It is important to get a good grip on what portions should look like.

Appropriate serving sizes:

3 oz. of meat looks like a deck of cards
1 oz. of cheese looks like three dice or almost 1/4 cup (3 tablespoons)

Fat—Recommended Daily Allowance:
10.7 to 17.8 grams of saturated fat (no more than)

Saturated Fat Examples:

Fat Source	Total Fat	Saturated Fat
2 bacon slices	6.4 grams	2.2 grams
1 tablespoon bacon fat	12.62 grams	5.73 grams
8 oz. whole milk	8 grams	5.1 grams
8 oz. 2% milk	4.8 grams	3.1 grams
8 oz. skim milk	0 grams	0 grams
3 oz. chicken	3 grams	1 gram
3 oz. red meat (flank steak)	7 grams	2.9 grams
3 oz. ground turkey	6 grams	2 grams
3 oz. rib eye steak	18 grams	8 grams
1 oz. feta cheese (just under ¼ cup)	6 grams	4.2 grams
1 oz. of cheddar cheese	9.4 grams	6 grams
1 tablespoon butter	11.5 grams	7.3 grams
1 tablespoon coconut oil	13.6 grams	11.8 grams
3 regular or 2 double stuffed Oreos®	7 grams	2 grams
1/2 cup Blue Bell® ice cream	8 grams	6 grams
1 tablespoon sour cream	2.4 grams	1.4 grams
1 large egg	5 grams	1.6 grams
1 Burger King Whopper® with cheese	45 grams	15 grams

Trans Fats
Steer clear of trans fats all together. A number of studies have observed an association between increased trans fatty

acid intake and increased risk of cardiovascular disease. This increased risk is due, in part, to its LDL cholesterol-raising effect.

Food producers hydrogenate products containing unsaturated fatty acids in order to make them solid at room temperature and extend the shelf life of the product. This process of hydrogenation, or partial hydrogenation, converts unsaturated fatty acids to saturated fatty acids. Trans fatty acids produced this way are referred to as "synthetic" or "industrial" trans fatty acids. Those words alone scream "chemicals." You will find these lab-manufactured trans fats in some margarines, snack foods and prepared desserts as a replacement for saturated fatty acids. They are also naturally occurring in small quantities in meat and milk products. Just as GMOs raise questions about whether their nutrients are metabolized properly for our health, synthetic trans fats raise questions about whether they are metabolized differently from those occurring naturally; therefore, we cannot be sure of health outcomes.

This is why knowing what you are eating is so important. If you decide you will have three Oreo™ cookies tonight, then you would want to pass on all other foods with trans fats today. These are the worst fats you can possibly consume. You will soon be able to look at some foods and think, "Not worth it." But guess what? Sometimes it WILL be worth it! Choosing what treats are worth it for you (in small amounts), and becoming more aware, are part of changing the way you think about food.

Once the USDA mandated labeling of trans fats on food packaging, there was a decrease in trans fats in manufactured food products. I speculate there are many reasons why this is happening, outside of the mandated labeling. It may be because organic products have gained market share, and organic processed foods do not contain hydrogenated fats. Also, palm oil/palm kernel oil, another saturated fat, is replacing hydrogenated oil in many processed foods. When you buy peanut butter, for example, look at the ingredients and see if it has palm oil or palm kernel oil in it. If it does, don't buy it. Buy the organic peanut butter that contains only organic roasted peanuts and salt (or no salt!).

CARBOHYDRATES

The right carbohydrates play a crucial role in keeping your body healthy, strong and functioning well. Carbohydrates are the body's main source of fuel, and they are easily accessed for energy. They are broken down and converted to glucose and other sugars that supply tissues and organs with the fuel they need to perform necessary functions. Your body will look to use proteins and fats as energy sources if you are not getting enough carbs as an energy source. This happens, for example, on low-carb diets. Carbs are your body's most efficient energy source, fats are the least efficient, and protein has more important work to do in maintaining muscle mass and keeping hormones in check, to name two significant protein functions.

Carbohydrates are needed for the proper functioning of the central nervous system, the kidneys, the brain and the muscles (including the heart—the heart is a muscle).

Simple and Complex Carbs

Carbohydrates are either simple (simple sugar) or complex (starch, fiber), depending on the food's chemical structure and how quickly the sugar is digested and absorbed. Complex carbohydrates are digested more slowly and supply a lower, more steady release of glucose into the blood stream. Some complex carbohydrate foods are better choices than others, as are some simple carbohydrate foods.

You want to stay away from simple sugars in the form of refined grains and sugars. These take a negative toll on our bodies. Refined grains are white breads, white rice, white pasta, and anything that has been processed, made with white flour and packaged such as, cookies, cakes, breakfast cereals, crackers and snack foods. Also, watch out for sodas, energy drinks and other sweetened beverages. Refined sugars spike your blood sugar—resulting in an energy high followed by an energy low—and make you crave more. This is, in part, the dopamine and insulin response that affect your brain. After they seemingly make you feel good, then they make you feel lousy, mess with your hormones and mood and help you store fat.

A simple sugar in the form of fructose—the sugar in fruit, for example—comes packed with complex carbohydrates in the form of fiber, and includes antioxidants, phytochemicals, vitamins and minerals. This, in no way, compares to a processed sugar in the form of a candy bar or soda. Make no mistake, fruit has *naturally occurring* sugar, and is an excellent nutrition choice and a great way to fulfill a sweet tooth craving.

For good health and for weight loss, choose complex carbohydrate foods that are high in nutrients and fiber. Fiber is found in fruits, vegetables, beans, grains and nuts. These foods, especially vegetables, are generally lower in calories, saturated fat and added sugars, provide abundant nutrients and help promote satiety. Starches are bread, grains, pasta, rice, cereal, potatoes and beans. The Institute of Medicine recommends choosing a diet with 45 to 65 percent of total daily calories from complex carbohydrates. For example, a 1,600 calorie diet would consist of 720-1040 calories per day (225-325 grams) of complex carbs. Do not get hung up or confused on this. I am including this information for perspective. Keep your focus on the food lists provided and control your portions.

Grains and Starches

Whole grains are complex carbohydrates (as opposed to refined grains that are simple carbohydrates): they are rich in fiber, flush cholesterol from your body and make you feel full longer—therefore, they're more satisfying. Studies show that a diet rich in whole grains lowers the risk of many chronic diseases and some cancers. Whole grains are packed with nutrients, including protein, fiber, B vitamins, anti-oxidants and trace minerals such as iron, zinc, copper and magnesium.

Every whole grain you choose in your diet over a refined grain helps your health. The USDA suggests that we need at least three servings of whole grains per day for good health, and a grain serving is half a cup. So, that is 1.5 cups of a whole grain per day. Mind your portions and servings!

The best-in-class choices for starchy carbs: Wild Rice, any Ancient Grain (Quinoa, Farro, Kamut, Amaranth, Chia seed), Brown Rice, Sweet Potato (starchy veggie), Lentils, any bean such as Garbanzo, Black or Kidney

Fruits and Vegetables
Studies show a diet rich in plant foods, colorful fruits and vegetables prevents disease. Fruits and vegetables are healthy complex carbohydrates that offer a winning punch of fiber, phytochemicals and antioxidants.

Phytochemicals are the non-nutritive plant chemicals in foods that we believe fight disease in humans, just as they do in plants. Plants produce these chemicals to protect themselves. This is why processed foods do not have the power to do for our health what real food does for us. Processed foods, even enriched and fortified, will not have these naturally occurring compounds that are found in real foods.

You will get what you need from real foods, and I am okay with supplements as part of a healthy diet to catch shortfalls.

Nothing can replace a healthy diet first, though. Certain populations may need supplements due to age, pregnancy, disease or even vegetarianism—people in these categories may not be able to get everything they need from their diet. There is no harm in taking a multivitamin, and calcium is one of the minerals that is most often lacking in the American diet. The other two supplements that are sometimes recommended are fish oil and Vitamin D. However, taking fish oil supplements does not provide the same health benefit as actually eating fatty fish weekly. Keep in mind that supplements are not regulated the same way that foods or over-the-counter and prescription drugs are, and supplements are about a $22 billion industry.

Currently, the hype is that many of us are not getting enough Vitamin D. I can ask two doctors the Vitamin D question and get two answers—because I have! One told me to take Vitamin D without even checking my Vitamin D levels. I should add that I get a safe amount of sun every day (I live in Texas!), I am active, and I eat dairy and plenty of greens. The other physician laughed about the Vitamin D recommendation. Get your Vitamin D levels checked if you are concerned. I vote for a multivitamin and calcium, depending on your age; but I primarily recommend a healthy diet.

Phytochemicals are found in all of the brightly colored fruits and veggies. Grapes have resveratrol, which you hear about in red wine. Blueberries, carrots, spinach, beets…bright is good!

Specific Phytochemicals are:

Phytochemical	Found In	Function
Allicin:	onions and garlic	onions and garlic
Phenolics	citrus, cereals, legumes, oils and seeds	slows aging, protects the heart, and protects against inflammation
Flavonoids	apples, blueberries, broccoli, cabbage, capers, dark chocolate, onions, strawberries, red grapes, tea and red wine (resveratrol is a polyphenol)	reduce inflammation, promote healthy arteries, help fight aging, repair cellular damage, may protect against dementia, Alzheimer's and some cancers
Antioxidants (Vitamin C, Carotenoids, and Beta Carotene)	carrots, sweet potatoes, cantaloupe, kale, spinach, turnip greens	prevent or slow oxidative damage to our body, prevent and repair damage done by free radicals
Isoflavones	soy	claim to imitate human estrogen and help reduce menopausal symptoms and osteoporosis (significance is up for debate)
Indoles	cabbage	interfere with DNA replication and are thought to prevent replication of cancer cells
Terpenes (similar function as Indoles)	citrus	interfere with DNA replication and are thought to prevent replication of cancer cells
Proanthocyanidins	cranberries	bind physically to cell walls and prevent the binding of pathogens to cell walls

We know from the activity in petri dish studies that these brightly colored fruits and vegetables slow cancer cell growth and prevent inflammation. You cannot single out one food as a magic bullet for disease prevention. We need to get over this idea that "this one food" will make us healthy. We tend to eat more of one food when we hear it is good for us. Instead, simply add that specified food to your overall healthy diet.

I provided all of this information to show you why fruits and veggies are what we are supposed to be eating. There is power in eating real foods. They positively affect your entire body, blood, hormones and brain chemistry, gene expression, body fat, weight, mindset, relationships, purpose, drive and love of life.

FIBER

It makes sense that the same foods rich in antioxidants and phytochemicals also have fiber. Fiber has consistently been clinically proven to lower the risks associated with specific cancers and heart disease. The benefits of fiber have withstood the test of time.

Telling someone to eat more fiber is another way of saying "eat your veggies, eat your fruits and eat your whole grains, eat fewer refined and processed foods and less sugar." Fiber is found in plant foods and, for the most part, is not digested by human enzymes. Fiber makes you feel full longer so you are not as hungry and, therefore, aids in achieving a healthy weight, helps control blood sugar levels, lowers cholesterol, helps maintain bowel health and normalizes bowel movements. It is divided into two categories: soluble (partially dissolves in water) and insoluble (does not dissolve in water).

Soluble fiber is found in fruits (apples and citrus), oats, barley and legumes. It:

- Delays GI transit so it benefits digestive disorders
- Is associated with lowering LDL (bad) cholesterol
- Regulates blood sugar
- Lowers risk of heart disease and type 2 diabetes

Insoluble fiber is found in whole grains such as wheat bran, corn bran, whole grain breads and cereals, vegetables (cabbage, green beans and Brussels sprouts). It:

- Accelerates GI transit
- Promotes bowel movements
- Delays glucose absorption

In a 2013 meta-analysis reviewing 22 studies specific to CVD and CHD, researchers found for every seven grams of dietary fiber eaten, the risks of CVD (Cardiovascular Disease) and CHD (Coronary Heart Disease) were each lowered by nine percent.[128] The analysis concluded, "Greater dietary fiber intake is associated with a lower risk of both cardiovascular disease and coronary heart disease." Greater intakes of insoluble fiber from cereal and vegetable sources reduced the risk of CHD and CVD, and fruit fiber intake was associated with a lower risk of CVD.[134]

When you are eating from the lists provided in this book, you will get the fiber that your body needs. The following list of "high fiber foods" includes foods that have been called "superfoods," "cancer fighting foods," "anti-inflammatory foods," "antioxidant and phytochemical foods." These foods all have health benefits, help you shed pounds and prevent disease. Find some foods that you like and add those to your weekly diet for extra fiber. If you have not typically eaten foods rich in fiber, then add fiber *slowly* to your diet or you will find yourself very uncomfortable.

The National Institutes of Health established these recommendations for daily fiber intake:

- Women: Under 50 = 25 grams; Over 50 = 21 grams
- Men: Under 50 = 38 grams; Over 50 = 30 grams

Food	Amount	Fiber in grams
Turnip Greens, Boiled	1 cup	5.0
Raspberries	1 cup	8.0
Bananas	1 medium	3.1
Apple, with skin	1 medium	4.4
Sweet Potato	1 medium, baked	3.0
Almonds	1 ounce or 23 nuts	3.5
Whole Wheat Bread	1 slice	1.9
Black Beans	1 cup	15.0
Broccoli, cooked	1 cup	5.1
Carrots	1 medium	1.7
Oatmeal	1 cup	4.0
Bran Flakes	1 cup	7.0
Raisin Bran	1 cup	8.0
Brown Rice	1 cup	4.0
Garbanzo Beans	1 cup	12.0
Peas and Carrots, cooked from frozen	1 cup	4.0

PROTEINS

Proteins are made up of about 20 common amino acids and amino acids are the building blocks of protein. Proteins make up every cell, tissue and organ in the body and are an important part of a healthy diet and are the building blocks of most body structures. They are building blocks of our bones, teeth, skin, muscles, cells, enzymes (build up and break down structures) and hormones; serve as regulators of fluid balance, as acid-base regulators, as transporters (of nutrients and other molecules, oxygen, lipids, vitamins and minerals); and act as a source of energy and glucose. Because proteins are the main substances the body uses to build and repair tissues and help with our hormones, adequate protein intake is essential. Too much is also not beneficial and can be harmful.

There are nine essential amino acids that the body cannot make, and these you need to get from the foods you eat. Your body (liver) can synthesize the 11 non-essential proteins even if you are not getting all of these from your diet each day, and as long as your diet is otherwise healthy. The optimal goal is to get the protein you need from a healthy diet so your body does not need to break down its own proteins to get it.

Consuming enough protein helps you increase your ratio of lean mass to body fat and look and feel your best. Consuming too little protein can lead to fatigue, irritability, decreased muscle mass, a protruding belly, changes in hair texture and a weakened immune system.

According to the Institute of Medicine, adults should get at least 0.8 grams per kilogram of body weight per day, generally speaking. Of course, endurance athletes will need more than that and as much as 1.2-1.6 grams/kg/day. Protein-rich foods should provide 10 to 35 percent of your total daily calories (this is quite a range—and a good reason to follow 0.8 grams per kilogram of body weight guide), and the right amount will obviously be a little different for each of us. Here is how you convert your weight in pounds to kilograms and determine your daily protein needs.

Step 1) Divide your weight in pounds by 2.2 to get your weight in kilograms (kg)

Step 2) Multiply your weight in kg by 0.8 to get how much protein you need each day

Example:
Step 1)130 lbs/2.2 = 59 kg
Step 2) 59 kg X 0.8 grams = 47 grams of protein

In this example, you would need 47 grams of protein, which could look like seven ounces of salmon or chicken, or seven eggs. This will help you understand the portion sizes you are choosing to eat and what they should look like. Remember that three ounces of meat, chicken or fish looks like a deck of cards. How big are your portions?

If your present weight falls outside a healthy weight range, use the midpoint of the range you know your healthy weight should fall within, and will be, to calculate your protein needs.

But don't let all of this confuse you. Just start with eating the right foods in the right portions and don't worry about the calculations. I'm providing this information to help with perspective.

Choose lean protein sources such as fish, chicken, turkey, (lean beef, if this is your preference, although it is not on the best in class list), and bake, broil or grill rather than fry. If you choose red meat, then choose a lean cut, and do not have it too often. Focus on healthy choices and the best in class lists.

You can also choose low- to non-fat Greek yogurt and low- to non-fat milk. There are plenty of healthy plant protein sources such as beans, quinoa, nuts and seeds, to name a few. Although brown rice is a carbohydrate, for example, one cup of it includes five grams of protein. Another example is corn tortillas. The ones I buy each have five grams of protein. All of your protein does not need to come from animal sources.

Choosing lean proteins is part of choosing a healthy diet. Just like eating too many calories or too much of anything, if you eat more protein than your body needs, it will be converted to fat and stored for later use, as well as interfere with other processes.

Healthy Protein Food Sources and Portions:

Food Source	Amount	Protein in grams
Skim milk	8 oz.	8.0
Greek yogurt	6 oz.	12.0
Egg	1 large	6.0
Chicken or fish	1 oz.	6.0-7.5
	3 oz. is a portion size and looks like a deck of cards	22.0
Whole grain brown rice	½ cup	2.5
Quinoa	½ cup	4.0
Wild rice	½ cup	3.25
Lentils	½ cup	8.2

A word about the egg

The incredible edible egg protein can be used as a standard for measuring protein quality. The egg is a high quality protein! Scientists give it a value of 100, and the quality of other food proteins is determined based on how they compare to the egg. This standard is called a "reference protein." A regular egg contains 70 calories, five grams of fat and six grams of protein.

Do you believe eggs are good or bad for you? The real question is, "How much saturated fat is in your overall diet?" Your answer to that question gives you the answer to the egg question. If you are eating more than the recommended amount of protein and getting it from saturated fats, then substitute some of that protein with plant-based sources and eat the right amounts. Moderation, moderation, moderation.

A word on sodium

On average, Americans consume more than 3,400 milligrams of sodium each day. Your body only needs a small amount of sodium (less than 500 milligrams per day) to function properly. Sodium contributes to high blood pressure, and high blood pressure destroys your arteries. Preparing your own food is one sure way to mind your sodium intake. Most people get too much sodium from processed foods or from eating out.

According to the American Heart Association: Do not consume more than 2,400 milligrams of sodium per day in order to lower your blood pressure. Even better, reduce it to 1,500 mg per day to lower your blood pressure even more.

- 1/4 teaspoon salt = 575 mg sodium
- 1/2 teaspoon salt = 1,150 mg sodium
- 3/4 teaspoon salt = 1,725 mg sodium
- 1 teaspoon salt = 2,300 mg sodium

A word on dairy alternatives

There is a huge push away from dairy for various reasons. Some people are lactose intolerant, and some are following the non-dairy fad. I enjoy some dairy, but in moderation. My personal preferences include real cheese on occasion, skim milk and nonfat yogurt. Whole milk (saturated fat) is not a wise choice. I never bought into the concept that we need three servings of dairy each day, as there are many other healthy plant-based sources of calcium. I might have a glass of skim milk sometimes, but not every day. I like feta cheese on my salads sometimes. Sometimes we have pizza. Low fat or nonfat yogurt is nice choice sometimes.

I am glad to hear from parents who have gone dairy-free that they still give dairy to their children. Unless parents know exactly how to get their children all of the calcium they need to grow up strong and healthy, then I am glad they are reaching for a reliable source of calcium. I would much rather see a child have a cup of milk at breakfast and at lunch than any sweetened artificial beverage. In addition, I could argue that a cheese stick with grapes is a much healthier snack than some processed and packaged "bar."

Drinkable dairy alternatives are almond milk, hazelnut milk, rice milk, soy milk, oat milk, hemp milk, coconut milk and cashew milk—at least that I know of. You should look for unsweetened options in these alternatives; but note, not all of them are abundant in calcium or protein (except for soy milk). They are simply a milk alternative. I do not recommend soy in abundance, yet I see that it is fine, like any other real and healthy food, in moderation. Soy is a complete protein and is a good protein option, especially for those of you who do not eat meat. However, I have a few good reasons for my reservations about soy.

The first reason I have concerns about soy is because 90 percent of the nation's soy crop is GMO. That tells me soy is in abundance and, therefore, soy is in everything processed and marketed heavily. There continues to be growth opportunity for soy products, and many studies are still being conducted on soy consumption. Because Americans have been listening to marketing and health claims, we have added a lot of soy products to our diets: soy milk, tofu, edamame and more. But as you know, I am always the skeptic when I hear about the health benefits of one food.

In the 1990s, studies claimed that regularly eating soy-based foods lowers cholesterol, helps calm hot flashes, can aid in weight loss, may prevent some cancers such as breast and prostate, and even help stave off osteoporosis. The FDA even allowed health claims in product marketing, such as "Eating soy as part of a low fat diet may reduce the risk of heart disease."[135] But the studies that led to those health claims have been contradicted since then. Initially it looked like regular consumption of soy might lower the bad cholesterol, but then researchers discovered, maybe not so much. Then scientists thought the isoflavones in soy, a type of plant-made estrogen (phytoestrogen), mimic estrogen and might help reduce hot flashes during menopause. They are not so sure now. The American Heart Association reviewed data on this claim and concluded that it was "unlikely" that soy isoflavones have enough estrogenic activity to have an important impact on symptoms of menopause including hot flashes.[136] The same reversal of claims occurred for cancer prevention and memory benefits.

Having said all of this, the real story most likely looks like this: Soy is a low-fat alternative to other foods. Choosing soy to replace red meat will most likely improve your health. A diet rich in plant foods has proven health benefits, and if soy replaces less healthy choices, and is part of that heart-healthy diet, then benefits will show up for all of those reasons. But practice moderation.

A word about sugar

Added sugars are in many processed foods. Avoid artificial sugars or too much sugar, in general. The American Heart Association recommends no more than six teaspoons of added sugar per day for women and children, which is 100 calories or 25 grams; and no more than nine teaspoons of added sugar per day for men, which is 150 calories or 37.5 grams. Read labels and know how much added sugar you are consuming. Be aware.

There are 4.2 grams of sugar in a teaspoon, so you can look at food labels and know how much ADDED sugar is in the product per serving. Fruit is your friend and is not considered "added sugar." For example, if your yogurt has fruit on the bottom, there will be sugar on the food label but that is not "added" sugar. However, if you find any of these words in the ingredients panel, that means there is added sugar:

- Brown sugar
- Corn sweetener
- Corn syrup
- Fruit juice concentrates
- High-fructose corn syrup (avoid completely and you will naturally eliminate some of the worst processed foods from your pantry or fridge)
- Honey
- Invert sugar
- Malt sugar
- Molasses
- Raw sugar
- Sugar
- Sugar molecules ending in "ose" such as dextrose, fructose, glucose, lactose, maltose, sucrose
- Syrup
- Cane Sugar
- Beet Sugar
- Brown Rice Syrup

Artificial sweeteners are made chemically in laboratories. Avoid these completely; they look like this on food labels:

- Acesulfame K (Twin Sweet™)
- Aspartame (Nutrasweet™, Equal™)
- Neotame, saccharin (Sweet'n Low™)
- Sucralose (Splenda™)
- Cyclamate
- Stevia rebaudiana (Stevia™) (even marketed "from a plant," it is still created in a chemical lab)

There is no single food or beverage that has created our health crisis. It is too much of the wrong foods, too much of the time, in the form of too much sugar, too much fat, too much refining. Our consumption has us in a hormonal, chemical, craving, overweight mess. Know what you are eating. If the ingredient list is long and you cannot pronounce some of the words, do not buy it.

Focus on the best-in-class food lists, and eat most of your foods from these lists, and mostly in the forms of fresh fruits and vegetables. Michael Pollen has it right: "Eat food. Not too much. Mostly plants." After a while, you will get over your cravings for sugar, fat and salt, and you will have more control over the things you want to have control over. As you form new habits and map new neuro-pathways, you will be less likely to fall back into old habits. Your decision and choices and conviction will grow stronger every day.

13

Eating Right: How to Make It Happen

"Truth is ever to be found in simplicity, and not in the multiplicity and confusion of things."

– Isaac Newton

Planning and preparing meals is a predictor of any successful weight loss strategy. Tips and suggestions for success and how to meal plan will get you through week after healthy week.

MEAL PLANNING AND PREPARATION

We have to get back into the kitchen for the sake of our health and our children's health. The pace of our lives has us turning to unhealthy convenience foods. Meal planning and preparation ensures that you have healthy meals and snacks available. A little time up front reduces waste and saves the stress of wondering what is for dinner and the stress of hitting a drive-through knowing it is awful for your health and your waistline. Eating at home also costs much less than eating out, and you will spend less on junk foods that stock your pantry. Putting time in the kitchen benefits your and your family's short-term and long-term health, the way you feel each day, your mental and physical strength, your healthcare spend, not to mention your quality of life as you age. If these are things you value, then this is the way to achieve them.

It is a myth that it costs more to purchase healthy foods than fast foods. An apple costs $.90 (healthy), and a protein bar costs $1.75 (less healthy). A dinner of grilled chicken ($10.00), spinach salad ($5.00) and brown rice ($3.00) for a family of four is much healthier and less expensive than take-out pizza ($20.00). You will also have leftover spinach in the container, and leftover brown rice in the bag for other meals. The food, itself, does not cost more, yet there is the cost of your time for shopping, prepping, cooking and cleaning. The more you plan and prep, the more efficient you will become, and the healthier you will get, and the better you will feel. Grocery stores now have prepared meats ready for the grill and sliced veggies ready to throw in a stir fry. These are time saving options that can get you eating better very quickly.

Remember Jeremiah? He and his wife plan their meals for the week every Saturday morning. He says his entire family eats healthier with planning, and they eliminate waste. Tricia said she cooks dinner every night and makes meals and sandwiches from leftovers. I always have go-to foods for my family and myself in the fridge. Planning and prep time are key to healthy eating. Meals come easily when foods are already prepped to use in the recipe. In general, a way to ensure you choose healthy meals is to have a few go-to foods that are healthy and easy to make. You want to plan and prepare each week, and it looks something like this.

How to plan and prepare each week:

1. Plan five breakfasts, five lunches and five dinners (and how/when to dine out)
2. Plan your go-to or snack foods
3. Make your list
4. Grocery Shop
5. Prep for your first few meals of the week and your go-to foods
6. Pack your snacks and meals to go

It is typical that people reach for what is available when they are hungry, and having the right foods prepared and available makes it easy to eat healthy. Write down what works for you and your family and start with five to get you rolling.

Journal Exercise: (download your free *Healthy Weight Success Journal* at healthinspires.com)
Meal Brainstorming

1) Write as many healthy breakfast foods you can think of that you know you can prepare or grab on your way out the door in the morning:

2) **Write as many healthy lunches you can think of that you know you can prepare or purchase each day:**

3) **Write as many healthy dinners you can think of that are easy for you to prepare and reuse leftovers from one night in another night's recipe. Think about good health, time and cost savings.**

Here are some examples...

Brainstorm breakfast (home or on the go):

- 1 whole egg plus one egg white scrambled plain or with any variation of veggies such as a handful of wilted spinach or sautéed onion. *I like to slice tomatoes and avocados on my eggs, very lightly salted.
- 1 hardboiled egg cut up with tomato and avocado slices, salted
- A 6 oz. yogurt with ½-1 cup of berries
- Homemade fruit smoothie with protein powder or yogurt; or just fruit, ice and spinach (see recipes)
- 1/2 cup real oatmeal (with cinnamon, diced apples, blueberries, raisins or walnuts)
- 1 slice of toast with peanut butter and sliced banana
- A baggie filled with adult cereal to take on the go
- Banana and a baggie with crushed peanuts for dipping
- One handful of almonds (12) and a piece of fruit

- One slice of Ezekiel® bread smeared with avocado, lightly salted
- Fruit

Brainstorm lunch:

- 3 oz. of chicken or fish (canned or fresh) grilled/broiled/baked/pan sautéed in olive oil with a salad or fresh vegetable
- Salad and soup
- Lentil or bean "chili" or soup
- Sandwich with lots and lots of veggies
- Pasta with mostly veggies and chicken or beans
- Wrap loaded with veggies
- Leftover dinner
- Trash can salad (everything healthy that's in my refrigerator—and this is one of my go-to foods anytime)

Brainstorm dinner:

What is good for you is good for your family. You are not on this journey alone, and you can prepare healthy foods and have enough options available for everybody to feel nourished and satisfied. Think of food you like and typically eat, and then look at ways to reuse leftovers or cook extra in order to make meals throughout a busy week. If you have leftover grilled chicken and fresh greens available, you can create many options with a few extra ingredients.

Let's break meal planning into steps, and I will explain what it looks like in greater detail.

Write your plan:

Step 1:
Learn to cook a little extra to use in other meals throughout the week or freeze for another time. For example, when you cook brown rice—make the entire bag of rice. It saves time. Another time saver to consider is having a sandwich and salad as a fast, easy and healthy dinner.

Examples…

Dinner:

Monday:	Grilled chicken, quinoa and a spinach salad
Tuesday:	Veggie tacos made with homemade black bean salsa, avocado, tomatoes and any other veggie you want
Wednesday:	Cut up leftover grilled chicken to throw in a pasta. Make homemade sauce with fresh tomatoes (or a large can of whole tomatoes) and garlic slices sautéed in olive oil and toss it all with pasta, salt and pepper and serve with a side salad
Thursday:	Grilled salmon, new potatoes and sautéed spinach
Friday:	Salmon croquettes and broccoli

Lunch:

Bring or buy salads and leftover chicken (two days)
Sandwiches (two days)
Sweet potato, salmon and salad (one day)

Breakfast:

Eggs (one or two days)
Peanut butter toast (one or two days)
Yogurt and fruit (one or two days)

Step 2: Write your grocery list

Create a grocery list from your menu. Check all ingredients, calculate how much you will need and write these on your list. Factor in nights that you will eat out or order in. The goal is to get good at preparing most of your meals at home, and to order healthier meals when you're out.

Tip: Add a few bags of frozen veggies and fruit to help you continue eating well throughout the week even when your fresh veggies and fruit run out, or when you are crunched for time.

Step 3: Go Grocery Shopping

Stick to your list. The best approach to a healthy diet is choosing real foods in their purest form. The best place to shop is around the perimeter of the grocery store where the produce, meat, fish, poultry and dairy are. Make sure to buy whole grains that are just the grain and nothing else. Use the food lists from Chapter 12.

Step 4: Meal Preparation

As soon as you get home from the grocery store is a good time to prep some of those meals. You can make a marinade and clean and prep your chicken, cook your quinoa, chop the ingredients for your black bean salsa and clean your new potatoes. Make your salad dressings when you make your marinade. Make your salads for your two salad lunches so all you have to do is add chicken after it's cooked. Make one or two go-to salads (beet salad and black bean mango salsa), or hummus, and slice some veggies. Allow time for all of this as soon as you get home, or plan for the best time soon after. Here is what it looks like.

Tips:
Salad dressings: Make one or two dressings for the week.

Fruit: Peel and cut fruit so it is ready and available to offer and eat. This helps your entire family eat more fruit. For example, peel mandarins, clean grapes, and have them in a bowl in the fridge. Cut mangos or pineapples and have berries where everybody can see them in the fridge. Apples and pears and bananas can stay out on the counter in a bowl.

Vegetables: Have tubs of pre-washed greens for salads available. Clean and cut broccoli for stir fry or roasting, and cut bell peppers for salads or for dipping. Slice veggies for whatever meals you are planning for the next few days. If you decide on stir fry, cut onion, broccoli and peppers. Then when you come home, all you have do is throw the veggies in the pan and stir fry and season them.

Step 5:

Each night, check your menu for the next day and prep what you can before bed, or early in the morning. Planning for the entire day helps, including what's going on with the kids, to make sure healthy foods are available for all schedules. There is a caveat. Sometimes we do not want to eat what we planned on eating, and that is okay too. Sometimes we plan on having a salad and we really prefer to have a sandwich. Have the sandwich and eat your salad tomorrow.

Step 6:

Repeat each week, choosing a new recipe at least twice a month. Keep what you need to keep the same and change what you need to change. Skip recipes with canned soups and heavy creams and those that are loaded with cheese. Choose recipes that call for olive oil, fresh vegetables and other foods from the lists in Chapter 12.

Tips: Consider replacing meat with lentils or a bean recipe for one dinner a week, or one lunch. You may not be able to imagine a meal without meat, but consider making just one meal a week a meatless. Keep an open mind. Know that your thoughts and tastes can change over time.

Journal Exercise:

4) **Make a list of your top five breakfasts that you can make and will stick to:**

5) **Write your top five lunches that you can make and stick to:**

6) **Write your top five dinners that you can make easily and healthily:**

General Healthy Eating Tips:

- Drink plenty of water and fill in with green tea. People confuse thirst with hunger. If you think you are hungry, try drinking a glass of water first. If the feeling of hunger dissipates, you only needed water. If drinking water is not an easy task for you, try adding a splash of juice or squeeze a lemon or lime in it.
- Green tea is a healthy option. The warmth of the tea is filling as well. Add a little honey for a treat.
- Be particular about your night time snacks. If after dinner time triggers mindless eating of high-calorie snacks for no other reason than to put something in your mouth, consider one or some of these solutions that you know will work for you:

- Close your kitchen after dinner (just like our parents did).
- Allow yourself only fruit or crunchy veggies before bedtime.
- Have small ramekin bowls on hand and fill one with your favorite snack for portion control...no seconds! You can buy 1/4 or 1/2 cup bowls for portions. Ramekin bowls are a staple in our household.
- Eat your favorites sometimes—this will eliminate weight gain over time because focusing on what you can't have will most likely lead to overeating later, and because it is important that we feel satisfied.
- Focus on adding fruits and vegetables each day to your diet rather than on cutting other foods out.
- Make half your plate vegetables.
- Make sure to pack fruit or veggies for a snack.
- Add a salad to your lunch or choose to eat crunchy red bell pepper slices as a side to your sandwich.
- Freezing foods in the right portions will help you get healthy meals on the table fast. As a working mom, I swear by advanced food preparation as the only way for my family to have healthy meals. As you plan your meals, remind yourself you are finding what works for you. There may be some things you are willing to change and other things that you simply will not want to do without. Recognize that time may change this too.
- Stock your kitchen with healthy, prepped and ready-to-eat convenience foods. Make sure you always have these in addition to your fresh foods:

- Frozen vegetables as a backup in case you run out of fresh
- Frozen fruit for smoothies
- Fresh pre-washed greens
- Canned tomatoes
- Canned beans
- Cooked whole grain, stored in fridge/freezer
- Grilled chicken breasts stored in fridge/freezer

Eating Out Tips:

Americans eat out more now than they used to, citing "lack of time" to cook healthy meals as the reason. Spending on food away from home increased from 25.9 percent of the American food budget in 1970 to its highest level of 43.1 percent in 2012.[137] The trends are leveling out as grocery stores are preparing more convenience foods. Because eating out is more frequent and not the "once every other pay check" event that it used to be, it is even more important to make healthy choices when you are out. Decide what you will have before you go, no matter what the other person orders, share an entree, or ask the waiter to box up half before he brings it to the table. Save half the meal for another day, not a late night snack. It will still be there tomorrow.

- Know what you are going to order ahead of time.
- Top salads with a lean protein.
- When ordering green salads, ask your waiter to add only fresh veggies and eliminate any added cheese, chips or

fried treats that may normally come on top (or get those on the side and have only a little: those toppings really mess up the calorie and nutrition content of a salad).

- Order olive oil and a lemon wedge for your salad dressing. If that is too drastic for you, then ask for the dressing on the side so you can control how much goes on your salad. Olive oil-based dressings are a better choice than the creamy ones. Add some avocado for a creamy treat.
- When ordering meals, skip the sauces all together that cover your otherwise lean protein.

From here, you can plan and enjoy your treats during the week. When you know you are going to lunch on Friday with work friends, that is a nice time to order a burger if that is what you enjoy. This does not mean you're falling off the track and going back to old habits. This is the time to enjoy a favorite, and then, it's back to eating healthy. If a burger is your favorite treat, then enjoy it, but it doesn't need to be a double bacon cheeseburger with large fries. That is not healthy! However, what if you split that insane burger with a friend (or two!)? That way, you've enjoyed something you love but stayed in control of your portion. Having your favorites sometimes and eating less of them might be one huge step toward a healthier lifestyle. Considerations for that burger (or other less healthy favorites that you want to be able to enjoy sometimes): Order a small one, skip the cheese, take off one bun, eat half of it, or split it with a coworker/friend/spouse.

Enjoy foods in moderation and mostly eat healthy foods, and sometimes have a favorite. If you know a food will trigger you, you need to decide on "no" and have your planned distraction fast!

Tips for rethinking your snacks:
Pack healthy snacks and keep them at work, in your purse, in your glove compartment, or in a cooler you are packing. We have a tendency to eat a processed food snack whether we are really hungry or not. These refined foods provoke our cravings and the dopamine response, and especially if you have struggled with weight in the past, it may trigger an old subconscious habit.

Journal Exercise:

7) **What are your favorite foods that are worth indulging in once in a while? These are what you are not willing to do without. There is room for these in your healthy diet.**

8) **What are the junk foods that you have been eating that you can easily do without and keep out of your diet? Write them down, and put those aside. These are what you are willing to do without.**

Plan a time each week where you sit down to meal plan. Remember that a sandwich and salad is easier than the drive-through when planning isn't enough. Creating these new habits will automatically change other things in your life. It is inevitable. Feeling good leads you to engage in new actions and results in new outcomes.

TIPS FROM PEOPLE WHO'VE DONE IT

The winners of a recent employer based health challenge in Austin were the male and female who lost the greatest percent of their body fat. We asked them how they were able to lose weight and here are some of the things that the winners and other participants said about how they succeeded in weight loss:

- "I quit eating crap."
- "I don't know about you, but I cannot have one cookie— I have to eat the entire tray, and so if I ate that entire tray, I might as well start on the next one. So now (showing off her slim new self), I can pass on the cookies altogether because it is not worth it. This is (her slim self)."
- "There is no quick fix. Consistency is the only way."
- "I read a book about the psychology of willpower and that helped me understand how the mind tricks us."
- "I cut out most breads, pasta and potatoes and focused on portion size."
- "Exercise has never been my problem. I always exercised…but I do not have the two hours to exercise like I used to with my new baby. You get really creative when you want something, and I found ways to exercise with my baby."

What is special about this particular challenge is that we do it with few resources. I jokingly call it the "Together but Separately Health Challenge." We use MyFitnessPal and send out e-mails to the participants. Essentially, it is a solo health initiative, but with the "support" of the other people around you who are making the same efforts. They all agree it creates self-awareness, and self-awareness allows for change. At the end of the day, it always comes down to being ready and willing to change.

Focus on healthy foods and plan and prepare to have these available and ready to eat. Investing time for your health is worth your time, and being healthy will change your life.

14

Exercise, Sleep and Rest: The Rest of the Story

"No man has the right to be an amateur in the matter of physical training. It is a shame for a man to grow old without seeing the beauty and strength of which his body is capable."

- SOCRATES

THE WHAT

Scientific evidence supports the obvious and not so obvious benefits of exercise as well as the fact that we might get edgy without it. Exercise is a proven mood booster, stress reliever, natural antidepressant, insulin metabolizer and fat burner. As a matter of fact, most clinicians would agree that exercise is the best mood enhancing thing you can do, and all it takes is 30 minutes a day. The good news is, if you haven't started exercising yet, then 10 minutes is all you need to get started to receive all of these benefits.

Sounds like a great investment! It requires no cash outlay, makes you stronger and happier, increases your energy and gives you an edge! Free!

But knowing that physical activity enhances overall wellbeing and is a natural antidepressant and positive mood booster isn't enough to get everybody moving. The CDC reports that only 49.2 percent of adults ages 18 and older met the Physical Activity Guidelines for aerobic physical activity, and only 20.8 percent met the guidelines for both aerobic physical and muscle-strengthening activity.[138]

The minimum recommendations from the 2008 Physical Activity Guidelines for Americans are that adults get either:

1. 150 minutes of moderate-intensity aerobic activity (i.e., brisk walking) every week and muscle-strengthening activities on two or more days a week that work all major muscle groups (legs, hips, back, abdomen, chest, shoulders, and arms); or

2. 75 minutes of vigorous-intensity aerobic activity (i.e., jogging or running) every week and muscle-strengthening activities on two or more days a week that work all major muscle groups; or

3. An equivalent mix of moderate- and vigorous-intensity aerobic activity and muscle-strengthening activities on two or more days a week that work all major muscle groups.[139]

That is the minimum. You can always do more.

The American Heart Association recommends 30 minutes of moderate activity most days, or 150 minutes per week. AHA also suggests other options such as being active for three 10-minute periods a day.[140]

The 10-minute push helps people get started, and new data shows that moving throughout the day is a health benefit, as sedentary jobs are now the norm. Getting up to move around, taking the stairs and parking far away from the front door all contribute to your health. All of it counts. Ten-minute bursts of activity are a necessary part of your day and a healthy way to take a break. Ten minutes is achievable, it gets you moving, and success breeds success. That is exactly what happened to Tricia, from Part I. She started with her 10-minute walk one Saturday morning. Motion equals emotion! Moving is magic.

You will want to get up to longer periods of continuous physical activity to get more health benefits than 10-minute spurts can give you. All movement is good, yet activity is different from physical activity. Start with 10 minutes, if that is where you are, and work up to more time. Always consult your doctor before starting any exercise regimen. As a matter of fact, if you have to wait for counsel before you start exercising, then call your doctor now and get the earliest appointment available. No excuses.

Most of us know that exercise is good for us. The hard part is getting started. The second hardest part is sustaining it until you cannot ever imagine not fitting it in as part of your daily routine (or at least five times per week). The funny part is that once you fall off for a few days, then you have to persuade yourself to get started again. Have you ever experienced that? It has been at least 20 years since I have felt that way; yet, I remember. Now I wouldn't miss it. It is part of who I am, and helps me think and feel better and strengthens my mind, body and spirit.

Starting an exercise regimen is a crucial part of weight loss and being healthy.

THE WHY

Strength training is as important as aerobic activity. Up until the age of about 30, we are able to more easily keep and grow muscle mass. Somewhere in our 30s, and as part of the aging process, we lose muscle mass and function if we are not doing something to keep it. As inactive adults, we can lose as much as three to eight percent of our muscle mass per decade.[141] Not doing anything to replace the lean muscle you lose, you'll increase the percentage of fat in your body. That makes it harder to burn calories. We all know by now that muscle burns calories more efficiently than fat. So, if you have ever found yourself wondering why a lean person seems to be able to eat more than you do without gaining weight, it's because he probably can. His hormones are in check because he may eat healthier, exercise consistently and have the occasional pleasure food in small amounts.

As we age into our 60s and 70s and beyond, it gets more difficult to maintain muscle mass because our bodies' ability to synthesize the protein that builds our muscles decreases and hormones change. There is also a reduction in nerve cells that send signals to the brain to initiate movement. We slow down. This is natural. It is our job to stay as healthy and strong as we can to prevent weakness and falls. Most of us can continue modified strength training and walking into our old age.

There are many other reasons you will want to start an exercise program. We know that exercise is good for your heart and your brain, your weight, your mood and more. It can also stave off dementia, a mild or major neurocognitive disorder that can be characterized by a decline in cognitive skills that affects a person's ability to perform everyday activities, including memory, language and problem-solving. A long-term study over three decades looking at midlife exercise and onset of dementia and Alzheimer's in older adulthood showed that exercise may reduce the odds of onset.[142]

Other studies show that exercise, along with other healthy lifestyle habits, can stimulate new brain cells. Exercise sends blood flow and oxygen to the brain, gives us better cognitive functioning and simply makes us FEEL GOOD. It makes sense, then, that not exercising is a depressant. As a matter of fact, studies have shown that depressed patients who engaged in physical activity had positive mood boosts. The trouble is in getting depressed patients to exercise. That would be a free health benefit for one out of every 10 U.S adults who are depressed, according to the CDC.

Studies also find that more active and fit individuals tend to develop coronary heart disease at a lower rate than their sedentary counterparts. If active and fit people do develop coronary heart disease, it occurs at a later age and tends to be less severe.[143]

A Women's Health Study, published in the Archives of Internal Medicine in 2008, looked at 39,000 women free of cardiovascular disease, cancer and diabetes at baseline. The study found that women who were normal weight and physically active had the lowest risk of developing coronary heart disease over more than 10 years of follow-up. Next up with good results were women who were lean, but not physically active; and then finally, women who were overweight but physically active. The findings demonstrate that having a healthy body weight might have more significance on your health than physical activity, although both play a role in lowering the risk of heart disease in overweight or obese women.[144]

Exercise also significantly benefits those with diabetes. It increases insulin sensitivity both short- and long-term, lowers blood sugar levels, reduces body fat and improves cardiovascular functioning.[145]

And let's look at the effect of exercise on cancer. A model constructed by cancer investigators showed that if the current overweight and obesity trends continue over the next 20 years, at least 500,000 cancers attributable to obesity will be diagnosed in the United States. From the model, they concluded, "If every adult in the United States decreased his or her weight by 2.5 lb, 73,000 to 127,000 fewer cancers would occur." They also mentioned that physical activity is associated with a healthier weight and better health, and yet only one-third of cancer survivors get the required amount of physical activity.[146]

We also know for a scientific fact that when a person with a BMI of 25 or above loses five percent of her body weight, she also may reduce her risk of heart disease and diabetes and may reduce her blood pressure and cholesterol and possibly get off some medications.[147] If you weigh 200 pounds and lose 10 pounds (5 percent), you will most likely see tremendous results in all the areas of your health and your life. That is significant! If this matches your personal profile, and you start walking every day for 30 minutes and change nothing else, you could lose that weight within three months. If you exchange one less healthy meal for a healthy, portion-controlled salad each day, the weight would come off even sooner.

Exercise simply makes you feel good, and once you get started, you will look forward to it. Find something you enjoy to get started. Of all the ways to exercise, walking has the lowest dropout rate. It is the simplest way to increase your health, and most of us can go for a walk right outside our front doors.

Research shows that exercising just 30 minutes a day:

- Improves your general well being
- Enhances mind-body coordination
- Boosts your mental wellness and stimulates your brain
- Relieves tension, anxiety, depression and anger
- Promotes optimism
- Improves your physical wellness and overall health
- Provides for a better quality of life and longevity

- Prevents disease and lowers risk for heart disease, stroke, type 2 diabetes, depression and some cancers
- Prevents bone loss
- Increases muscle mass and strength
- Helps with weight loss
- Helps maintain a healthy weight
- Promotes a peaceful sleep
- Increases your sex drive, body confidence and arousal
- Reduces LDL cholesterol
- Increases HDL cholesterol
- Increases insulin sensitivity
- Improves muscular function
- Reduces Blood Pressure

After you are cleared by your doctor, your goal is to start and sustain an exercise routine.

HOW TO GET STARTED

You want to choose something you enjoy doing. Your preferences matter if you want to remain engaged. Decide what it is for you and start. Know your motivators so you remember why you started and to help you stay on track. I have exercised for more than 20 years at 5:00 a.m., or close to it. I often jog with a girlfriend, nurturing our relationship and getting some good girl time as well as my exercise. Use the buddy system for accountability and the sheer enjoyment that it brings. Many people starting a new exercise program need the accountability to stick with it. This support system could be your spouse, your friend or a trainer.

You want a consistent plan, exercising at the same time each day, or most days of the week, in order to create a habit. Some people are able to fit it in whenever they can, but that leaves it up to chance if you are not in the habit yet. Eventually, you will not want to miss your exercise time because it will make you feel amazing. Continue to focus on what you want, read about the health benefits of exercise, and stay in the zone. Remember how good you feel when you exercise, so that when you are tired, you go anyway, and you will be so glad that you did! If you can remember a time in your past that you enjoyed exercising and the way that it made you feel, focus on that and simply start.

Know your numbers so you can measure improvement (waist circumference, BMI, cholesterol (HDL, LDL, Triglycerides), blood glucose, weight). And know your goals. Seeing your hard work pay off is a strong motivator.

All activity counts, but there is a difference between activity and physical activity. Make it intentional. Find what works for you, and focus on how good you feel after achieving your daily goal. Find your meaningful motivator to get started. Your motivation could be the health cost savings, the fact that you feel amazing, or that you look and feel sexy!

Maybe you want to join a gym and maybe you don't. I have been working out in my home for most of 25 years. From time to time I join a gym to change things up, but usually I like to wake up early and do my own thing. I enjoy jogging, lifting weights, yoga, Pilates, jump rope, and any combination that I feel like doing. It depends on the day. I sometimes cycle, and I swim in the summer. In my home, I have nothing fancy or extravagant: workout clothes and good running sneaks, a bike, a jump rope, hand weights, a weighted ball, free weights and a bench, a Pilates stability ball, yoga mat and music.

Soon enough you will not want to miss your workouts. This will be your stress reliever when stress hits. It can be your planned distraction. Go for a walk if you find yourself walking toward the pantry. Act quickly! This change in your normal routine can break a mindless eating habit at home. At work, go for a walk around your office instead of hitting the breakroom vending machine. This is a diet trick. Maybe you just needed to get up and move your body.

Physical activity is as essential as brushing your teeth. If you want or need help with a workout schedule, contact your local gym and ask for a certified personal trainer to help you get started and on track. When you feel strong, you act strong, and you have more confidence. Your strength and health is not only good for you, it is good for all of us.

SLEEP

More than 25 percent of U.S. adults report that they occasionally don't get enough sleep, and 10 percent experience chronic insomnia. Not getting enough sleep is associated with a number of chronic diseases and conditions such as diabetes, cardiovascular disease, obesity and depression. You see, this is all the same story, no matter how we write it. Proper diet, regular exercise and sufficient sleep are all crucial for good health, and they all affect our mind, body and spirit.

The most prevalent sleep disorders are insomnia, Restless Legs Syndrome and sleep apnea. Insomnia is characterized by an inability to initiate or maintain sleep. You may wake up in the early morning hours and cannot go back to sleep. Restless Legs Syndrome (RLS) is a neurological disorder characterized by an unpleasant "creeping" sensation, often feeling like it is originating in the lower legs, and associated with aches and pains throughout the legs. RLS contributes to sleep loss because symptoms are activated at night when a person is relaxing or trying to sleep. It is interesting that abnormalities in the neurotransmitter *dopamine* have often been associated with RLS. An estimated 10 percent of the population has RLS and the incidence is twice as high in women than in men.

Sleep Apnea needs your attention if you think you have it. If you have sleep apnea, you are not breathing consistently, leading the oxygen level in your body to fall. In response, your blood pressure rises to increase blood flow to your brain and heart. Thus, the condition can cause or worsen high blood pressure, elevate blood lipid levels, contribute to insulin resistance and diabetes, and markedly increase the risk for heart attack and stroke. Snoring may be a sign of sleep apnea as well as making periodic snorting noises that interrupt sleep. Daytime sleepiness often follows, as sleep is interrupted and not restorative.

An estimated 18 million Americans have sleep apnea, and it is often associated with people who are overweight. With extra weight in the trunk and neck area, the risk of sleep-dis-ordered breathing increases due to compromised respiratory function.[148]

If you are eating right and exercising, you are more likely to sleep better. Exercise reduces stress, and therefore, helps you sleep. Eating right helps regulate your hormones, steady your blood sugar, and have better digestion and, therefore, helps you sleep. Sleep makes you more likely to want to exercise and eat well. If you are not sleeping well, your hormones are not regulating properly, and you may eat to perk up your energy, even when you are not truly hungry. When you are not sleeping, you are not dealing with stress appropriately; and being rested helps cognition, the processing of thoughts and managing stress better. Everything is connected!

There is a correlation between being overweight and los-ing sleep. In one sleep poll, 77 percent of adults who were obese reported sleep problems.[149] Some data show that if you get your sleep under control, you may lose weight easier. This is because the hormone response is more regulated and that, combined with less fatigue, will make you more likely to exer-cise, and less likely to reach for sugary foods to boost energy. When you are tired, you are more likely to skip exercise. Unhealthy habits are a vicious cycle.

Recent research has focused on the link between sleep and the peptides ghrelin and leptin, which regulate appetite. Ghrelin stimulates hunger, and leptin signals satiety to the brain and suppresses appetite. Studies have found that less sleep is associated with the elevation of ghrelin, and a decrease in leptin. Not only does sleep loss appear to stimulate appetite. It also stimulates cravings for high-fat, high-carbohydrate foods.[150] We also know that studies show elevations of evening cortisol levels in people with chronic sleep loss, and that is likely to promote the development of insulin resistance, a risk factor for obesity and diabetes.[151]

There are also practical reports that say we get used to functioning on less sleep, but in truth, we are not functioning fine. We just think we are because we get used to that as our normal.

The national sleep foundation recommends that adults get seven to nine hours of sleep each night. Getting less than six hours of sleep:

- Causes cognitive impairment—you can't think clearly
- Decreases your sex drive
- Changes your appetite
- May cause health issues relating to your heart
- Makes you more likely to be in an automobile accident

I found myself watching Rachel Ray over Christmas break 2014. One of her guests was a dermatologist who talked about the importance of sleep and what lack of sleep can do to your skin over time. We know that sleep restores and gives our skin elasticity and makes us look younger. From my perspective, the solution is to make sleep a priority and to get more sleep. The dermatologist's solution was this new fun toy she had in her office, and for several hundreds of dollars, you could get your face zapped to make it look tighter. I sense the better long-term solution is to learn to meditate, eat better, exercise, practice breathing techniques and try other things that lead to better sleep such as wearing an eye mask or earplugs. Find what works for you to help you get more sleep, and make it a priority. Can you think yourself back to sleep with my mantra: "Sleep is the most important thing right now"?

Sleep experts tell us other ways to get enough sleep include:

- Keep the same bedtime routine
- No computer blue light screens before bed
- If you wake up, read a book for a few minutes until you get sleepy again
- Only use your bed for sleep and sex
- No heavy meals three hours before bedtime
- No alcohol—it causes sleep disturbances
- No caffeine late in the day

REST

Leisure time is powerful. One of many studies shows that people who engage in physical activity as part of their leisure time are less likely to become unhappy, and those who are inactive are more likely to become unhappy.[152]

A study of 115 men and women from different racial and age groups looked at how the body reacts to leisure activities, defined as anything a person does in his or her free time such as exercise, socializing, listening to music, doing puzzles or watching movies. Virtually all the participants reported reduced stress and had a lower heart rate during their leisure activities, as compared to parts of the day when they weren't involved in leisure. The study participants said they were 34 percent less stressed and 18 percent less sad. On top of that, participants' heart rates dropped an average of three percent while engaged in leisure activities. These are the positive benefits of leisure activities, and they can last longer than the leisure activity itself.[153]

Leisure activities keep you focused on healthy habits and distracted from less healthy habits. I know a woman who lost weight because she started knitting. She said. "My hands were occupied."

Know that exercise, sleep and rest are as equally important as proper nutrition, your sense of purpose and the practice of gratitude. These affect how you feel, and we have learned that we must feel good first in order to take positive actions and affect positive outcomes. Exercise makes us feel good, and so does getting plenty of sleep and rest. Decide what physical activity will work for you, and do it until you feel so good that you can't imagine a day without it.

"Exercise is king. Nutrition is queen. Put them together and you've got a kingdom."

—Jack LaLanne

Final Thoughts

Every health talk I have ever given has the same message. Whether it is about stress management, sugar intake, cardiovascular disease, superfoods, fitness, overall health, nutrition or mind, body, spirit—the solutions are essentially the same.

Believe that you are healthy already in this present moment. See it as if it were already happening. "I am healthy. I am strong. I am lean. I am magnificent. I am here to be all that I can be. I have control over my thoughts and my actions." This starts with your beliefs and the story you tell yourself. Even if the story you're telling yourself is not accurate, is your reality—so make it accurate!

The only difference between a person who can accomplish what he hopes to accomplish, including weight loss and keeping it off, is the belief that he can.

I have done my best to dispel every weight loss myth, every gimmick, and every excuse and story you have relied on in the past that kept you stuck. No more excuses, and no more self-berating talk. You have learned by now that your psychology is your physiology, your spirituality and your emotionality. Thoughts rule your emotions, moods, feelings, hormones, reactions and more. I will say it again; your psychology is your physiology. Everything in life is 80 percent psychological and 20 percent mechanics and execution. You have to have your story right.

Do not conform to the ways of this world. Instead, be transformed by the renewal of your mind. You know what to do and that you are fully capable. Whether you choose to believe that, as Michael Shermer put it, "…depends on your own belief journey and how much you want to believe."[154]

Appendix A
Recipes: A Few to Get Started

Salad Dressings:
Basic Balsamic Vinaigrette Dressing
1/4 c Balsamic vinegar
3/4 c olive oil

Optional:
1/4 tsp salt (or more to taste)
1/4 tsp pepper (or more to taste)
pinch of sugar (or more to taste)

Basic olive oil dressing
2 tsp extra-virgin olive oil
1/2 tsp lemon juice from a lemon
Sea salt and ground black pepper, to taste

Apple Cider Vinaigrette
3 T apple cider Vinegar
1/2 cup extra virgin olive oil
1 tsp oregano
1/4 tsp sea salt
1/8 tsp fresh ground pepper

Dijon and Lemon
2/3 cup olive oil
1/4 cup lemon juice (3 T is about one large lemon)
1/4 cup water

1 T Dijon mustard
1 clove garlic minced (optional)
Herbs to taste

Simple Lime
2 T olive oil
1 lime zested and juiced
1/2 tsp salt

Greek
3 T freshly squeezed lemon juice
1 T red wine vinegar
¼ cup extra virgin olive oil
1/4 tsp dried oregano
1/4 tsp paprika
1 garlic clove minced
Salt and ground black pepper to taste

Honey Sweetie
1 T plus 2 tsp fresh lemon juice
1 T honey
1/4 cup extra-virgin olive oil
Sea salt or Kosher salt and ground black pepper to taste

Salads:
A salad can include anything you can imagine in the world of greens, beans and colorful vegetables. You cannot go wrong. A salad is more than lettuce, tomatoes, cucumber

and carrots. You can add beans, avocado, grilled meats, feta cheese, carrots, bell peppers, mandarins, blueberries and any fresh vegetable on the list. Use your imagination and here are some ideas:

Baby Spinach, Avocado and Pumpkin Seed Salad
Salad:
10 cups baby spinach
1/2 cup green pumpkin seeds
2 avocados
4 oz. Smoked or canned salmon

Dressing:
2 T olive oil
1 lime zested and juiced
1/2 tsp salt

Toss spinach and pumpkin seeds in a large bowl. Slice avocado and salmon over salad. Whisk the salad dressing ingredients together, pour over salad and gently toss. Makes two dinner portions or six side portions. I like to toss dressing and spinach then allow guests/family to add their own amounts of seeds, avocados and salmon on top.

Another Fabulous Spinach Salad:
3 T (1/4 cup) feta cheese
1 cup cherry or grape tomatoes
1 cup fresh cooked or canned chickpeas, rinsed
3 cups fresh baby spinach

2 tsp extra-virgin olive oil
1/2 tsp juice from a lemon
Sea salt and ground black pepper, to taste

Instructions:
Combine first four ingredients in a medium to large bowl.
Combine olive oil and lemon in a separate small bowl until blended. Add salt and pepper to taste.
Pour olive oil mixture over spinach combination and toss until well coated. Serves 2-4

Spinach or Kale Salad

Spinach or Kale
Mandarins or fresh blueberries
Roasted slivered or chopped almonds (optional)
Sweetie Honey dressing

Beet Salad

3 beets roasted, peeled and chopped
5 mandarin oranges, peeled and broken into slices
3 celery stalks, cleaned and diced

Dressing
1.5 T apple cider Vinegar
1/4 cup extra virgin olive oil
sea salt and fresh ground pepper to taste

Add first three ingredients to a bowl. Whisk together the dressing ingredients and add as much as you like for taste.

Greek Quinoa Salad
If you are a fan of traditional Greek Salad and you are not sure if you like quinoa or have never tried it, this will make you a quinoa-a-holic!

Step 1
Greek Dressing:
3 T freshly squeezed lemon juice
1 T red wine vinegar
¼ cup extra virgin olive oil
1/4 tsp dried oregano
1/4 tsp paprika
1 garlic clove minced
Salt and ground black pepper to taste

Whisk dressing ingredients together

Step 2
Quinoa:
1 cup Quinoa
Salt and pepper

Rinse quinoa in a strainer per package instructions. Combine quinoa, 2 cups water, 3/4 tsp salt and 1/4 tsp pepper in a small saucepan, bring to a boil and cook to package instructions (about 15 minutes), until water is absorbed and quinoa is tender.
Transfer quinoa to a bowl, fluff with a fork and let it cool slightly while you finish prepping next ingredients.

Step 3

Add all these ingredients:
2 cups red grape or cherry tomatoes halved
3/4 cup pitted Kalamata olives coarsely chopped or halved
2 green onions (green part only–thinly sliced)
1 small red onion (halved and thinly sliced)
1 cucumber seeded and cut into crescent moons

Step 4

Feta for sprinkling
Cover and refrigerate for at least 1 hour to allow flavors to expand. Just before serving, transfer to a serving bowl or platter and sprinkle with feta cheese.

Additional thoughts: Use what you have in your refrigerator. I have added carrots and diced pepperoncinis, tomatoes, cucumbers, some Kalamata olives and sprinkled it with feta. Yum! Be creative!

Basic Mango Salsa

1-2 Mangos
1 Red Bell Pepper
1 can of Black Beans
Lemon
Olive oil (variation is to squeeze twice as much lime juice than lemon and skip the olive oil)

Chop up mango and bell pepper and place in a bowl. Rinse the can of black beans and stir into the mango and red bell pepper bowl. Squeeze lemon, (and possibly lime), and drizzle in a little olive oil. Mix all ingredients. Add salt and pepper to taste but it is unnecessary for this salsa. Add a finely chopped jalapeño and cilantro for REAL flavor! Let the mango be the most abundant ingredient, and add the other ingredients for color, your taste and more nutrition!

Serve over fish or chicken, eat as a snack or side dish, or as a chip dip.

Meat and Fish:

Basic Chicken Marinade
15 minutes to make, 8 hours to marinate. This marinade will give you restaurant-grade tender and tasty chicken. This is no fail with a 6 to 8 hours of marinating!

3 skinless boneless chicken breast halves
1 T lemon juice
2 T canola or olive oil
1/2 tsp salt
1/4 tsp pepper
1/2 tsp tarragon or rosemary
(I prefer rosemary and olive oil)

Grill Chicken

Easy Pan Sauté Chicken or Fish for Two (multiply to serve more)

2 - 4 oz piece of Fish or Chicken (cut up)

4 Campari tomatoes or your choice of tomatoes (or more, your preference)

2 small garlic cloves

4-5 tsp olive oil

salt, pepper, Italian seasonings to taste

Steps:

Cut up and seed Campari tomatoes

Slice or mince garlic cloves

Heat oil in a skillet

Add tomatoes and garlic to soften

Add meat or fish to skillet and cook through

Season to taste

Salmon or any fish: Grill, bake or broil with skin side down with a little olive oil. Add any relish, any herb, any seasoning to taste.

Asian flare: Mix a little soy sauce with a little brown sugar and a little ginger. Baste the top of your salmon before grilling or baking.

Fancy flare: Serve with traditional capers and sour cream (use plain Greek yogurt instead of sour cream), or top or pair with mango salsa.

Vegetables:
Roasted Prosciutto Wrapped Asparagus Bundles
(Preheat Oven 400 Degrees) I like to bundle three medium to large asparagus stalks per person by wrapping them in a slice of prosciutto. Bundle more if you'd like, especially if you decide to use thinner stalks.

Ingredients:
Olive oil (enough to generously coat asparagus)
Medium to thick stalk asparagus (I like 3 per person)
Package of thinly sliced prosciutto or deli sliced thin (you need a slice for each bundle)
Salt to taste

Step 1
Wash asparagus and bend each spear until it naturally breaks at the tough end of the stalk. Toss tough end away

Step 2
Toss asparagus in a bowl with olive oil, and lightly salt

Step 3
Bundle three asparagus stalks and wrap with one slice of prosciutto

Step 4
Place asparagus/prosciutto bundles, single layer in a baking dish

Step 5
Roast 20 minutes, then check with a fork for desired tender-ness, roasting longer, until you like the texture

Steamed Asparagus:
Aparagus, lemon, olive oil, salt and pepper

Step 1
Wash asparagus and bend each spear until it naturally breaks at the tough end of the stalk. Toss tough end away

Step 2
Place asparagus spears in a steamer on the stove, steam to desired doneness (not too much)

Step 3
Remove from heat, place in a serving dish and toss to coat with a little olive oil, squeeze a little lemon, and salt and pepper to taste

Roasted Broccoli (Broccoli and Cauliflower, or even add baby carrots):
(Preheat oven to 400 degrees) Toss vegetables with a little olive oil, salt and pepper and put in a roasting pan in the preheated oven. Check on veggies in about 20 minutes and then turn/stir. Keep your eye on them until desired doneness.

You can do this same recipe for almost any vegetable: green beans, Brussels sprouts, zucchini, eggplant, etc.

Quick veggie tips:
It is easy to steam broccoli or any other veggie, and the same goes for roasting. When you steam, toss your veggies with a little olive oil salt and pepper or sauté garlic in a pan with olive oil and toss that on your veggies. When roasting, toss in a bowl with a little olive oil to lightly coat and then salt and pepper. You may choose to add garlic or not. Roast in pan at 400 degrees until ready to desired doneness.

Traditional Hummus
2 cups canned garbanzo beans, drained—but save some liquid to add in mixing if dry (or cook garbanzo beans from dried beans)
1/3 cup tahini (start with a little less)
1/4 cup lemon juice (might want to add more for your taste)
1 teaspoon salt
2 cloves garlic, cut in half (might want to add more for your taste)

Blend above ingredients in a blender, transfer to a serving bowl and decorate with 1 T olive oil drizzled on top, sprinkle with paprika. Slice carrots and bell peppers and eat hummus as a dip or spread for sandwiches.

Tomato and Basil Bruschetta
Bruschetta is an open-faced sandwich, bread rubbed with garlic and topped with olive oil, salt and pepper. The toppings are endless.

Most recipes call for plum tomatoes. I like the Campari tomatoes because of their sweeter taste.

Ingredients:
5-6 tomatoes, seeded and diced small
1 clove garlic minced
3 T extra-virgin olive oil
2 T fresh basil leaves, sliced into ribbons
1 T balsamic vinegar
1/2 baguette, sliced into 1/2-inch rounds
Extra olive oil for drizzling on toasted bread

Directions:
Preheat the oven to 350 degrees F

Step 1
Tomatoes:
In one bowl, add the tomatoes and basil. In a smaller bowl, mix together the garlic, 3 tablespoons extra-virgin olive oil and balsamic vinegar. Pour olive oil mixture over tomatoes and basil, toss, and season to taste with salt and pepper. Let sit at room temperature while you toast the bread.

Step 2
Bread:
Slice bread in 1/2 inch slices and add to a baking sheet in a single layer. Toast in the oven until hardened on top, barely turning golden brown. I like to turn over and toast both sides.

Remove from oven and rub each toast piece with garlic clove and drizzle with olive oil.

Step 3
Top:
Either serve the tomatoes in a bowl and have toast on the side for self-serving and topping; or top toast and serve immediately.

Variation: Make it a meal. Chop up grilled chicken and toss with the tomato and basil topping, sprinkle with parmesan or mozzarella cheese and top the toast. Heat in oven at 350 degrees F, and serve warm.

Fruit Smoothies:
Directions for All Smoothies
Thoroughly blend all ingredients together, adding ice cubes, cold water or unfiltered apple juice until the shake reaches desired consistency.

Tips for Delicious Smoothies

- Using frozen fruit eliminates need for more ice and water and makes a thicker smoothie
- Try creating your own. Mangos or peaches add a nice flavor, and pineapple adds sweetness
- Slice and freeze your extra ripe bananas to use for making fruit smoothies

- Adding a handful of fresh spinach to your smoothies increases your antioxidant intake, nutrition and just makes you feel like you are doing something good for yourself
- Adding a 6 oz. container of Chobani yogurt has been a crowd pleaser. It adds protein without protein powder and a nice creamy texture. Depending on the fruit ingredients, we have used blueberry the most, then strawberry, mango and peach yogurts
- When you add protein powder, your smoothie will expand, so some smoothie recipes produce portions from one to two smoothies

Banana Berry Blast
Makes two

- 1 banana
- 1/2 cup blueberries
- 1/2 cup strawberries
- 1/2 cup apple or cranberry juice
- Optional-add 6 oz. blueberry Chobani Greek yogurt (taste creamy and yummy for kids) OR, protein powder
- Ice cubes and cold water to your desired consistency

Lean and Green
Makes two

- 1 banana
- 1/2 cup frozen mangos

- 1/2 cup frozen peaches
- One or two handfuls of fresh spinach
- Ice cubes and water to desired consistency
- Protein powder optional

Peanut Butter, Chocolate Banana
Makes one fruit smoothie (better than a milkshake!)

- 1 frozen sliced banana
- 1 T unsweetened cocoa powder
- 1 T natural peanut butter
- 1/2 cup skim milk
- Ice cubes to desired consistency

Pumpkin Pie
Makes one

- 1 banana
- 1/2 cup pumpkin puree
- 1/2 tsp ground cinnamon
- 1/8 tsp ground ginger or all spice
- Ice cubes and water to desired texture
- Protein powder optional, handful of spinach optional

Bibliography

INTRODUCTION

1. National Weight Loss Control Registry, Research Findings. December 12, 2015. Retrieved from http://www.nwcr.ws. May 10, 2015.

2. Seligman, Martin E.P., Ph.D. *What You Can Change and What You Cannot.* New York: Random House, Inc., 2007. Print. Page 184.

3. O'Meara, Alex. The Percentage of People Who Regain Weight After Rapid Weight Loss and the Risk of Doing So. November 07, 2015. Retrieved from http://www.livestrong.com/article/438395-the-percentage-of-people-who-regain-weight-after-rapid-weight-loss-risks/. December 1, 2015.

4. Seligman, Martin E.P., Ph.D. *What You Can Change and What You Cannot.* New York: Random House, Inc., 2007. Print. Page 189.

CHAPTER 1

5. Sir Roger Bannister: Breaking the 4-minute mile-Academy of Achievement. November 26, 2013. Retrieved from http://www.achievement.org/autodoc/page/ban0int-2. September 22, 2015.

6.   Sir Roger Bannister: Breaking the 4-minute mile- bibliography of article from journal

7.   Academy of Achievement. November 26, 2013. Retrieved from http://www.achievement.org/autodoc/page/ban0int-1. September 24, 2015,

8.   Shermer, Michael. *The Believing Brain*. New York: Henry Holt and Company, LLC. 2011. Print. Page 258.

9.   Nutrition Advertising Targeting Children. August 21, 2015. Retrieved from http://www.cdc.gov/phlp/winnable/advertising_children.html. October 20, 2015.

10. Bailey, Sharon. The Role of Branding and Advertising in the Soft Drink Industry- Market Realist. November 20, 2014. Retrieved from http://marketrealist.com/2014/11/role-branding-advertising-soft-drink-industry/. October 11, 2015.

11. Mallett Clifford J., Hanrahan Stephanie J. *Elite Athletes: Why Does the 'Fire' Burn so Brightly? I don't know but you can find it.* Psychology of Sport and Exercise Volume 5, Issue 2, April 2004: Pages 183–200. Print.

12. Bandura, Albert. *Self-Efficacy: Toward a Unifying Theory of Behavioral Change.* Psychological Review 1977, Vol.84, No.2: 191-215. Print. http://www.uky.edu/~eushe2/Bandura/Bandura1977PR.pdf

13.   Butler-Bowden, Tom. *50 Psychology Classics*. New York: Gildan Media, LLC. 2007. Audio. Disc 3.

14.   Seligman, Martin E.P., Ph.D. *What You Can Change and What You Cannot*. New York: Random House, Inc., 2007. Print. Page 189.

15.   Sharkey, Wendy. Erik Erikson (May 1997) Retrieved October 1, 2015 http://www.muskingum.edu/~psych/psycweb/history/erikson.htm

16.   Shermer, Michael. *The Believing Brain*. New York: Henry Holt and Company, LLC. 2011. Print. Page 333.

CHAPTER 2

17.   Butler-Bowden, Tom. *50 Psychology Classics*. New York: Gildan Media, LLC. 2007. Audio. Disc 3.

18.   Burns, David, MD. (September 5, 2014) Feeling Good. Retrieved from https://www.youtube.com/watch?v=H1T5uMeYv9Q

19.   Burns, David, MD. Feeling Good. September 5, 2014. Retrieved from https://www.youtube.com/watch?v=H1T5uMeYv9Q. September 20, 2015.

20.   Burns, David, MD. Feeling Good. September 5, 2014. Retrieved from https://www.youtube.com/watch?v=H1T5uMeYv9Q. September 20, 2015.

21. Ledgerwood, Alison. Getting Stuck in the Negatives (and How to Get Unstuck). June 22, 2013. Retrieved from https://www.youtube.com/watch?v=7XFLTDQ4JMk. Dec. 03, 2015.

22. Ledgerwood, Alison. Getting Stuck in the Negatives (and How to Get Unstuck). June 22, 2013. Retrieved from https://www.youtube.com/watch?v=7XFLTDQ4JMk. Dec. 03, 2015.

23. Ledgerwood, Alison. Getting Stuck in the Negatives (and How to Get Unstuck). June 22, 2013. Retrieved from https://www.youtube.com/watch?v=7XFLTDQ4JMk. Dec. 03, 2015.

24. http://www.loni.usc.edu/about_loni/education/brain_trivia.php. Education Retrieved September 20, 2015.

25. Bargh, John and Morsella, Ezequiel. The Unconscious Mind Perspective Psychology Science 2008 Jan; 3 (1): 73-79. Retrieved from http://www.ncbi.nlm.nih.gov/pmc/articles/PMC2440575/. September 20, 2015.

26. Robison, Esther. Scientific American: Can We Control Our Thoughts? Why Do Thoughts Pop into My Head as I'm Trying to Fall Asleep? March 1, 2013. Retrieved from http://www.scientificamerican.com/article/can-we-control-our-thoughts/. August 10, 2015.

27. Lewis, Thomas M.D., Amini, Fari M.D., Lannon, Richard, M.D. *A General Theory of Love.* New York: Random House, Inc., 2000. Print. Page 44.

28. Thuret, Sandrine. You can Grow New Brain Cells. Here's How. June 2015. Retrieved from https://www.ted.com/ talks/ sandrine_thuret_you_can_grow_new_brain_cells_ here_s_how?language=en. December 5, 2015.

29. Patten SB, Williams JV, Lavorato DH, Eliasziw M. A longitudinal community study of major depression and physical activity. Gen Hosp Psychiatry 2009;31(6):571-575. Retrieved from http://www.ncbi.nlm.nih.gov/pub-med/19892216. December 6, 2015.

30. The American Institute of Stress. What is Stress? Retrieved from http://www.stress.org/what-is-stress/. February 15, 2016.

31. The American Heart Association. Stress and Heart Health. June 13, 2014. Retrieved from http://www.heart. org/HEARTORG/HealthyLiving/StressManagement/ HowDoesStressAffectYou/Stress-and-Heart-Health_ UCM_437370_Article.jsp#.V98cdjuq30c. August 12, 2016.

32. Tovee, Martin J. Neuronal Processing: How Fast is the Speed of Thought? Current Biology 1994, Vol. 4 No. 12.

Retrieved from http://www.science.smith.edu/depart-ments/neurosci/courses/bio330/pdf/94CurrBiolTovee.pdf. July 21, 2015.

33. Bandura, Albert. *Self-Efficacy: Toward a Unifying Theory of Behavioral Change.* Psychological Review 1977, Vol.84, No.2: 191-215. Print. http://www.uky.edu/~eushe2/Bandura/Bandura1977PR.pdf

CHAPTER 3

34. Burns, David, MD. Feeling Good. September 5, 2014. Retrieved from https://www.youtube.com/watch?v=H1T5uMeYv9Q. September 20, 2015.

35. Burns, David, MD. Feeling Good. September 5, 2014. Retrieved from https://www.youtube.com/watch?v=H1T5uMeYv9Q. September 20, 2015.

36. Seligman, Martin E.P., Ph.D. *What You Can Change and What You Cannot.* New York: Random House, Inc., 2007. Print. Page 232.

37. Seligman, Martin E.P., Ph.D. *What You Can Change and What You Cannot.* New York: Random House, Inc., 2007. Print. Page 232.

38. Sheldon, Kennon M., Lyubmirsky, Sonja. How to Increase and Sustain Positive Emotion: The Effects of Expressing

Gratitude and Visualizing Best Possible Selves. The Journal of Positive Psychology, April 2006; 1 (2): 73-82.

39. Sheldon, Kennon M., Lyubmirsky, Sonja. How to Increase and Sustain Positive Emotion: The Effects of Expressing Gratitude and Visualizing Best Possible Selves. The Journal of Positive Psychology, April 2006; 1 (2): 73-82.

40. Sheldon, Kennon M., Lyubmirsky, Sonja. How to Increase and Sustain Positive Emotion: The Effects of Expressing Gratitude and Visualizing Best Possible Selves. The Journal of Positive Psychology, April 2006; 1 (2): 73-82.

41. Sheldon, Kennon M., Lyubmirsky, Sonja. How to Increase and Sustain Positive Emotion: The Effects of Expressing Gratitude and Visualizing Best Possible Selves. The Journal of Positive Psychology, April 2006; 1 (2): 73-82.

42. Emmons, Robert. Greater Good. Why Gratitude is Good. November 16, 2010. Retrieved from http://greatergood.berkeley.edu/article/item/why_gratitude_is_good. March 1, 2016.

43. Katterman SN, Kleinman BM, Hood MM, Nackers LM, Corsica JA. Mindfulness meditation as an intervention for binge eating, emotional eating, and weight loss: a

systematic review. Eating Behaviors 2014; 15(2): 197-204.47. Retrieved from http://www.ncbi.nlm.nih.gov/pubmed/24854804. February 12, 2015.

CHAPTER 4

44. Maslow, Abraham. *Motivation and Personality*. New York: Harper & Row, Publishers. 1954. Print.

45. Maslow, Abraham. *Motivation and Personality*. New York: Harper & Row, Publishers. 1954. Print.

46. Adkins, Amy. Employee Engagement in U.S. Stagnant in 2015. January 2016. Retrieved from http://www.gallup.com/poll/188144/employee-engagement-stagnant-2015.aspx. April 24, 2017.

CHAPTER 5

47. Lewis, Thomas M.D., Amini, Fari M.D., Lannon, Richard, M.D. *A General Theory of Love*. New York: Random House, Inc., 2000. Print. Page 161

48. Maslow, Abraham. *Motivation and Personality*. New York: Harper & Row, Publishers. 1954. Print.

49. Lewis, Thomas M.D., Amini, Fari M.D., Lannon, Richard, M.D. *A General Theory of Love*. New York: Random House, Inc., 2000. Print. Page 161.

50. Lewis, Thomas M.D., Amini, Fari M.D., Lannon, Richard, M.D. *A General Theory of Love*. New York: Random House, Inc., 2000. Print. Page 203-204.

51. Covey, Stephen. *The 7 Habits of Highly Effective People*. New York: Simon & Schuster. 1989. Print.

52. Covey, Stephen. *The 7 Habits of Highly Effective People*. New York: Simon & Schuster. 1989. Print.

53. Lewis, Thomas M.D., Amini, Fari M.D., Lannon, Richard, M.D. *A General Theory of Love*. New York: Random House, Inc., 2000. Print. Page 144.

CHAPTER 6

54. Brainy Quote. Retrieved from http://www.brainyquote. com/quotes/quotes/d/dwightdei164720.html. September 18, 2016.

55. The Stress Theory of Hans Selye. May 20, 2007. Retrieved from https://www.youtube.com/watch?v=YJCeDtNh_ Aw. November 13, 2015.

56. Dingfelder, Sadie F. Solutions to resolution dilution. American Psychological Association January 2004, Vol 35, No. 1 Print version: page 34. Retrieved from //apa. org/monitor/jan04/solutions.aspx. December 3, 2015.

CHAPTER 7

57. Fredrickson, B.L. (2006) The broaden and -build theory of positive emotions. In Csiksgentmihalyi, M. & Csikszentmihalyi, I.S. (eds.) A Life Worth Living: Contributions To Positive Psychology (85-103). NY: Oxford Press.

58. VIA Institute on Character. VIA Classification of Character Strengths. Retrieved from http://www.viacharacter.org/www/Character-Strengths/VIA-Classification. December 8, 2015.

59. Rath, Tom. *Strengths Finder*. New York: Gallup Press, 2007. Print.

CHAPTER 8

60. Clarey, Christopher. Olympians Use Imagery as Mental Training. Embedded video by Donaldson, Nancy, Saget Bedel, Ward Joe, Sablich, Justin. Emily Cook, of the United States freestyle ski team, visualizes each aerial jump as part of her training for the Olympics. February 22, 2014. Retrieved from http://www.nytimes.com/2014/02/23/sports/olympics/olympians-use-imagery-as-mental-training.html. January 10, 2016.

CHAPTER 9

61. Carmona, Richard H., Vice Admiral M.D., M.P.H, FACS. June 10, 2003 12:30 p.m. Retrieved from http://www.

surgeongeneral.gov/news/speeches/obesity061003.html. January 10, 2016.

62. Press release. Controlling the global obesity epidemic. March 3, 2003. Retrieved from http://www.who.int/ nutrition/topics/obesity/en/. January 10, 2016.

63. CDC. Childhood Obesity Facts. August 27, 2015. Retrieved from http://www.cdc.gov/healthyschools/obe-sity/facts.htm. December 12, 2015.

64. CDC. Obesity and Overweight. June 13, 2016. Retrieved from http://www.cdc.gov/nchs/fastats/obesity-overweight.htm. July 15, 2016.

65. Cheryl D. Fryar, M.S.P.H.; Margaret D. Carroll, M.S.P.H.; and Cynthia L. Ogden, Ph.D., Division of Health and Nutrition Examination Surveys. Prevalence of Obesity Among Children and Adolescents: United States, Trends 1963–1965 Through 2009–2010 (September 2012) Retrieved from http://www.cdc.gov/nchs/data/hestat/ obesity_child_09_10/obesity_child_09_10.pdf. July 15, 2016.

66. CDC. Obesity and Overweight. June 13, 2016. Retrieved from http://www.cdc.gov/nchs/fastats/obesity-overweight.htm. July 15, 2016.

67. Cheryl D. Fryar, M.S.P.H.; Margaret D. Carroll, M.S.P.H.; and Cynthia L. Ogden, Ph.D., Division of Health and Nutrition Examination Surveys. Prevalence of Obesity Among Children and Adolescents Aged 2-19 Years; United States, 1963-1965 Through 2013-2014. Retrieved from http://www.cdc.gov/nchs/data/hestat/obesity_child_13_14/obesity_child_13_14.htm. July 30, 2016.

68. Source: CDC. Vital and Health Statistics: Series 10, number 260, Feb 2014. Summary Health Statistics for U.S. Adults: National Health Interview Survey, 2012. 10/19/2015

69. National Institute of Diabetes and Digestive and Kidney Diseases. Retrieved from http://www.niddk.nih.gov/health-information/health-topics/Diabetes/diabetes-heart-disease-stroke/Pages/index.aspx. March 17, 2016

70. Ogden, Cynthia L., PhD. Prevalence of Childhood and Adult Obesity in the United States, 2011-2012. Journal of American Medicine (JAMA). February 26, 2014 Vol 311, No 8. Retrieved from http://jama.jamanetwork.com/article.aspx?articleid=1832542. December 10, 2015.

71. CDC. Adult Obesity Causes and Consequences Retrieved from http://www.cdc.gov/obesity/adult/causes.html. March 17, 2016.

72. Moss, Michael. *Salt Sugar Fat.* New York: Random House, Inc. 2014. Print. Page 4.

73. Consumption of Sugar Drinks in the United States, 2005-2008. NCHS Data Brief No. 71, August 2011. Retrieved from http://www.cdc.gov/nchs/data/databriefs/db71.htm. January 15, 2016.

74. Edwards, Nicholas Murphy; Pettingell, Sandra; Borowsky, Iris Wagman Where Perception Meets Reality: Self-Perception of Weight in Overweight Adolescents. Pediatrics, March 2010, VOLUME 125 / ISSUE 3 Retrieved from http://pediatrics.aappublications.org/content/125/3/e452. January 3, 2016.

75. Duncan, Dustin T.; Wolin, Kathleen Y. Wolin; Scharoun-Lee, Melissa; Ding, Eric L.; Warner, Erica T. Warner; Bennett, Gary G. Bennett Does perception equal reality? Weight misperception in relation to weight-related attitudes and behaviors among overweight and obese US adults. *International Journal of Behavioral Nutrition and Physical Activity*, March 2011, 8:20, Retrieved from http://ijbnpa.biomedcentral.com/articles/10.1186/1479-5868-8-20. January 20, 2016.

76. Baughcum, Amy E.; Chamberlin, Leigh A.; Deeks, Cindy M.; Powers, Scott W.; Whitaker, Robert C. Moms misperception that child might be overweight. Pediatrics, December 2000, VOLUME 106 / ISSUE

6. Retrieved from http://pediatrics.aappublications.org/content/106/6/1380.short. February 26, 2016.

77. Pratt Laura A, PhD Brody Debra J., MPH Depression in the U.S. household population, 2009–2012. National Center for Health Statistics Data Brief, No. 172. December 2014. Retrieved from http://www.cdc.gov/nchs/data/databriefs/db172.htm. March 18, 2016.

78. Pratt, Laura A., Ph.D.; Brody, Debra J., M.P.H. Depression and Obesity in the U.S. Adult Household Population, 2005–2010. NCHS Data Brief, No. 167, October 2014. Retrieved from http://www.cdc.gov/nchs/data/databriefs/db167.htm. January, 2016.

79. Pratt, Laura A., Ph.D.; Brody, Debra J., M.P.H; Gu, Qiuping, M.D., Ph.D. Antidepressant Use in Persons Aged 12 and Over: United States, 2005–2008 NCHS Data Brief, No. 76 (October 2011). Retrieved from http://www.cdc.gov/nchs/data/databriefs/db76.pdf. January, 2016.

80. Brooks, Megan. 'Alarming' New Stats on US Heroin Epidemic. July 08, 2015. Retrieved from http://www.medscape.com/viewarticle/84765. July 12, 2016.

81. Preda, Adrian, MD; Chief Editor: Dunavevich, Eduardo, MD Opioid Abuse (June 7, 2016) Retrieved from http://

emedicine.medscape.com/article/287790-overview. June 20, 2016.

82. A Comprehensive Review on Metabolic Syndrome Jaspinder Kaur* Cardiol Res Pract. 2014; 2014: 943162. Published online 2014 Mar 11. Retrieved from http://www.ncbi.nlm.nih.gov/pmc/articles/PMC3966331/. February 3, 2016.

83. Ferrie, Jane E., PhD; Shipley Martin J., MS; Akbaraly, Tasnime N., PhD; Marmot, Michael G., MD.; Kivimäki, Mika, PhD.; Singh-Manoux, Archana, PhD. Change in Sleep Duration and Cognitive Function: Findings from the Whitehall II Study Sleep. 2011 May 1; 34(5): 565–573. Retrieved from http://www.ncbi.nlm.nih.gov/pmc/articles/PMC3079935/. March 4, 2016.

CHAPTER 10

84. U.S. Food Retail Industry - Statistics & Facts. Retrieved from https://www.statista.com/topics/1660/food-retail/. April 24, 2017.

85. Food Marketing Institute. The Voice of Food Retail Supermarket Facts. Retrieved from http://www.fmi.org/research-resources/supermarket-facts. April 24, 2017.

86. What to Do When There Are Too Many Product Choices on the Store Shelves? January 2014. Retrieved from

http://www.consumerreports.org/cro/magazine/2014/
03/too-many-product-choices-in-supermarkets/index.
htm. April 24, 2017.

87.   Clifford, Stephanie. At Stores, Making 5 for $5 a Bigger
       Draw Than 1 for $1. New York Times. July 17, 2011.
       Retrieved from http://www.nytimes.com/2011/07/18/
       business/grocery-stores-use-big-quantities-to-entice-
       shoppers.html?_r=0. March 20, 2016.

88.   Strom, Stephanie. A Big Bet on Gluten-Free. New
       York Times, February 17, 2014. Retrieved from http://
       www.nytimes.com/2014/02/18/business/food-industry-
       wagers-big-on-gluten-free.html. November 12, 2015.

89.   Mintel Gluten -Free Foods Surge 63% in Last Two
       Years. November 18, 2014. Retrieved from http://www.
       mintel.com/press-centre/food-and-drink/gluten-free-
       foods-surge-63-percent. November 12, 2015.

90.   Mintel Half of Americans Think Gluten-Free Diets Are
       A Fad While 25% Eat Gluten -Free Foods. December
       4, 2015. Retrieved from http://www.mintel.com/press-
       centre/food-and-drink/half-of-americans-think-gluten-
       free-diets-are-a-fad-while-25-eat-gluten-free-foods.
       April 29, 2017.

91.   Mintel Gluten-Free Foods Surge 63% in Last Two Years. November 18, 2014. Retrieved from http://www.mintel. com/press-centre/food-and-drink/gluten-free-foods-surge-63percent. November 12, 2015.

92.   Mintel Gluten-Free Foods Surge 63% in Last Two Years. November 18, 2014. Retrieved from http://www. mintel.com/press-centre/food-and-drink/gluten-free-foods-surge-63percent. November 12, 2015

93.   Mintel Gluten-Free Foods Surge 63% in Last Two Years. November 18, 2014. Retrieved from http:// www.mintel.com/press-centre/food-and-drink/ gluten-free-foods-surge-63percent. November 12, 2015

94.   Celiac Disease Foundation. What Can I Eat? Retrieved from https://celiac.org/live-gluten-free/glutenfreediet/food-options/#DikOr4VxP5UmwtDE.99. November, 2015.

95.   USDA. Organic Agriculture. Retrieved from http:// www.usda.gov/wps/portal/usda/usdamobile?navid= organic-agriculture. November 20, 2016.

96.   USDA. Organic Agriculture. Retrieved from http:// www.usda.gov/wps/portal/usda/usdamobile?navid= organic-agriculture. November 20, 2016.

97. Environmental Working Group. The "Dirty Dozen". Retrieved from http://www.organic.org/articles/show-article/article-214. January 20, 2016.

98. Fernandez-Cornejo, Jorge; Wechsler, Seth J.; Livingston, Michael; Mitchell, Lorraine Genetically Engineered Crops in the United States. USDA Economic Research Report No. (ERR-162) 60 pp, February 2014. Retrieved from http://www.ers.usda.gov/publications/err-economic-research-report/err162.aspx. November12, 2015.

99. Shelby, Ginger. How GMO Foods Damage Human DNA. Retrieved from http://www.ecopedia.com/health/how-gmo-damage-human-dna/. August 18, 2016.

100. Foss, Arlid S. Growing Fatter on a GM Diet (July 17, 2012). Retrieved from http://sciencenordic.com/growing-fatter-gm-diet. June 25, 2016.

101. Weise, Elizabeth. Fishy Fakes Common in Restaurants. USA Today, February 21, 2013. Retrieved from http://www.usatoday.com/story/news/nation/2013/02/20/fish-seafood-fraud-common-oceana-report/1927065/. June 25, 2016.

102. Cutler, Jacqueline. Parmesan cheese from many top brands may contain wood by product. New York Daily News (February 17, 2016). Retrieved from http://www.

nydailynews.com/life-style/eats/woody-filler-parmesan-cellulose-article- 1.2534707. June 25, 2016.

103. Alban, Deane Fake Olive Oil What you need to Know. Retrieved from http://eatlocalgrown.com/article/12300-is-your-olive-oil-lying-about-its-virginity.html. January 8

104. Federal Trade Commission Leibowitz, Jon; Rosch, J. Thomas; Ramirez, Edith; Brill, Julie; Ohlhausen, Maureen.Review of Food Marketing to Children and Adolescents. FTC Follow-Up Report December 2012, page ES-1 https://www.ftc.gov/sites/default/files/documents/reports/review-food-marketing-children-and-adolescents-follow-report/121221foodmarketingreport.pdf. December 2, 2015.

105. Federal Trade Commission Leibowitz, Jon; Rosch, J. Thomas; Ramirez, Edith; Brill, Julie; Ohlhausen, Maureen. Review of Food Marketing to Children and Adolescents. FTC Follow-Up Report December 2012, page ES-2. Retrieved from https://www.ftc.gov/sites/default/files/documents/reports/review-food-marketing-children-and-adolescents-follow-report/121221foodmarketingreport.pdf. December 2, 2015.

106. Federal Trade Commission Leibowitz, Jon; Rosch, J. Thomas; Ramirez, Edith; Brill, Julie; Ohlhausen, Maureen. Review of Food Marketing to Children and

Adolescents. FTC Follow-Up Report December 2012, pages 5-6. Retrieved from https://www.ftc.gov/sites/default/files/documents/reports/review-food-market-ing-children-and-adolescents-follow report/121221food marketingreport.pdf. November 20, 2016.

107. Federal Trade Commission Leibowitz, Jon; Rosch, J. Thomas; Ramirez, Edith; Brill, Julie; Ohlhausen, Maureen. Review of Food Marketing to Children and Adolescents. FTC Follow- Up Report December 2012, page 104. Retrieved from https://www.ftc.gov/sites/default/files/documents/reports/review-food-marketing-children-and-adolescents-follow-report/121221foodmarketingreport.pdf. November 20, 2016.

108. Harris, JL, Bargh, JA, Brownell KD Priming effects of television food advertising on eating behavior Health Psychol. 2009 Jul;28(4):404-13. Retrieved from http://www.ncbi.nlm.nih.gov/pubmed/19594263. December 15, 2015.

109. Nestle, Marion. What to Eat: An Aisle-by-Aisle Guide to Savvy Food Choices and Good Eating. New York: North Point Press, 2006. Print. Pages 71-72.

110. USDA HHS and USDA Release New Dietary Guidelines to Encourage Healthy Eating Patterns to Prevent Chronic Diseases January 7, 2016. Retrieved from https://

www.usda.gov/media/press-releases/2016/01/06/hhs-and-usda-release-new-dietary-guidelines-encourage-healthy. April 29, 2017.

111. Schlosser, Eric. Fast Food Nation: The Dark-Side of the All-American Meal. New York, NY: HarperCollins Publishers, 2001. Print. Pages 51-53.

112. Federal Trade Commission Leibowitz, Jon; Rosch, J. Thomas; Ramirez, Edith; Brill, Julie; Ohlhausen, Maureen. Review of Food Marketing to Children and Adolescents. *FTC Follow-Up Report* December 2012, page ES-3. Retrieved from https://www.ftc.gov/sites/default/files/documents/reports/review-food-marketing-children-and-adolescents-follow-report/121221foodmarketingreport.pdf. November 20, 2016.

113. Nutrition facts. Chick-fil-A. Retrieved from http://www.chick-fil-a.com/Food/Menu-Detail/ChickfilA-Nuggets#?details=nutrition. June 10, 2016.

114. Nutrition facts. McDonalds. Retrieved from https://www.mcdonalds.com/us/en-us/about-our-food/nutri-tion-calculator.html. August 18, 2016.

115. Nutrition facts. McDonalds. Retrieved from https://www.mcdonalds.com/us/en-us/about-our-food/nutri-tion-calculator.html. August 18, 2016.

116. Nutrition facts. McDonalds. Retrieved from https://www.mcdonalds.com/us/en-us/about-our-food/nutrition-calculator.html. August 18, 2016.

CHAPTER 11

117. Threapleton, Diane, et al. Dietary Fibre Intake and Risk of Cardiovascular Disease: Systematic Review and Meta-Analysis. British Medical Journal, December 19, 2013, pages 80-81.

118. Schardt, David Coconut Oil: Lose Weight? Cure Alzheimer's? Clog your Arteries? Nutrition Action Newsletter June 2012. Retrieved from http://cspinet.org/nah/pdfs/feature-coconut-oil.pdf. February 17, 2015.

119. Schardt, David Coconut Oil: Lose Weight? Cure Alzheimer's? Clog your Arteries? Nutrition Action Newsletter June 2012. Retrieved from http://cspinet.org/nah/pdfs/feature-coconut-oil.pdf. February 17, 2015.

120. American Heart Association. Monounsaturated Fats. Retrieved from http://www.heart.org/HEARTORG/HealthyLiving/HealthyEating/Nutrition/Monounsaturated-Fats_UCM_301460_Article.jsp#.V4JMmldlzPk. June, 2016.

121. Gray, Nathan What is a Health Benefit? Researchers issue Probiotic Guidance for EFSA applications September 11, 2013. Retrieved from http://www.nutraingredients. com/Research/What-is-a-health-benefit-Researchers-issue-probiotic-guidance-for-EFSA-applications?utm_source=copyright&utm_medium=OnSite&utm_campaign=copyright. December 12, 2015.

122. Stang M, Wysowski DK, Butler-Jones D. Incidence of lactic acidosis in metformin users. Diabetes Care. 1999 Jun;22(6):925-7. Retrieved from http://www.ncbi.nlm. nih.gov/pubmed/10372243. January 3, 2016.

123. FDA Drug Safety Communication: FDA evaluating risk of stroke, heart attack and death with FDA-approved testosterone products. Retrieved from http://www.fda. gov/Drugs/DrugSafety/ucm383904.htm. November 25, 2015.

124. Tanner, Lindsey. A landmark study suggests that testosterone treatment is no fountain of youth. February 17, 2016. U.S. News. Retrieved from http://www.usnews.com/ news/business/articles/2016-02-17/study-finds-testosterone-gel-is-no-fountain-of-youth. February 12, 2016.

125. Mousumi Bose, Blanca Oliván, and Blandine Laferrère. Stress and obesity: the role of the hypothalamic–

pituitary–adrenal axis in metabolic disease. Curr Opin Endocrinol Diabetes Obes. 2009 Oct; 16(5): 340–346. Retrieved from http://www.ncbi.nlm.nih.gov/pmc/articles/PMC2858344/. March 20, 2016.

126. Frellick, Marcia. AMA Declares Obesity a Disease. Medscape, June 19, 2013 Retrieved from http://www.medscape.com/viewarticle/806566. November 25, 2015.

127. CDC. Smoking and Tobacco Use. Retrieved from http://www.cdc.gov/tobacco/data_statistics/fact_sheets/cessation/quitting/. March 11, 2016.

128. CDC. Smoking and Tobacco Use. Retrieved from http://www.cdc.gov/tobacco/data_statistics/fact_sheets/cessation/quitting/. March 11, 2016.

129. CDC. Smoking and Tobacco Use. Retrieved from http://www.cdc.gov/tobacco/data_statistics/fact_sheets/cessation/quitting/. March 11, 2016.

130. Centers for Disease Control and Prevention. Overweight and Obesity, September 21, 2015. Retrieved from http://www.cdc.gov/obesity/data/adult.html. February 25, 2016.

131. Krajmalnik-Brown, Rosa, PhD.; Dehra-Esra, Ilhan; Dae-Wook, Kang, PhD.; DiBaise, John K., MD. Effects

of Gut Microbes on Nutrient Absorption and Energy Regulation. Nutrition in Clinical Practice 2012 April 27: 27 (2):201-214. Published online February 24, 2012. Retrieved from http://www.ncbi.nlm.nih.gov/pmc/articles/PMC3601187/. June 30, 2016

132. New Procedure Estimates for Bariatric Surgery: What the Numbers Reveal. Connect, May 2014. Retrieved from http://connect.asmbs.org/may-2014-bariatric-surgery-growth.html. February 20, 2016.

133. Kell, John. Lean Times for the Diet Industry. Fortune, May, 22, 2015. Retrieved from fortune.com/2015/05/22/lean-times-for-the-diet-industry/. January 13, 2016.

CHAPTER 12

134. Threapleton, Diane, et al. Dietary Fibre Intake and Risk of Cardiovascular Disease: Systematic Review and Meta-Analysis. British Medical Journal, December 19, 2013, pages 80-81.

135. Phates, Emily H. Straight Talk about Soy. The Nutrition Source, February 12, 2014. Retrieved from https://www.hsph.harvard.edu/nutritionsource/2014/02/12/straight-talk-about-soy/. June 29, 2016.

136. Phates, Emily H. Straight Talk about Soy. The Nutrition Source, February 12, 2014. Retrieved from https://www.

hsph.harvard.edu/nutritionsource/2014/02/12/straight-talk-about-soy/. June 29, 2016.

CHAPTER 13

137. USDA Food Away From Home December 30 2016. Retrieved from https://www.ers.usda.gov/topics/food-choices-health/food-consumption-demand/food-away-from-home.aspx. April 29, 2017.

CHAPTER 14

138. CDC. Exercise and Physical Activity July 20, 2015. Retrieved from http://www.cdc.gov/nchs/fastats/exercise.htm. December 12, 2016.

139. 2008 Physical Activity Guidelines for Americans. Retrieved from https://health.gov/paguidelines/pdf/paguide.pdf. November2, 2015.

140. American Heart Association Recommendations for Physical Activity in Adults, July 27, 2016. Retrieved from http://www.heart.org/HEARTORG/HealthyLiving/PhysicalActivity/FitnessBasics/American-Heart-Association-Recommendations-for-Physical-Activity-in-Adults_UCM_307976_Article.jsp#.V-B2PTuq30c. August 20, 2016.

141. English, Kirk L., Paddon-Jones, Douglas. Protecting muscle mass and function in older adults during bed rest. Curr Opin Nutr Metab Care 2010 Jan; 13 (1): 34-39.

Retrieved from http://www.ncbi.nlm.nih.gov/pmc/articles/PMC3276215/. July 25, 2016.

142. Andel, Ross; Crowe, Michael; Pedersen, Nancy L; Fratiglioni, Laura; Johansson, Boo; Gatz, Margaret. Physical Exercise at Midlife and Risk of Dementia Three Decades Later: A Population-Based Study of Swedish Twins. The Journals of Gerontology March 31, 2007. Retrieved from http://biomedgerontology.oxfordjournals.org/content/63/1/62.full. July 23, 2016.

143. Chen J, Millar WJ. Heart disease, family history and physical activity. Health Report 2001 Aug;12(4):23-32. Retrieved from http://www.ncbi.nlm.nih.gov/pubmed/15069809. June 23, 2016.

144. Weinstein AR, Sesso HD, Lee IM, Rexrode KM, Cook NR, Manson JE, Buring JE, Gaziano JM. The joint effects of physical activity and body mass index on coronary heart disease risk in women. Archives of Internal Medicine 2008 April 28;168 (8) :884-890. Retrieved from http://www.ncbi.nlm.nih.gov/pubmed/18443265. March 28, 2016.

145. American Diabetes Association. Physical Activity/Exercise and Diabetes. Diabetes Care 2004 Jan; 27(suppl 1):258-s62. Retrieved from http://care.diabetesjournals.org/content/27/suppl_1/s58. July 10, 2016.

146. Goodman, Alice. 'The Skinny' on Obesity, Cancer and Losing Weight. Medscape, July 09, 2015. Retrieved from http://www.medscape.com/viewarticle/847573. June 4, 2016.

147. Rena R. Wing, PHD1⌷, Wei Lang, PHD2, Thomas A. Wadden, PHD3, Monika Safford, MD4, William C. Knowler, MD, DRPH5, Alain G. Bertoni, MD6, James O. Hill, PHD7, Frederick L. Brancati, MD8, Anne Peters, MD9, Lynne Wagenknecht, DRPH6 and the Look AHEAD Research Group. Benefits of Modest Weight Loss in Improving Cardiovascular Risk Factors in Overweight and Obese Individuals With Type 2 Diabetes. Diabetes Care 2011 July; 34(7): 1481-1486. Retrieved from http://care.diabetesjournals.org/content/34/7/1481.short. June 10, 2016.

148. National Sleep Foundation. Sleep Apnea. Retrieved from https://sleepfoundation.org/sleep-disorders-problems/sleep-apnea. May 20, 2016.

149. National Sleep Foundation. Obesity and Sleep. Retrieved from https://sleepfoundation.org/sleep-topics/obesity-and-sleep. May 20, 2016.

150. Cauter, Eve Van PhD, Knutson, Kristen PhD, Leproult, Rachel PhD, Spiegel, Karine PhD. The Impact of Sleep Deprivation on Hormones and Metabolism. Medscape

April 2005. Retrieved by http://www.medscape.org/viewarticle/502825. May 3, 2016.

151. Cauter, Eve Van PhD, Knutson, Kristen PhD, Leproult, Rachel PhD, Spiegel, Karine PhD. The Impact of Sleep Deprivation on Hormones and Metabolism. Medscape April 2005. Retrieved by http://www.medscape.org/viewarticle/502825. May 3, 2016.

152. Wang F, Orpana HM, Morrison H, de Groh M, Dai S, Luo W. Long-term association between leisure-time physical activity and changes in happiness: analysis of the Prospective National Population Health Survey. American Journal of Epidemiology 2012 Dec. 15;176(12): 1095-100. Retrieved from http://www.ncbi.nlm.nih.gov/pubmed/23171884. May 2, 2016.

153. Wang F, Orpana HM, Morrison H, de Groh M, Dai S, Luo W. Long-term association between leisure-time physical activity and changes in happiness: analysis of the Prospective National Population Health Survey. American Journal of Epidemiology 2012 Dec. 15;176(12): 1095-100. Retrieved from http://www.ncbi.nlm.nih.gov/pubmed/23171884. May 2, 2016.

154. Shermer, Michael. *The Believing Brain*. New York: Henry Holt and Company, LLC. 2011. Print. Page 333.

Acknowledgments

We accomplish nothing alone and we are greater together. I am fortunate to be surrounded by amazing, caring people who help me along the way, and specifically for the completion of this book. This book began with my desire to make a difference in people's lives as I have been an observer, learner, participant and contributor of health behaviors and people's food choices and lifestyle habits over the years. I have complete awareness about health and nutrition, and a healthy skepticism about health claims—depending on the messenger. My beliefs have evolved over time and by evidence of what my memory holds on to, I feel I am on the right path.

I owe thanks to my late grandmothers—Mamaw—for walking three miles a day before it was cool and smearing avocado right onto her arm to show me real food serves many purposes (inside and out)—and Nannie—for having three freezers and one refrigerator stocked with real food she prepared on weekends to have food ready to thaw and serve in a pinch. Even she didn't have time to cook during the work week back then, as a single working mother of twins! To my parents, Carol and Sam King, who never had soda available in our home (unless company was coming), planted a garden some seasons, kicked us out of the house to play outside, and for a time, banned sugar, kids' cereals and white bread from our kitchen. I panicked then, and I am forever grateful now. Thank you for your never ending love and support. I love you Mom and Dad.

My greatest thanks and gratitude goes to my husband of 22 years, John Scoblick, for his never ending love and support, guidance and encouragement. He is solid. I thank him for listening to me talk about my book in excess, for helping me achieve my dreams and for believing in me. To my children, Luke and Dayne—from them I learn the most because they are my heart and responsibility. They give me insight every day as I learn from their youthful kindness, strength, genius and authenticity. It is because of my children that I became hyper aware of food and nutrition. To Melissa, my stepdaughter, for teaching me through the years with her grace, courage and strength to make good choices—now working full time, earning her PhD and raising two healthy children of her own, and showing us by example that we are capable of many great things. I love you all.

To my amazing editor, Pam Bixby—this book would not be coherent without her! I cannot thank her enough for being the brilliant editor that she is and the friend that she has been. She is kind, intelligent, professional, honest and fun to work with. Thanks to Tom for telling me that Pam is an amazing editor with 25 years of editing experience! She is the reason my book flows, and she saved readers from redundancy and wordiness. I feel it is safe to say that we all thank her! It is Pam about whom I was referring at the close of Chapter 4. She has the big picture and helps people where she can, using her strengths and talents. I am forever grateful—it enhances the experience to have somebody walk with you. Thank you.

I have had the opportunity to learn from some of the brightest minds over the past 20 years. From physicians to researchers in the realm of cardiology, bariatrics and other surgeries and including orthopedics, oncology, primary care physicians, childhood obesity experts, registered dietitians, as well as healthcare leaders and leaders in the non-profit world who focus on healthy living and obesity prevention. I have asked many of them through the years about their thoughts on diet, disease, statistics and behavior change. Their opinions are based on science, statistics, current protocols and mostly, their experience and their beliefs. That is to say, not all of the answers are the same, and most agree the answers are a culmination of things. Thank you to the physicians who have taken time to share with me over the years their views on diet and disease and what it takes for their patients to change health behaviors in the face of surgery or a health crisis. There are a few I'd like to mention: Gordon Marshall, MD; Bill Kessler, MD; Eric Hoenicke, MD; Jim Yegge, MD; James Muntz, MD; Ana Roman, MD; Kevin Spencer, MD; Bill Hogan, MD and childhood obesity expert Stephen Pont, MD.

I have learned from observing office staff and nurses and even physicians who have dieted over the past 20 years and hearing their stories, struggles, moans and groans, while munching on carrot and celery sticks or embarking on the Atkins diet. I have learned through them how to make it easier for people to be healthy. You know who I am talking about if you worked at the nationally recognized Texas Medical Center in Houston, Texas from 1995 to 2004. I continue to learn every day.

Thank you to childhood obesity research and intervention experts Sandra Evans, PhD, and Deanna Hoelscher, PhD, for their continued support, and for the opportunity to intern at the nationally recognized Dell Center at the University of Texas School of Public Health. There I learned more about childhood obesity and interventions, food insecurity and our nations' food and exercise habits. I am also grateful to those who have helped me in my professional development over the years and who have provided me with opportunities to grow. Those thanks go to Amanda Frye, Denise Bradley, James Finck, Jim Pacey, Lauren McPhail, Kathleen Hassenfratz, Christopher Kennedy and the late Barbara Lewis. Thanks to my web and book cover designer, Mark Collier of BigBlueDesigns, for his help and support for these things that I have no skill set for. Thanks to Dana Abramovitz for her friendship, support and for helping me create awareness of my work and my hope to make a difference for people. Also, to Kelly and Adria Rebbecchi and Lynne Henderlong-Rhea for being my sounding boards along the way. I owe many thanks to Jeremiah Bentley, Tricia Casler and Cinnamon Henley for sharing their stories and giving hope to anybody who has ever struggled with his or her weight, has a desire to be healthy and/or to be a healthy role model for their families. Anecdotal stories move the soul and provide hope to others so they might finally realize that we can do whatever we put our minds to.

Anything is possible. Nurture and lean on your support systems and take care of yourselves. Your health matters. We accomplish nothing alone and we are greater together.

Kathryn Scoblick volunteers her time as vice chair for the Austin Metropolitan YMCA Board of Directors and serves on the board of directors for the Austin Mayor's Health and Fitness Council, is on the School Health Advisory Council (SHAC) for her children's school district and is a proud graduate of the 2015 Leadership Austin Essential Class. She is a lifelong health advocate, co-created nutrition education tools for Baylor College of Medicine and feels

Kathryn Scoblick
Health Inspires, LLC

fortunate to have interned at the nationally recognized Dell Center at The University of Texas School of Public Health. Kathryn is owner of Health Inspires, LLC working as a trained and certified health and wellness coach, helping people reach their full potential and master their wellbeing and serves as Director of Employer Health and Wellness for a large Central Texas healthcare conglomerate in Austin, Texas, working with employers on wellness strategies and employee engagement. She is wife to John Scoblick for 22 years and mother of 16-year-old twin boys, Luke and Dayne.

Made in the USA
San Bernardino, CA
10 November 2017